BUBISHI
THE CLASSIC MANUAL
OF COMBAT

Translated with Commentary by
Patrick McCarthy

BUBISHI
THE CLASSIC MANUAL
OF COMBAT

With new contributions from Jesse Enkamp,
Cezar Borkowski, Evan Pantazi,
Joe Swift and Andreas Quast

TUTTLE Publishing

Tokyo │Rutland, Vermont│ Singapore

Published by Tuttle Publishing, an imprint of Periplus Editions (Hong Kong) Ltd.

www.tuttlepublishing.com

This Revised and Expanded Edition
ISBN 978-4-8053-1384-8

Library of Congress Cataloging-in-Publication Data
Names: McCarthy, Pat (Patrick)
Title: BuBishi : the classic manual of combat / translated with commentary by Patrick McCarthy, with new contributions from Jesse Enkamp, Cezar Borkowski, Evan Pantazi, Joe Swift and Andreas Quast.
Description: Rutland, Vermont : Tuttle Publishing, [2016] | ©2008. | Includes bibliographical references and index.
Identifiers: LCCN 2015044728 | ISBN 9784805313848 (paperback)
Subjects: LCSH: Karate--History. | Karate--Philosophy. | Karate--Japan--Okinawa-ken. | Martial arts.
Classification: LCC GV1114.3 .B82 2016 | DDC 796.815/3--dc23 LC record available at http://lccn.loc.gov/2015044728

"Books to Span the East and West"

Tuttle Publishing was founded in 1832 in the small New England town of Rutland, Vermont [USA]. Our core values remain as strong today as they were then—to publish best-in-class books which bring people together one page at a time. In 1948, we established a publishing outpost in Japan—and Tuttle is now a leader in publishing English-language books about the arts, languages and cultures of Asia. The world has become a much smaller place today and Asia's economic and cultural influence has grown. Yet the need for meaningful dialogue and information about this diverse region has never been greater. Over the past seven decades, Tuttle has published thousands of books on subjects ranging from martial arts and paper crafts to language learning and literature—and our talented authors, illustrators, designers and photographers have won many prestigious awards. We welcome you to explore the wealth of information available on Asia at **www.tuttlepublishing.com**.

Distributed by

North America, Latin America & Europe
Tuttle Publishing
364 Innovation Drive, North Clarendon,
VT 05759-9436 U.S.A.
Tel: 1 (802) 773-8930; Fax: 1 (802) 773-6993
info@tuttlepublishing.com
www.tuttlepublishing.com

Japan
Tuttle Publishing
Yaekari Building, 3rd Floor, 5-4-12 Osaki,
Shinagawa-ku, Tokyo 141 0032
Tel: (81) 3 5437-0171; Fax: (81) 3 5437-0755
sales@tuttle.co.jp
www.tuttle.co.jp

Asia Pacific
Berkeley Books Pte. Ltd.
3 Kallang Sector #04-01, Singapore 349278
Tel: (65) 6741-2178; Fax: (65) 6741-2179
inquiries@periplus.com.sg
www.tuttlepublishing.com

26 25 24 23   11 10 9 8 7   2312VP
Printed in Malaysia

TUTTLE PUBLISHING® is a registered trademark of Tuttle Publishing, a division of Periplus Editions (HK) Ltd.

✦ Table of Contents ✦

Part Two: Chinese Medicine and Herbal Pharmacology

Articles on Chinese Medicine and Herbal Pharmacology

Part Three: The Vital Points

Articles on Vital Points

Part Four: Fighting Techniques

Articles on Fighting Techniques

❧ Note on Romanization ❧

In this text I have opted to use the pinyin romanization system for all Chinese words. As such, kung fu is *gongfu, ch'i* is *qi, ch'uan fa* is *quan fa,* etc. I have also elected to refer to the Chinese unarmed civil fighting traditions using the popular Cantonese term *gongfu* rather than *quan fa, wushu,* or *kuoshu.* Although *gongfu* is a general term meaning "hard work" or a "work out" that does not specifically refer to the unarmed civil fighting traditions, I felt its common use justified my using it in this text.

⋙ Acknowledgments ⋙

The voluminous nature of my research has brought me into contact with virtually hundreds of people over the years. I would especially like to acknowledge the following people:

In America, I would like to thank my teacher Richard Kim, Hanshi of the Dai Nippon Butokukai. Through Mr. Kim's continued efforts, patience, and perseverance, I ultimately came to perceive that which lies beyond the physical boundaries of karate-do.

In Taiwan, I am deeply grateful to Liu Songshan Shifu for sharing his "family treasure" with me, the *Shaolin Bronze Man Book* (Shaolin Tong Ren Bu).

In China, I am very grateful to Li Yiduan from the Fuzhou Wushu Association who, at my request, was able to gather several herb experts and *gongfu* masters to study and help translate the Bubishi. Resolving many of the grammatical errors in the Bubishi, Mr. Li's immeasurable contributions and support continue to be of enormous benefit to my research. I would also like to thank Colin Whitehead for supplying a copy of *The Secrets of Wudang Boxing*. I am also indebted to Xie Wenliang, White Crane *gongfu* master and great-grandson of Ryuru Ko, for sharing so much of his knowledge with me.

In Japan, I am grateful to the following: Konishi Takehiro *Sensei* of the Ryobukai, who provided me with an original copy of Mabuni Kenwa's Bubishi; Otsuka Tadahiko Shihan, author of the Japanese translation of the Bubishi and a myriad of other related research projects, whose extensive analysis and deep knowledge of the Bubishi have had a profound effect upon my understanding of this obscure treatise; Dr. Iokibei Tsutomu, an expert in the Chinese healing arts of acupuncture, herbal medicines, and *qigong*, who helped me decipher the mysteries surrounding the internal organs, their corresponding meridian channels, and vital points; and Alexander Kask for fundamentally revising and editing this presentation of the text.

In Okinawa, I am indebted to: Dr. Hokama Tetsuhiro Shihan, master of both Goju-ryu karate-do and kobu-jutsu and the curator of Okinawa's only museum dedicated to the preservation and promotion of its native civil fighting heritage, for his many contributions and support; Nagamine Shoshin Soke and his son Takayoshi *Sensei*, of Matsubayashi-ryu karate-do, for their considerable assistance; Professor Takara Kuraiyoshi, for his help with my research; and Tokashiki Iken, director of the Goju-ryu Tomari-te Karate-do Kyokai, for his continuing assistance.

In Canada, my thanks go out to my colleague and friend, Ken Low Shifu, president of the Canadian Chinese Kung Fu Association. Low Shifu helped me translate some of the Bubishi's most enigmatic Chinese ideograms.

In Australia, I would like to express my appreciation to Carole Rogers for granting permission to use the illustrations from her *Acupuncture Point Dynamics Manual* and to Kevin Brennan of *Australasian Fighting Arts Magazine* for his assistance in publicizing my research throughout Australian and New Zealand.

In England, I would like to thank Graham Noble and Terry O'Neill from *Fighting Arts International* magazine for their assistance in publicizing my research in Europe, the UK and around the world.

I would also like to thank my lovely wife, Yuriko, without whose endless patience, love, and support, this work would never have been made possible.

Finally, it is unfortunate that I am unable to appropriately extend my personal gratitude to all the others who assisted with this research; as there have been so many, nonetheless, their assistance was very much appreciated, and sincerely hope this publication may reflect favorably upon them.

⪻ Foreword to the 2016 edition ⪼

Studying the art of karate has been likened to conquering a mountain.

You start off by hiking around the foot of the mountain. Birds are singing and everything is going great. What a wonderful adventure!

Gradually, as you reach higher altitudes, you need to start climbing. No problem—you love a challenge! So you climb and climb, steadily ascending Mt. Karate.

But after a while you find yourself struggling to find a foothold. It's getting harder now, and you're not sure which way to go. Are you even on the right path?

Doubt creeps in.

You look up at the sky. The birds have disappeared. That's when you realize it...

You're lost.

We've all been there; that uncomfortable place where we're no longer sure how to proceed in our karate journey. That place where nothing feels quite right.

This is where the Bubishi can help—as a guide for finding the right direction in your journey up the mountain of karate.

Hailed by the old masters as "karate's most sacred treasure," the Bubishi was an essential text in Okinawa, the birthplace of karate, directly influencing the formation of what we today refer to as karate do—the way of the empty hand.

Miyagi Chojun, (1888–1953) even referred to it as his "bible of karate".

So, why not use it as a guidebook in your personal quest for karate mastery?

I believe no other book can do it better, and the reason was best stated by Steve Jobs (1955–2011):

> You can't connect the dots looking forward. You can only connect them looking backwards.

Now, some people might argue that an old document such as the Bubishi couldn't possibly hold relevance in today's world—where the question of whether something works in the cage against a trained MMA fighter, or not, seems to be the main measure of determining a martial art's worth. But I beg to differ.

The Bubishi's message is timeless, its wisdom boundless.

Although some of the information contained in the Bubishi might very well be difficult to apply in your everyday life, like the herbal remedies or "death touch" techniques, the underlying principles can, and should, be applied in your karate life.

By understanding the past, you can find harmony in the present and go confidently into the future.

This is why the Bubishi, despite its ancient origins, still has relevance today.

All you need to do is study it with an open mind and connect the dots—so that one day you may look down from the summit of karate's proverbial mountain and enjoy the view.

It's not always easy, but it's always worth it.

This way, the Bubishi becomes more than a mere historical artifact.

It becomes a practical tool in your search for karate mastery, empowering you to rediscover the path when you're lost, to assume your quest of conquering Mt. Karate.

But only if you use it right.

On ko chi shin.—To learn from the old is to understand the new.

Good luck my friend—I believe in you!

Jesse Enkamp
Stockholm, 2015
www.karatebyjesse.com

✁ The Bubishi Project ✂
Leaving no Stone Unturned, and the Importance of Kimochi

by Cezar Borkowski
Hanshi, 9th Dan
www.northernkarate.com

I first met Patrick McCarthy in 1972 at a local tournament in Buffalo, New York. Over the next 15 years, this highly-skilled and formidable competitor and I often crossed paths, at local, national and eventually, international martial arts competitions.

As much as I respected his martial prowess, I appreciated his sense of humor and quick wit. Whether distilling information to its most fundamental essence, or interpreting it with a broader, richer point of view, he had an uncanny ability to see things in a multi-dimensional way.

We became, and remained, fast friends, even when time, life commitments and geography took us in different directions. I had the distinct pleasure of visiting his home in Japan on several occasions, and enjoyed traveling to Okinawa together. More on this later.

After McCarthy *Sensei* relocated to Australia nearly two decades ago, I watched his research, practice and teaching entertain and educate martial artists around the world. Although his first book, *Classical Kata of Okinawan Karate* (Ohara Publications, 1987), established him as a researcher of note among martial artists and opened many doors, it was his ground-breaking *Bubishi—the Bible of Karatedo* that solidified his reputation in the "budo community." In the early 1990s, I was honored to receive a self-published, advanced copy, its light brown cover *hanko*-stamped by the author. I still regard this tome as a precious treasure. While I don't think deep secrets can be gleaned from a singular book, it was McCarthy *Sensei*'s insightful explanations, observations and practical application that resonated then and now. Rather than a stale, academic retelling of a well-known subject, his was a genuine *bugeisha*'s take on an ancient text.

Although I had no role in the research, writing or editing of Patrick McCarthy's books, perhaps it was kismet, fate, or simply good luck that I happened to be present at meetings that would eventually lead to the publication of several of his now popular texts. One such exchange took place during a joint visit to Okinawa in October, 1994, where the seeds of the *Bubishi—The Bible of Karatedo*—were further harvested during interviews with renowned martial artists and historians.

Our first visit was to Hokama Tetsuhiro, in his Nishihara dojo and Budo Museum. A 10th Dan boasting a remarkable martial lineage, Hokama *Sensei* heads a large, international group, the Kenshikai. He started makiwara and bojutsu practice with his grandfather, and continued his formal training in high school under the watchful eye of the legendary Higa Seiko, Fukuchi Seiko and Matayoshi Shinpo. Hokama *Sensei* shared rare manuscripts and presented exotic training implements associated with the original Chinese Bubishi. A master of Shodo (brush and ink calligraphy), he also created calligraphy invoking selected concepts.

Our second port of call was Kumoji at the Kodokan dojo of Nagamine Shoshin. Nagamine *Sensei* remains one of Okinawa's leading karate masters. He studied with the who's who of the golden-age of fighting tradition including Kuba, Shimabukuro, Arakaki, Motobu and Kyan, all of whom deeply influenced this grand master of Matsubayashi. We enjoyed a warm welcome from Nagamine *Sensei* and his son Takeyoshi. During a discussion that focused on the introduction, dissemination and usage of the original Chinese text, they were cordial and forthcoming, readily sharing information, offering their opinions, and presenting private artifacts. At this meeting, Nagamine *Sensei* also asked McCarthy *Sensei* if he would translate his *Tales of Okinawa's Great Masters*, a request to which McCarthy *Sensei* humbly and enthusiastically agreed.

Our next expedition took us to the *honbu dojo* of the Gohaku-Kai. Tokashiki Iken is the headmaster of this unique international group that offer a syllabus combining the practice of Goju-ryu and Tomari-te into a highly dynamic system of Karatedo that honors the principles of his teachers—Higa Seiko, Fukuchi Seiko of Goju, and Nakasone Seiyu of Tomari-te. Tokashiki *Sensei* has made several research trips to China, including Fujian province. He possesses a wealth of unique information on ancient Chinese martial texts and combative practices, with special emphasis on Southern Crane fist-boxing methods. Tokashiki *Sensei* offered information, advice, and technical training. While visiting his dojo he introduced us to the great-grandson of Xie Zhong Xiang, also known as RuRuKo, the famed master of Whooping Crane Kung-fu. He was employed by Tokashiki *Sensei* for the purpose of adding his great grandfather's curriculum to the Gohaku-Kai catalog. Observing Mr. Xie teaching McCarthy *Sensei* several obscure forms was a priceless, indelible experience.

On our last excursion, we made our way to the Shimbukan dojo of Akamine Eisuke, Grand Master of The Ryukyu Kobudo Shinkokai, where we explored the weapon arts of China and Okinawa in the Ryukyu kingdom, and the Chinese influence on teachers like Chinen Umikata, Chinen Sanda, Chinen Masami, Yabiku Moden, and Taira Shinken. Throughout our visit, Akamine *Sensei* was gracious and engaging. At one point, he disappeared, only to resurface a few minutes later holding a valuable pair of *sai* that had once belonged to Yabiku and had been used by Taira. He presented McCarthy *Sensei* with this cherished set as a token of his esteem, and also discussed McCarthy *Sensei* serving as an editor and translator for the works of Taira Shinken and Akamine *Sensei*. It was an unforgettable episode in my martial arts life.

Although the research for the seminal work the *Bubishi—The Bible of Karatedo* was conducted throughout the late 1980s, McCarthy *Sensei* has continued his quest for additional information, traveling far and wide, exploring every source and resource. He will leave no stone unturned in his passionate pursuit.

Why would so many famous masters willingly reveal information previously guarded? Why would they disclose proprietary research, and share rare, museum-quality manuscripts and artifacts with Patrick McCarthy? The answer is simple: *Kimochi*, a Japanese term that may be translated as feeling or mood, optimism, and the anticipation of joy. Through a lifetime of dedicated practice, these masters had cultivated a highly-developed sense of intuition. Whether faced with the threat of a blade or fists, they had a sixth sense about the outcome of many situations. In this case, they'd likely experienced joy and optimism at the realization that McCarthy *Sensei* would preserve and propagate what they held precious, and lead future generations along a bright, new martial path.

Cezar Borkowski
Hanshi, 9th Dan, Okinawa Karatedo
Hanshi, 9th Dan, Ryukyu Kobudo

Sharing a moment with my dear friend and respected colleague, as we examine two antique Ryukyu kingdom era *wakizashi* with unique Ryukyu style pommel and the straight doubled-edged *jian*. The two weapons represent duality of martial and socioeconomic influences of Japan and China on the islands of Okinawa.

⧏ Preface ⧐
No Time Like the Past

Reflections

I remember sitting in the Burbank office of Geri Simon, then publisher at Ohara Publications, late in 1985 when she declined my offer to publish the Bubishi. Instead, she encouraged me to write the book, *Classical Kata of Okinawan Karate*. I suppose her choice was based upon the idea that a Top-Ten rated kata competitor, with whom their sister publication—*Karate-Illustrated* magazine—co-supported, represented the potential for more commercial success than taking a chance on a abstract project like the Bubishi. While I was certainly disappointed by Ohara's lack of interest in such an important work

Patrick McCarthy Hanshi.

they did allow me to introduce a summary of its articles with the publication of *Classical Kata*, released in 1987. That was, to the best of my knowledge, the very first time such details had ever been translated into English and published in the Western world.

Although my book *Classical Kata* was noteworthy for its time, it did little to attract any widespread attention. By 1989 a Tokyo-based colleague of mine, named Gene Pelc, arranged for me to meet a friend of his who was in the publishing business. Delivering an improved edition of my work, which also included a foreword by Higaonna Morio, Gene's friend offered some important advice about how I might better present the work.

Paying heed to the advice given at that encounter, I subsequently made many important changes to the manuscript. By this time, I had generated interest in the translation through the small research group I had established in Japan, and was receiving requests from all over to release a limited edition. As such, I released the first 109-page translation of my work in the fall of 1990, complete with the foreword by IOGKF Director, Higaonna Morio, which did much to attract additional attention.

Patrick McCarthy's 1992
edition of the Bubishi.

Patrick McCarthy at the Shaolin
Temple in 1992.

Returning from a trip to Fujian in late November 1990, my wife informed me that the vanity press-style edition had sold rather quickly. It became evident that another edition had to be produced immediately. Using what little money we generated from sales of the first edition, I went on to produce an even better quality and larger publication 18 months later. By the summer of 1992 I had released a 140-page version of the same work, which now included a foreword by Li Yiduan, and the support of the Fuzhou Martial Arts Association.

Over the next two years I made several trips back to Okinawa, Yongchun, Fuzhou, the Shaolin Temple, Shanghai, Taiwan and SE Asia in connection with the book. I also began teaching seminars, which did much to further promote interest in the Bubishi. With a significant improvement, and more than fifty pages of supporting research, we released a 244-page special edition Bubishi in 1994. Featuring a highly informative introduction, complete with several forewords by leading authorities, photos, diagrams and illustrations, the edition was a big success and caught the attention of Tuttle publications.

Patrick McCarthy's 1994
edition of the Bubishi.

Introducing a summary of the Bubishi in 1987, and three subsequent self-published editions, before being produced by Tuttle in 1995, this project has been remarkably rewarding.

Revising and editing my work, and publishing it under the new name, *Bible of Karate,* was an excellent marketing strategy. The new title and strength of Tuttle's worldwide distribution network soon made the book an instant success and a martial art's bestseller. What's even more pleasing is to learn that my work has since been translated into several languages, including Spanish, Italian, German, Russian, and Czech.

Changes

Much has changed since the publication of my original work more than twenty years ago. Most noticeably is the effortless way with which we are now able to locate, collect, and process information. The Internet's information highway has not only provided instantaneous access to incredible sources of online information, it has also made worldwide networking with like-minded learners a virtual walk in the park. These days, it's even possible for a person with absolutely no foreign language skills to translate Chinese script into English with just a few strokes of the keyboard. Isn't that amazing? Computers, the Internet, and some pretty awesome software now allow for things that were simply not possible during the early years of working on this project.

There's no denying that the development and popularity of the Internet has certainly made subsequent research much less troublesome. Contrasted with traditional research methods I can't help but wonder how such technology might have otherwise influenced the final outcome of this project, had it then been available. That said, I remain confident nothing could ever replace the indelible experiences and wonderful memories collected during my journey throughout Japan, China, and Southeast Asia. Delivering the essence of what appears in this publication required things that the Internet is still incapable of reproducing, such as hands-on experience, feeling the pulse of the culture and the spirit of those people most responsible for keeping it alive.

What is the Bubishi?

Undated and unsigned, the Bubishi—武備志/誌—A Record of Martial [Art] Preparation—is an abstract collection of Chinese writings about Fujian *gongfu*-based fighting arts and related subjects. Hand-brushed in old Chinese script, and linked to turn-of-the-century karate in Okinawa, its articles range in variety from *gongfu* history, attacking anatomically vulnerable targets, tactical strategy, and moral philosophy to identifiable acts of physical violence, prescribed application practices, escapes and counters, herbal concoctions, and medicinal remedies. Far from being the definitive book on karate the Bubishi is, nonetheless, a treasure trove of information. In the right hands, this penetrating work tells us much about what the Okinawan pioneers of karate valued most. In a modern tradition, where mimicking overly-ritualized styles and "fighting" in rule-bound contests have taken precedence over functional application practices, I am reminded of the wisdom of Matsuo Basho: *Don't [blindly] follow in the footsteps of the old masters, but rather seek what they sought.*

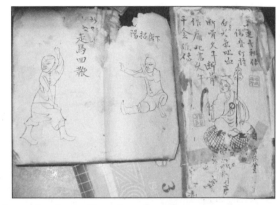

Older hand-drawn books on Yongchun Quanfa.

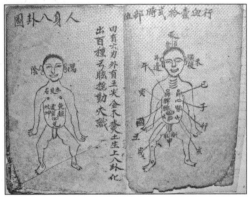

Another mid-nineteenth century hand-drawn Bubishi-like manual from Fujian Province

Bubishi located at the library of Kyushu University.

A Document of Great Historical Importance

Credible pre-twentieth century documents explaining the history and evolution of Karate are virtually non-existent. Until the publication of Funakoshi Gichin's first book on the art, in 1922, and the few pre-war publications which followed, the only known testimony in existence were a haphazard collection of rare writings; i.e., a single quote by the seventeenth century Ryukyuan statesman, Junsoku, dated 1683; a brief passage in the 1761 *Oshima Hikki*; abstract comments from a few visitors (Hall, Mcleod, Bettelheim, Perry) of various nineteenth century foreign ships; two mid-nineteenth century illustrations about mikiwara and hand-conditioning which appeared in the *Nagoku Zatsuwa (Tales of the Southern Kingdom)* by the Satsuma samurai, Nagoya Sagenta; a copy of an 1867 program outlining a demonstration of the fighting arts at Shuri's Ochayagoten; a letter written in 1882 by Matsumura Sokon, and a motto he later penned in 1885; the 1904 testimony of Noma Seiji; a single page from a book written in 1905 by Hanashiro Chomo; and the ten-items of Itosu Ankoh written in his October 1908 letter to the Ministry of Education.

If nothing else, the sheer scarcity of early documentation should demonstrate the enormous historical value the Bubishi represents. I suppose for some, the value of this old compilation can only be measured by knowing that Okinawan karate pioneers, such as Funakoshi Gichin, Mabuni Kenwa, Miyagi Chojun, and Shimabuku Tatsuo, used it in their own personal studies. In spite of the rich and penetrating information, which lies within its pages, this fact that Okinawan karate pioneers used the Bubishi seems enough to reinforce its historical significance.

A Lifetime Study

I actually obtained my first copy of the Bubishi in Toronto's Chinatown in 1973 while shopping for books on karate. Unknowingly, I purchased the Chinese (Taiwan) pirate copy of Mabuni Kenwa's 1934 publication, entitled *Karate Kenpo (The Study of Seipai)*, in which the second half of this book contains what he describes as Itosu Ankoh's Bubishi.

Mabuni 1934 Bubishi.

I never really understood just how important the old text actually was until an Okinawan karate teacher, named Teruo Chinen, later explained it to me at a 1985 karate tournament in Bermuda. Promising to show me his hand-drawn copy of the Bubishi the next time we met, it wasn't until a Las Vegas tournament, hosted by Osamu Ozawa, that I finally got the chance to see his treasured book. Since that awakening, the task of understanding this monumental work became a virtual obsession.

Patrick McCarthy at his Vancouver dojo with Teruo Chinen.

Left: Taiwan pirate copy of Mabuni's 1934 book; Right: An illustration from inside the book from the 48 Postures

Meaningful Journey

How fortunate I was to have stumbled across a book of such magnitude never knowing what impact it would ultimately have upon me. From beginning to the end and beyond, this project has brought me into contact with many interesting sources of information from which I've enjoyed wonderful learning opportunities. It's no exaggeration to say that the Bubishi has led me down a fascinating path of learning, enriching my entire life.

As someone with more than just a passing fancy in the history of karate, the Bubishi became a window through which to identify a cultural landscape and social mindset diametrically opposite to the lifestyle we take for granted today. Through studying the past, understanding local knowledge, and becoming familiar with those personalities most responsible for pioneering this art, it became possible to identify their original aims and spirit. By linking the past to the present I discovered the original contextual premise upon which this art was forged, what forces affected its evolution, why such variations upon common themes unfolded, and how such secrets fell quietly dormant into an abyss of ambiguity.

As a student of the fighting arts, and fully understanding its original contextual premise, I was able to glean crucial foundation knowledge about the human body, its mechanics and those immutable principles that underpinned how application practices work. Armed with this information, I established a working theory—*Habitual Acts of Physical Violence* [HAPV]—from which to help eliminate the ambiguity shrouding the original meaning of kata. Modifying the original Shaolin-based empty-handed, "one-on-one," 36 acts of physical violence scenarios, I developed an easy-to-learn (-teach and -practice) structure of two-person reenactment drills. Applying this knowledge to the HAPV-premise resulted in astonishing discoveries. Using passive resistance as the preliminary basis from which to introduce a learner to the prescribed mnemonic-like application rituals found in kata, I used rote repetition, and a gradual to exponential ascent to aggressive resistance, as the definitive mechanism to nurture instinctive, rather than cognitive, response capabilities against the unpredictability of physical violence.

HAPV-theory

Gongfu pioneers responsible for establishing early ways through which to impart their lessons found success using mnemonic-like physical rituals. By recreating the kind of violent scenarios common to their society and era, *quanfa* teachers introduced learners to real-life contextual premises and prescribed fighting techniques through ritualised two-person drills. Using the safety of a private practice venue, learners rehearsed their prescribed fighting techniques against passive resistant partners until growing familiarity, indomitable fortitude, and physical skill afforded them combative functionality against unpredictable aggressive resistance. Separating the two-person drills into identifiable attack scenarios and prescribed response sequences [as exampled in the Bubishi's forty-eight diagrams], *quanfa* teachers successfully established solo reenactment models and called the ritual practices *Hsing* (型 Kata in Japanese). By linking together individual models into collective routines, *quanfa* innovators developed unique and complex solo exercises through which to not only culminate the lesson imparted but also express one's individual prowess while strengthening their overall mental, physical, and holistic conditioning.

Introduced to Okinawa during the later part of its Ryukyu Kingdom Period, kata ultimately found its way into the school system. Simplified for the sake of exercising large groups of school children at one time, this process removed its contextual premise-based two-person drills, thereby reducing the original art, which quietly fell dormant. With the focus upon form over function, kata became a vehicle through which to cultivate physical fitness and social conformity, in support of Japan's war efforts during a radical era of military escalation. Kata practiced in modern karate have been so affected by the simplification process, the reverse influence of pre-war Japanese Budo culture, and its post-war rule-bound competitive agenda, that their introduction and practice throughout the twentieth century has literally been without a realistic contextual premise.

Not surprisingly, my theory has been ridiculed by some and opposed by others, before a general consensus argued such conclusions were self-evident. For a while, I almost believed there was a prize being awarded for trying to discredit my work. Because of this, I came to better understand Schopenhauer three stages of truth: *All truth passes through three stages: First, it is ridiculed. Second, it is violently opposed. Third, it is accepted as being self-evident.*

Two-person Drill Practice Simplified

#1. The habitual acts of physical violence (i.e., headlock, bear-hug, strangle, being impacted, or tackled from behind, etc.) are identified as the contextual premise of kata. Each is identified and methodically introduced to the learner in order of distance and simplicity (i.e. kicking, punching, trapping, and clinching distance). There are 36 habitual acts of physical violence and no fewer than 72 variations on these common themes, representing a total of 108 different scenarios.

#2. The habitual acts of physical violence are taught individually so that each learner can understand its dynamics, what makes them dangerous and which prescribed defensive tactics are best suited to effectively negotiate them.

#3. A single prescribed application is practiced with a partner back and forth at passive resistance, before variations are considered, thereby promoting familiarity with both the act of physical violence and its prescribed counter. Once an acceptable level competency is reached the attacker and defender are encouraged to gradually increase the intensity of the attack until the two-person scenario can be performed with aggressive resistance, and confidence about understanding and effectively negotiating unpredictability is established.

#4. Learners are then asked to practice the prescribed application by themselves in solo re-enactment rehearsals. Shaped into template-like rituals these solo rehearsals become the individual composites which, when linked together into choreographed routines, become something greater than the sum total of their individual parts: kata.

In spite of the diametrically opposite way that kata are taught today, I believe this formula best represents the way they were originally conceived and passed on.

More than Self-defense?

There are certainly many other examples indicating just how wonderfully accommodating kata truly is. Serving several other purposes, the most obvious include kata serving as a tool through which to impart a style's curriculum, a creative competitive routine, an abstract form of shadow boxing, a way to hone one's fighting skills, an alternative form of holistic exercise, and a form of meditation in motion.

Rediscovering the lost contextual premise of kata awakens a sleeping Dragon and breathes life back into an otherwise dormant ritual. When I finally worked out how mnemonic mechanisms not only accumulated the lessons already imparted but, when linked together, clearly offered something greater than the sum total of its individual parts, the mystery was solved. Sadly, disbelievers need such words to be uttered by an oriental Master to reverberate truth. However, for those readers who don't require such validation you will find the HAPV-theory and two-person drill concept a workable formula with which to put the fight back into kata.

Pedagogical Perspective

As a teacher of the fighting arts, I was able to look at the Bubishi from a pedagogical perspective. By this I mean the whole context of instruction, learning, and the actual operations involved in the science of education. Teachers provide the link between the past and the future. What is imparted, and how it's taught, profoundly influences what a learner will retain. Retention rates vary disproportionately with different learners. The classic categories all learners fall into are identified as *auditory*, *visual*, and *kinesthetic*. Such knowledge provides the basis upon which teachers appropriately determine what combinations of these communications best suit each learner to achieve the desired outcome.

Source of the Bubishi English Translation

Over the years there have been questions concerning the source of my translation. Originally, I found such criticism rather odd as it was made perfectly clear in the acknowledgements that many people assisted with the overall translation of this work. It was my original intention to publish the work under the name, *International Ryukyu Karate Research Society*, but the publisher felt that having taken the lead from beginning to end with this project that identifying me as the translator would be more appropriate. My infatuation with this work, and passion for fighting arts, had brought me into personal contact with numerous senior Japanese/Okinawan and Chinese authorities who, in one way or another, helped me unlock many doors of understanding.

Most notably were: Li Yiduan, President of the Fuzhou Wushu Association; Hokama Tetsuhiro, author, historian, museum curator, and karate master, who dedicated fifty or so pages to the study of the Bubishi, in chapter nine, pp 294-343, of his 1984 book, *Okinawa Karatedo no Aiyumi*; Ken Low, a Vancouver-based politician, President of the Western Canadian Kung Fu Association, and Southern-style Quanfa Master; my lovely wife, Yuriko, without whom I simply could not have completed this project; and, a bunch of other folks from whom dribs and drabs came over the years.

Perhaps, this is a good opportunity to mention those people. First are the Chinese sources: Tang Shifeng Shifu, Shanghai Chin Wu oldboy; Si Yanpu, then chief instructor of Monk Fist boxing at the main Shaolin monastery; Liang Yiquan, retired Shaolin monk and director of the Shaolin Quanfa Research Society, Dengfeng County; Gao Shifu, Yangshuo Quanfa academy Guangxi; Guo Kongxi, third generation Tiger *quanfa* and the grandson of Zhou Zihe; Jin Jingfu, third generation lineage head master of Whooping Crane; Liu Songshan, third generation head master of Feeding Crane; Siaw Joonfa, fourth generation White Crane teacher, Persatuan Kebudayaan Jasmani Ming Chung Hok, East Malaysia; Cai Chuxian, Fujian, Cai family fist; Wu Bin, China's MA's Federation of Asia "Research & Teacher's Dept."

Japanese/Okinawan sources included: Yamaguchi Gogen, founder of the Goju Kai (who had previously published one version of the Bubishi); Otsuka Tadahiko, President of the Goju Kensha, and IMO, one of three leading Japanese authorities of the Bubishi; Nagamine Shoshin, historian, author, and the founder of Matsubayashi Ryu; Konishi Takehiro, second generation head master of Shindo Jinen Ryu and my source of Mabuni's completely hand-written copy of Itosu's Bubishi; Kinjo Hiroshi, widely regarded as one of Japan's senior most Okinawan masters of karate; Dr. Iokibei Tsutomu, a TCM practitioner; Prof. Takara Kurayoshi, University of the Ryukyus; Higaonna Morio, of the IOGKF, who also wrote the foreword for my 1990 edition; Hisataka Masayuki, President of the Shorinji Ryu Kenkokan, who wrote a foreword in my 1994 edition; Fujiwara Ryozo, a highly regarded Japanese martial art's historian/

author; Takamiyagi Shigeru, a highly regarded Okinawan martial arts historian/co-authored with Uechi Kanei, *Karate-do, Sono Rekishi To Gihon*; Miyagi Tokumasa, a highly regarded Okinawan martial arts historian/author; Kinjo Akio, a highly regarded Okinawan martial arts historian/author; Tokashiki Iken, a highly regarded Okinawan martial arts historian, president of the Gohakukai and Bubishi author; Nakamoto Masahiro, a highly regarded Okinawan martial arts historian/author, and president of the Bunbukan; and, Iwae Tsukuo, a highly regarded Japanese martial arts historian/author.

I could also add Dr. Misao Batts, then a professional translator at the University of British Colombia, whom I contracted in 1985 to translate the Bubishi section of the big Uechi Ryu blue book, and parts of the Taiwanese pirate copy of Mabuni's Bubishi. It was from these two works that my 1987 summary of the Bubishi came. There was also Egawa Machiko, principal lecturer at the Japanese Educational Centre, where I had been enrolled studying Japanese in 1985. Machiko san helped me understand little odds and ends here and there.

Patrick McCarthy in Naha with Tokashiki Iken.

Collectively, there have been many sources from which I drew liberally, but only I was responsible for the overall delivery of a finished product. It took nearly ten years of continual effort before my work finally caught the attention of Charles E. Tuttle. To be more precise, it was Alex Kask, then Tokyo editor for Tuttle's martial arts titles, who recognized the value of the Bubishi and helped me transform it into the work that lies before you today.

Summary of Bubishi Contents

There has also been some criticism about the manner in which I had presented the Bubishi articles. It is my hope the reader understands why this writer found it necessary to reorganize the order in which I originally received the articles. I am sure it may come as a surprise to learn that the original document I received from the Konishi family was unbound and in random order allegedly as received from Mabuni Kenwa. As such, I found it necessary to reorganize the order of the articles in which I received them for the sake of producing a coherent publication.

Order of Bubishi Articles

To say that the Bubishi contains abstract information about the fighting arts is to acknowledge the obvious. In addition to the difficulty experienced while trying to decipher its abstract nature I also found the disjointed way its articles were presented terribly distracting. After discussing this issue with several colleagues I decided to present the information in a more coherent way.

As such, articles were grouped together by association in the following way. I included the origins of White Crane, observations of Monk Fist Boxing and related material, along with advice on correct etiquette, in a section on history and philosophy and called it part one. Grouping together those articles dealing with Traditional Chinese Medicine (TCM), I brought meridian channels, herbal pharmacology, prescriptions (ointments, medicines and pills), and 12-hour based theories for blood circulation, (incurable) diseases, injuries, and recuperation, along with related charts and diagrams into an organized section where one had not previously existed. I brought all the vital point-related information, charts, and diagrams into a single chapter in order to isolate it from the rest of the material so they could be best studied in association with each other. I took the rest of the work that related directly to fighting and grouped it together, except for Happoren, which I left in Part One's history article, its original place.

With the help of Li Yiduan, Wu Bin, Chen Zhinan, Tokashiki Iken and Otsuka Tadahiko, I felt confident bundling the rest of the articles into a section entitled, *Fighting Techniques*. With the help of these authorities I identified Yongchun Crane and Monk Fist as the most likely nineteenth century precursor sources from which Okinawan Karate [kata] sprang. I defined the holistic value of kata and describe its contextual premise while identifying *qinna* as an adjunct practice and concluded the introduction to this section with a capsule history of Monk Fist *quanfa* and the principal variations of crane boxing: Jumping Crane (Zonghe Quan), Whooping Crane (Minghe Quan), Sleeping Crane (Suhe Quan), Feeding Crane (Shihe Quan) and Flying Crane (Feihe Quan), as they had not been previously identified for a western karate-based audience.

I saw fit to feature the following articles in the second component of Part Four: Articles #6, #7 and #32 [featured the *Rakanken* and *Nepai* kata along with general postures used in those routines], Article #13 [*The Eight Precepts of the Fist*—from which Miyagi Chojun chose the name Goju to identify his interpretation of the fighting arts], Article #14 [*The Principles of Ancient Law*], Article #15 [*Maxims of Sun Zi*], Article #16 [*Grappling and Escapes*], Article #20 [*Rokkishu*—Six Ji Hands of the Shaolin Style], Article #29 [The Forty-Eight Self-Defense Diagrams]. Although I was able to translate the two diagrams, identified as Articles #27 and #28 [Zheng's 24-Iron Hand Applications and White Monkey Style, and Eighteen Scholars White Crane Fist and Black Tiger Style Fifty-Four Step *Quan*], there was no supporting text to explain their contextual premise.

The hand-drawn Bubishi included no subsequent list of sources, so I saw fit to conclude the work by producing a bibliography of those principal written sources I used, a list of over 300 Chinese and Japanese names, terms and ideograms, along with a complete index to cite their location in the text, in an effort to help subsequent research.

TCM-based Articles

At the time I undertook the task of overseeing this translation I had little knowledge of classical Chinese writing and no formal education in TCM, whatsoever. I am not in the least embarrassed to say that trying to understand the abstract nature of these articles, especially with such inadequate preparation, posed more than just a challenge, it was damn near impossible. Had it not been for the unselfish assistance of my Chinese colleague, Li Yiduan, and some help from Dr. Iokibei, Dr. Manaka, Otsuka Tadahiko, and Hokama Tetsuhiro in Japan, along with studying a bunch of research material, the entire section may very well have been skipped over altogether. Posing the most difficulty were the articles on herbal pharmacology. It wasn't enough that some of the recipes were no longer in use, or several of the animal-related components were now on the endangered list, but also that the organic ingredients were frequently described using local jargon rather than correctly identified terms. Admittedly, even after the nearly two years it took to complete this most fascinating, yet perplexing, section I wondered just how much of it I truly understood.

Today's widespread availability of medical care, and general knowledge of first aid, should in no way reduce the importance of learning such a study. If anything, such studies certainly illustrate the importance once placed upon them, especially during a time when the medical conveniences we enjoy today in the West were unheard of in old Okinawa. Just as difficult to grasp were the articles referring to attacking vital points, commonly known as Dim Mak.

Dim Mak

My original introduction to Dim Mak was more than three decades ago when I read Bruce Tegner's 1968 publication, *Nerve Centers & Pressure Points*. However, coming up in fighting arts during the "blood 'n guts" era of the 60s/70s, little emphasis was ever placed on such things as pressure points. Moreover, hard-to-swallow advertisements about mas-

tering the secret art of Dim Mak, by "Count Dante" (aka John Keehan)—the *Deadliest Man Alive*, featured in comic books for $5.95, *plus shipping*, did little to encourage serious learn-ers of that era to venture beyond a cursory look. It really wasn't until I began training un-der Professor Wally Jay, pioneer of Small Circle Theory Jujutsu, in the 1970s, that I developed more of an interest in vital points. Of course, undertaking the Bubishi translation project changed the way I came to look at this secret art altogether.

"Count Dante" advertisement.

By the time I migrated to Japan during the mid-1980s, I was fortunate enough to meet Dr. Manaka Yoshio (author of the *Layman's Guide to Acupuncture*) through my senpai, Aladdin Timur, of Odawara, along with other experts like Otsuka Tadahiko (Author of the Japanese Bubishi) and Dr. Iokibei Tsu-tomu (TCM practitioner), all of whom were instrumental in my struggle to better understand its abstract nature. Even now, years later, it has only been because of subsequent studies that I am able to better under-stand the most ambiguous sections of the Bubishi; that, of course, being Dim Mak, the art of attacking of anatomically vulnerable structures and the so-called "delayed death touch."

That said, resolving such abstract practices would have been much easier had I access to the kind of research which has been subsequently carried out by Prof. Rand Cardwell, Bruce Miller, and Dr. Michael Kelly. I simply can't say enough good things about their work. Information that I myself was unable to glean from years of studying the Bubishi is now available thanks to the pioneering efforts of these researchers.

Prof. Rand Cardwell

Prof. Rand Cardwell's publication, *The Western Bubishi*, is simply a must have book. His insightful analyses of the Five-Element and Yin-Yang theories, bioelectrical energy, meridians and the diurnal cycle, will pro-vide the Bubishi reader with a clear understanding of how to attack the thirty-six essential vital points. I assure the reader that whatever is not evident about TCM-based theory through reading the Bubishi will be brutally apparent in his research.

Rand Cardwell wrote, "Cherished and highly guarded by pre-mod-ern martial arts pioneers in Okinawa, the Bubishi presents the modern reader with a number of tactical concepts which have great importance even today. Divided into various sections the Bubishi also includes foundational skills and an abstract presentation on attacking anatomically vulnerable structures through the art of Dim Mak. Upon examination it becomes evident that someone with superior knowledge and experience, in the laws and theories of Traditional Chinese Medicine (TCM), composed the Dim Mak-related articles. The unknown author(s) of this valuable anthology cites specific acupuncture locations as targets for attacking to produce various levels of incapacitation, even death. One major focus of my research was to verify the methodology used through a process referred to as 'reverse engineering.' The Bubishi includes a list of acupuncture point locations without providing the reasons why those points were selected. By examination of the laws and theories of TCM a much clearer picture of the actual depth of knowledge emerges. My research not only compliments McCarthy *Sensei*'s presentation of this old work, it also illuminates the ambiguity of TCM concepts while providing a simplified learning process. Rather than attempt to explain the effects of this Dim Mak from an occidental perspective, I chose to stay within the confines of the Eastern paradigm, which is how the Bubishi was presented. My research and conclusions rest solidly on the foundation provided by McCarthy's work, but also strives to push beyond the abstract information contained in the Bubishi. This complementary work provides the modern martial artist a means to develop an advanced understanding of the material presented in the Bubishi and eliminates the tedious task of researching numerous TCM-related textbooks for the hidden answers. My work has been reviewed and accepted by both academically trained acupuncturists and serious martial artists throughout the world. I was particularly pleased that McCarthy *Sensei* became such an outspoken supporter of this work making it mandatory reading for any and all Bubishi readers."

Bruce Miller

Bruce Miller's voluminous works include, *Essential Anatomy for the Martial Artist, Secrets of Power, Pressure Points – The Deadly Touch, The System of Pressure Points, Poison Hands – Truth, Techniques and Reasons, The Complete Book of Light Force Knock Outs*, and *Dim Mak – The Final Reality*.

Bruce Miller wrote, "A wonderfully insightful publication, the Bubishi appears to be more of a compilation of fighting art-related knowledge than it does a 'how-to' manual. What really confused me were its abstract articles on Dim Mak. Once considered secret, much of this vital point and death-touch theory is antiquated, highly abstract and based upon folklore with little or no medical-science to support it. My hands-on medical experience, and subsequent publications in this field, effectively clarify the ambiguity of what the Bubishi addresses. By using the modern principles of anatomy, physiology, and kinetics, readers are better able to understand the so-called secrets. Master McCarthy is not only likeminded in this area he also vigorously supports and promotes my work within his worldwide organization as the only rational way to compliment the Bubishi."

Dr. Michael Kelly

Death Touch, The Science Behind the Legend of Dim-Mak by Dr. Michael Kelly, delivers more than just a brutally honest explanation of this once secret art. An osteopathic physician by profession, Dr. Kelly's penetrating study of Dim Mak presents a simplified understanding based on sound medical science.

According to legend, Dim Mak formed the basis upon which both Shaolin and Wudang Chinese fighting arts unfolded. Hidden amidst the techniques of its elegant fighting routines (*hsing/kata*) these legendary fighting arts subsequently influenced the development of Karate in Okinawa. As the traditional kata of Okinawan karate are based upon the classical routines of Chinese *quanfa*, so too, with them comes the secrets of Dim Mak. Addressing all aspects of attacking vital points, knockouts, death, and even delayed death, Dim Mak is an extremely dangerous discipline, which has been passed on only in secrecy, until quite recently. Simplifying the mystery of Dim Mak in western terms, Kelly's work explains its true dangers and deadly effects through modern medical science. In addition to identifying lethal points on the body and teaching how to attack them and the internal organs, his work also includes quick knockouts, revival techniques, and the legendary delayed death touch. In old China, such learning was only ever imparted to the most loyal of disciples and never intended for public consumption. Having spent years thoroughly researching the medical implications of Dim Mak, I can hardly recommend a single work more comprehensive than Dr. Michael Kelly's.

Personal Recommendation

It has only been during this generation that the ironclad ritual of secrecy has been broken and the knowledge of Dim Mak seeped out into the public domain through books, DVDs, and seminars. While revealing such secrets have explained much, it remains obvious that the art of Dim Mak is still a highly dangerous practice. Hence, the need for sound medical science-based reference books on the subject. Readers not familiar with the work of these three credible sources are encouraged to study their publications and/or attend the many workshops they frequently teach. Not only will this compliment your study of the Bubishi, I guarantee it will also help you locate Dim Mak applications contained within your own styles, and deepen your overall understanding of the fighting arts. I have long supported the work of these three researchers and recommend their books as companion texts to the Bubishi.

Funakoshi Gichin

Prior to Mabuni Kenwa publishing much of the Bubishi in his 1934 book, the *Study of Seipai* (Kata), Karate pioneer, Funakoshi Gichin, had already included a word-for-word reproduction of articles 13 (The Eight Precepts of Quanfa), 14 (The Principles of Ancient Law), 15 (Maxims of Sun Zi), and 16 (Grappling and Escapes), in his 1922 (*Ryukyu Kenpo Karate*, pp274-276), 1925 (*Rentan Goshin Karate-jutsu*, pp296-298) and 1934 (*Karatedo Kyohan*, pp300-302) publications. He also used articles 8 (Discussions on Seizing and Striking Veins and Tendons Using the Hard Fist Method), 9 (Twelve-Hour Vital Points Revealed), 17 (Seven Restricted Locations), 21 (Delayed Death Touch Twelve-Hour Diagrams) and 24 (Bronze Man Statue), the principal sections on vital points, to describe the medical implications of Dim Mak, in *Karatedo Kyohan* (pp263-277). In fact, I was particularly taken by the English translation of these articles as they appear in Oshima Tsutomu's interpretation of this text (pp237-244, Kodansha International, 1973) and even more so with Neptune publication's 2005 English translation of the same work (pp231-245). For the purpose of cross-comparative study, I hope readers of this Bubishi will also consider looking at Ken Penland's Bubishi translation; articles 8 (p18-23), 9 (pp24-25), 13 (pp37-38), 14 (pp39-40), 15 (p41), 16 (pp42-44), 17 (p45), 22 (pp66-79), and 24 (pp83-86): John Teramoto's articles 13 through 16, which can be located in his English translation of Funakoshi's 1925 *Rentan Goshin Karate-jutsu*, entitled *Karate Jutsu* (pp175-177, Kodansha International 2001) and Neptune Publication features the same articles 13 (p260), 14 (p261), 15 (pp260-261), and 16 (p262) of Neptune's English translation of *Karatedo Kyohan*.

Bubishi Illustrations and Diagrams

One of the biggest problems I encountered trying to fully understand the amateur quality illustrations and diagrams that appear in the Bubishi was the inadequate explanations accompanying them. Of course, several drawings were rather straightforward, requiring little explanation, while others were far less accommodating. The diagrams featured in Article #21, concerning the delayed death touch, particularly challenged me, as did the posture-related illustrations located in Articles #27, #28, #29, and #32. I suppose the tradition of copying hand-drawn illustrations might be best left to professionals! Wherever possible, I provided as much supplementary information as I could. Adamant about not using the original illustrations and diagrams, apparently because of their poor reproduction quality, the publisher arranged for an in-house artist to reproduce the images more clearly. I believe this was very helpful.

The International Ryukyu Karate Research Society

After migrating to Japan from Canada I began writing articles for several international martial art magazines, about the Bubishi, the subsequent research it inspired into the unknown application practices of kata, and the history and personalities of the pioneers through whose hands it passed. My writing gradually attracted a small but loyal following of likeminded enthusiasts from all over the world. In time, the trickle of monthly mail became a deluge of weekly correspondence that made several things quite evident: how many people were interested in such studies, how few people had access to primary sources of research, the need to establish such a source—and, I was in a position to take the lead and establish such a source.

The Journey

After more than a decade of 3K-based karate training, participating in rule-bound tournaments, and searching unsuccessfully for more than just the physical aspect of the fighting arts, one of my tournament coaches, Wally Slocki, recommended that I meet Richard Kim, Hanshi of the Dai Nippon Butokukai. In October of 1977, Wally arranged for Don Warrener to invite me to attend a seminar he was sponsoring with Kim Hanshi in Hamilton, Ontario (Canada). After attending the seminar, and enjoying a lengthy discussion about obligation and responsibility, Kim invited me to become one of his students. Not without its own set of problems, learning under the Master changed the way I would embrace the fighting arts, set me upon a new and challenging journey, and literally change my life.

Kim advocated that, *As actual fighting was not bound by rules, one's training should not be limited by style.* In the strictest sense of the word the Master viewed styles as incomplete, limiting, and counterproductive. Using an abstract Zen-based formula of Eastern philosophy and instinctive action, the Master encouraged thinking outside the box, the learning of principles and the application of concepts rather than dogma and cognitive response. Most importantly, he taught that one's true adversary lay within and that mastering "The Way" required a synergy between the physical, mental, and spiritual. A classical teacher frequently referred to as the Harvard Professor of the fighting arts, to this end Richard Kim inspired me to embrace *Bunburyodo*—academic study in support of physical training [文武両道]—in order to achieve my desired outcomes.

Researching my first book, *Classical Kata of Okinawan Karate*, the Master encouraged me to read E.J. Harrison, Nagamine Shoshin, Nakamoto Masahiro, Nakaya Takao, George Mattson, Bruce Haines, C.W. Nicol, Ratti and Westbrook, R.W. Smith and Donn F. Draeger. During my studies I became particularly interested in Draeger's work. Like Kim, I found Draeger a practical advocate of the *Pen and Sword* (i.e., *Bunburyodo*). Through his work I learned of his organization, the International Hoplology Society (IHS), its many periodicals and publications and about Sir Richard Burton, the chosen patriarch of the IHS. This valuable experience inspired me to look beyond the obvious and into the culture, language, and ethos of the fighting arts to discover what forces affected its evolution. That new door of learning led me to the Japan Martial Arts Society (JMAS).

Although JMAS principally attracted Aikido and Koryu-based enthusiasts, as a karateka I was not discouraged from taking out a membership in the mid-1980s. While JMAS was another great source of learning it did not cater much to the Okinawan fighting arts. Yet, in its absence I was able to learn something quite unexpectedly by turning my attention to swordsmanship and Japan's old fighting arts. Just about the time JMAS fell quietly dormant from a lack of interest, in 1991 the annual seminars of martial arts culture began to grow in popularity, especially for *we foreigners* residing in Japan.

Sponsored by the Nippon Budokan Foundation and hosted by Japan's Budo University in Chiba, the International Seminars of Budo Culture project was launched in 1989. Developed to improve one's understanding of the historical, philosophical, and scientific aspects of Budo, the annual seminars attracted foreigners from both in and out of Japan. This wonderful forum not only provided the opportunity to deepen one's understanding of all aspects of the fighting arts in general, it also focused on traditional Japanese culture, and offered fabulous networking opportunities from which many new friendships came.

The Society

Collectively, these events, and a growing desire for some kind of separate *Kenkyukai* (study group) through which to specifically study the original fighting arts of Okinawa's old Ryukyu Kingdom, compelled me to consider taking the lead by establishing just such a group. Mentoring and guiding others was important to me not just because it played such an important role in my own progression, but because I also saw it as a bridge-building opportunity. In 1989, with more than ample encouragement, and the support of both my Okinawan teacher, Kinjo Hiroshi—fourth generation grandmaster of the Okinawan fighting arts, noted author and historian—and wife Yuriko, I established the Ryukyu Karate Kokusai Kenkyu Kai (International Ryukyu Karate Research Society, IRKRS).

Responsible for the translation and publication of some valuable historical documents—Matsumura's 1882 *Seven Precepts of Bu*, and his 1885 *Zaiyunomei*; Itosu's 1908 *Ten Lessons*; Miyagi Chojun's 1934 *Outline of Karatedo*; the minutes of the famous 1936 *Meeting of the Okinawan Masters*; Motobu Choki's *Watashi no Karate-jutsu*, Taira Shinken's 1964 *Encyclopedia of Kobudo*; Funakoshi Gichin's early (1914 thru 1934) writings, and Nagamine Shoshin's *Biographies of Karate & Tegumi Masters*—the Society developed a reputation as a reliable and credible source of learning. With no other Japan-based non-political study group reaching out to a foreign karate-based audience at the time, the IRKRS was able to attract an international membership.

Unexpected Opportunity

Amidst our strongest supporters during the early 1990s was John Halpin. A practitioner of Traditional Chinese Medicine (TCM), the president of the Australian Karate Federation, and an executive committee member of the WKF, John was a forward thinker who had closely followed my work, and hosted me twice in his country, where I lectured on the Bubishi and taught application-based seminars. Seeking to establish the country's first under-graduate accreditation program in the fighting arts, Mr. Halpin made an offer "I couldn't refuse." Chronologically speaking, the idea of using an early nineteenth century text as the principal source from which to deliver the core curriculum of a late twentieth century undergraduate program may have seemed anachronistic, but it was my opinion its wealth and richness could very well start a renaissance resurrecting the splendor of the old-ways.

In 1995 my family and I migrated to Australia where I succeeded in developing the first undergraduate program of its kind using the Bubishi and related materials. Hosted by the Australian College of Natural Medicine, the country's leading institute of TCM, the original idea was to introduce the two-year program at its principal campus in Brisbane and later throughout its branches in Melbourne, Perth, and the Gold Coast. While the pilot program did set a precedence, and attract both domestic and overseas students for more than five years, the college ultimately brought it to an end, citing "challenges in its profit margin"(!). Obviously, such a concept was ahead of its time and not anywhere near as profitable as the more trendy gladiatorial-style disciplines, then reaching the apex of international popularity.

Yet, to say that the Bubishi provides something about the fighting arts that is simply not available elsewhere would be to grossly understate its value. In spite of Australia's turn-of-the-century martial arts industry not being ready to support an academic-based program of this nature, I remain hopeful that it may serve as something more than just a source referencing the old fighting arts. An age-old tradition, the Bubishi remains a classic in the annals of the fighting arts and hopefully the republication of this work might serve to inspire a new generation to reconsider its application. I would be pleased to learn that this work opens as many doors of learning for you as it has for me.

Conclusion

This small but powerful document on the fighting arts provides a window through which the reader is better able to perceive the cultural landscape and social mindset of those people who shaped its practice. One mistake many make when trying to grasp the historical and technical ambiguities of the early art of karate, is to depend too much upon contemporary assumption. The truth is, how we "do it" today is not how it we did it originally. One's inability to understand such a thing will most definitely condemn them to remain forever in the dark. Einstein once said, *You cannot solve the problem with the same kind of thinking that created it.* Knowing something about the culture and local thinking of the time and place in which karate unfolded as a practice provides a huge advantage to those interested in understanding what forces affected its growth and direction. Moreover, delving into the evolution of this wonderful tradition allows us to learn more about the interesting personalities who shaped its practice. In doing so, a message of more important proportions unfolds. By studying the history and philosophy of the fighting arts, and by vigorously embracing its austere physical practice we not only honor the heritage passed on by its pioneers, we form a link with the past and help keep alive its culture and spirit. What could possibly improve our overall understanding of this art more than by walking in the footsteps of those people most responsible for pioneering it? Great people should never be forgotten, if only to remind us of the potential latent in ourselves. By studying the evolution of this tradition it becomes evident that many of its pioneers established a symbiosis with it, so that their lives became as much a product of the art as was the art a product of their lives.

With learning the art comes a responsibility to keep this knowledge alive, a responsibility that extends beyond karate and into society as a whole. Pioneers maintained that karate conditions the body, cultivates the mind, and nurtures the spirit. However, an even more important message reveals that the source of human weakness lies within, and it is there where all of our battles must be first fought and won before this art can ever improve the quality of our daily lives. In the provocative words of Krishnamurti, *All of us are working together in the spirit of real co-operation in which there is no single authority: it is our interest in the teachings which brings us together and helps us to work in harmony.* I am absolutely certain that this message is far more in line with the spirit and aims of the pioneers of karate than it is with today's commercial-based propaganda and conceit associated with one's "style" being the "THE ONE & ONLY CORRECT WAY!"

In 1995 I wrote, *The Bubishi is like reading a translation of Musashi's* Go Rin No Sho (Book of Five Rings) *or Sun Zi's* Art of War; *the more it's read, the more one gets from it.* More than a decade later, I am pleased to say that this wonderful old work continues to provide and inspire as much now as it did then. Always the constant learner and never one to rest on "knowing enough," this latest work is a better reflection of my current thinking. If nothing else, I sincerely hope that the Bubishi makes you realize that by going outside your art you're really going deeper inside it. I wonder what there is to discover when we're able to finally let go of those pre-conceived notions that style-based indoctrination has forced upon us?

What's New in the Revised Edition?

In addition to this preface to the revised edition, you will find thought-provoking words from several colleagues of mine who I invited to comment on the Bubishi. I am certain their remarks will provide interesting food for thought and help open a few new doors of consideration. I am including some of the most reproducible Chinese script from the original Mabuni Bubishi, wherever possible, several photographs of Bubishi-related research sources, the only known image of Itosu Ankoh in existence—discovered in 2007 by my teacher, Kinjo Hiroshi, and Itosu's "Ten lesson," written in October 1908. I have also made a handful of grammatical corrections that were missed in the original edition.

Appreciation

I need to thank my friends and colleagues, Roland Haberzetser, Joe Swift, Harry Cook, and Victor Smith, for taking the time to support this revised edition with their important comments. These gentlemen are noted experts in the fighting arts, along with the first three also being authors of important publications. Thanks to Bruce Miller, Rand Cardwell, and Hokama Tetsuhiro for their additional commentary. I am also most grateful to my American-based attorney, Mr. Jim Goss, who was instrumental in making this revision happen. As I bring the introduction of the revision to an end I am reminded of just how much time and sacrifice went into this labor-of-love and I hope it reflects favorably upon everyone.

Patrick McCarthy
Brisbane

The only known photo of Itosu Ankoh. He is seated in the second row,
second from the left, in this 1910 photograph taken at
Okinawa's First Prefectural Middle School.

Patrick McCarthy and Hokama Tetsuhiro visiting the daughter of Yabu Kentsu.

by Hokama Tetsuhiro
PhD, Hanshi, 10ᵗʰ Dan, Goju-ryu Okinawa, Japan

It is known to martial artists across the world that the Bubishi is an extremely important book for all who study the fighting traditions (Karate, Toudi, Kobujutsu). If there is anything else to be added to this understanding, it is that the Bubishi was, for the people alive during the time it was written, a book that contained the deepest secrets of both medical and martial arts.

The reason this can be said is that the contents of the Bubishi consist of many facets, including medicines, resuscitation techniques, energy flow meridians, acupuncture, vital points, and much more. Regarding the empty-hand martial arts techniques, the Bubishi details how to use methods of pliability when attacked by someone utilizing external physical strength, in both written form and through specific illustrations. Also included are explanations of strategies such as Sen no Sen and Go no Sen, which are important even before the physical portion of a violent confrontation even begins. In other words, the contents of the Bubishi are very practical from a martial arts point of view.

The longer one studies Karate-jutsu, the more important a martial arts text the Bubishi should become. In this regard, it is rightly considered the "Bible of Karate."

By studying the Bubishi and learning to read between the lines, I also believe that the practitioner will come to the realization that, generally speaking, Karate-jutsu uses attacks to the trunk of the body; Kyusho-jutsu utilizes attacks to the nerve centers; and Kobujutsu techniques are aimed at the nearest part of the opponent to the defender, such as the forward hand.

Hand techniques, leg-based grappling techniques and the use of the hips are all detailed. The fact that this tome represents the use of the hands, legs, hips, and Ki, along with 45 degree angles of impact and circular movement to defeat an opponent, shows that the Bubishi indeed does disclose ancient secrets that are just as important today as they were when the Bubishi was first penned.

by Roland Habersetzer
Hanshi, Soke Tengu-no-michi (Budo Kenkyukai–Tengu Gakuin),
www.tengu.fr Chemnitz, France

I think it is rather presumptuous to believe that mere contemporary assumption is the key to deciphering the ancient knowledge left to us by the pioneers of books such as the Bubishi. By studying the cultural landscape and social mindset of nineteenth century Fujian-China and Okinawa-Japan, along with cross-comparative analyses of traditional Fujian-based *quanfa* and classical Okinawan-Japanese fighting arts, does it then become possible to penetrate more deeply the historical and technical ambiguities of this important writing. In doing so, not only are we linking the past to the present, we are also keeping alive an important piece of cultural heritage while honoring the spirit of those responsible for passing it on.

In spite of its rather innocuous fighting diagrams, prescribed application practices, philosophical lessons and TCM-based remedies, this invaluable hand-drawn record is a classic example of old-school Chinese learning linking all traditional Karate styles to an identifiable source. Based predominately upon Yongchun Crane and Monk Fist Boxing, two principal southern *quanfa* styles, this knowledge gradually found its way from Fujian to Okinawa and ultimately to the mainland of Japan through an underground network of dedicated enthusiasts, some of whom we are familiar with. Thanks only to such conscientious effort has this illustrated manuscript been preserved and is now available to anyone who chooses to study the art of the empty-hand. The Bubishi may not be the definitive text of the empty-handed fighting arts but it undisputedly represents the source from which karate comes.

Patrick McCarthy is an authority on the Bubishi and his organization, The International Ryukyu Karate Research Society, is known throughout the world by serious researchers concerned with the history, evolution and application of authentic Okinawan fighting arts. Simply put, his unique experience, long-standing studies, and published work make him an authority in this field. Having researched and studied this ancient manual myself for many years, it was my teacher, Otsuka Tadahiko, Karatedo Hanshi, founder of Gojukensha, and lineage-based inheritor of this manual, who asked me to publish my French translation of his Bubishi in 1995. It was Otsuka Hanshi who brought McCarthy *Sensei* and I together prior to the publication of my work. I was pleased to learn that both he and I had been influenced in similar ways. The Bubishi had provided a clearer path to enlightenment and it was evident we were both moving in the same direction.

That said, I believe such a journey is not an easy task these days especially in a tradition so distorted by sport, commercial exploitation, and misunderstanding. Such things reflect poorly upon the technical and holistic richness of these fighting arts. I am, however, confident that Mr. McCarthy's revised publication of the Bubishi is timely and will certainly help the many passionate followers of traditional martial arts culture.

I applaud Mr. McCarthy's continued efforts and hope that it receives the attention it deserves.

by Harry Cook
Sunderland, England

When Robert W. Smith and Donn F. Draeger wrote their iconic work *Asian Fighting Arts* in 1970 they observed that Chinese boxing literature "is uneven, full of gaps, and smothered in places by ambiguities." While that is true of Chinese methods of fighting, it is even more so when applied to the combat arts of Okinawa. The tradition of secrecy meant that little was written down by Okinawan masters, and all we really have before the first karate books written in the 1920s are brief collections of aphorisms written by famous teachers, such as Matsumura and Itosu.

While the various codes and maxims are very valuable in helping us to understand the morals and values of Okinawan karate, they do not help us to grasp the technical aspects of the various forms of attack and defense or the tactics used by traditional Okinawan karateka. The various traditional kata transmitted by the schools of Okinawan karate can be a record of how techniques were performed, but when we try to grasp the applications or sense of the kata, problems of interpretation can arise.

Fortunately a number of Okinawan masters preserved and transmitted the Bubishi, a collection of articles on southern Chinese boxing systems, principally from Fukien, which help us immensely in gaining a realistic understanding of the techniques and rationale of traditional Okinawan karate. This work is the only known manual of what we might loosely call classical Okinawan karate and as such it is a unique window into the past. Traditionally it was hand copied by senior practitioners from versions owned by their own teachers and was highly valued by Okinawan karate masters; both Gichin Funakoshi and Kenwa Mabuni included sections of the Bubishi in their works and the Japanese master of Goju Ryu *Gogen Yamaguchi* wrote that the Bubishi "is the author's treasured book."

While the Bubishi is unique in Okinawan martial arts, in the wider context it is very similar to many hand-written martial arts manuals produced by Chinese martial arts teachers. The earliest hand-written Chinese works date from the beginning of the eighteenth century, although there are earlier wood block-printed military manuals such as general Chi Chi Kuang's *Chi Hsiao Hsin Shu* (1584). Although many of these works were considered to be secret, by the end of the nineteenth century printed versions were available, a process which gained momentum in the early years of the twentieth century, when books illustrated with photographs instead of drawings began to appear.

Information very similar to that found in the Bubishi can be found in Chin I Ming's *Wu Tang Ch'uan Shu Mi Chueh* (Secrets of Wu Tang Boxing, 1928) especially with reference to the vital points. In 1929 Li Tsai Luan wrote *Fukien Hou Ch'uan Mi Yao* (Secrets of Fukien Crane Boxing), which uses terminology very similar to expressions found in the Bubishi. The techniques and self-defense applications are very similar to the 48 self-defense techniques shown in the Bubishi. As more and more southern Chinese boxing manuals become available, I believe the place of the Bubishi in the wider context of the history of the spread of Chinese methods to Okinawa and other parts of Southeast Asia will become clearer.

In the same way that the deciphering of the Rosetta Stone opened up the world of Egyptology, grasping the ideas and concepts preserved in the Bubishi can open the doors of Okinawan karate. Close study of the 48 self-defense techniques will prove to be of great assistance to the reader who is trying to uncover the applications of the kata, and the principles that underpin the applications. Even a cursory analysis of the winning techniques shows that 39% are strikes or grabs with the hands, 29% are throws or escapes, and 17% are locks or immobilizations. This in turn points to the fact that the methods shown are derived from a close range system based on hand techniques; only 4% of the winning techniques feature kicking methods.

In an article I wrote many years ago I referred to the Bubishi as the "secret treasure" of Okinawan karate. Well it is a secret no longer.

Patrick McCarthy's masterful translation of the text makes it fully accessible to anyone genuinely interested in understanding the history and background of traditional Okinawan karate, and the inclusion of related Chinese material defines the background and context from which the Bubishi developed. I congratulate Mr. McCarthy for producing this translation and commentary of the Bubishi, which I believe will be a great help to karateka for many years to come.

by Victor Smith
Derry, NH

In your hands lies a contemporary translation of the Bubishi by Patrick McCarthy. Just a short 100 years ago, when even the wildest speculation could barely imagine karate becoming public, let alone being exported past the tiny shores of Okinawa, who would have ever considered their copy of the Bubishi becoming a public commodity sold at local bookshops?

The karate of that era was passed from instructor to student through oral and physical transmission. There were no karate texts and even the unique terminology used by instructors made it difficult for outsiders to understand the inner-workings of what was being imparted. Entrusted to senior instructors, to what extent the role of the Bubishi actually played remains obscure.

In 1922, Funakoshi Gichin let the cat out of the bag when he included several articles from the Bubishi in his first publication, *Ryukyu Kenpo Karate-jutsu*. Again, in 1925 with his book, *Karate-jutsu*, and *Karatedo Kyohan*, in 1934, Funakoshi continued to highlight the importance the Bubishi by republishing several of its articles. So, too, did Mabuni Kenwa see fit to publish Bubishi-related material in his 1934 book, *Seipai No Kata*. As Karate found its way to the four corners of the world, the content of these unique publications became sought after. So it was that the Bubishi first came to be known beyond the tiny shores of Okinawa.

When, why, and who actually composed the Bubishi remains unknown. However, the application of Occam's Razor is one approach that might offer us the simplest explanation. It seems conceivable that the 32 articles found within the covers of this hand-written document, could simply be the private notes of a Chinese student of the fighting arts. After all, it contains information about the use of medicinal herbs, some history of crane-based *quanfa*, a description of vital point striking timed to the hour, healing techniques to counter all of those vital point strikes, and a description of prescribed responses in defense of various attack scenarios, etc.

Written in an older style Chinese script, it must have been a difficult task to translate without having access to the original writer or direct lineage-based students to help decipher code-like phrases. Without accompanying commentary or side notes on how the Bubishi articles were meant to be used, I am left wondering if the document remained on a shelf where it may have never become such a vital key in the research of the fighting arts.

Making this information widely available to the general public today has been a very long and difficult journey. Hokama Tetsuhiro, Tokashiki Iken, and Otsuka Tadahiko represent the three principal sources from which various Japanese analyses and commentaries have been rendered. Tokitsu Kenji and Roland Habersetzer are responsible for different works in French, with the latter also publishing his comprehensive work in German. Of course, thanks to the independent efforts of researchers Ken Penland and Patrick McCarthy, their separate interpretations of the Bubishi have been widely distributed throughout the English-speaking world. Mr. McCarthy's work has also been translated into several other languages including Italian, Spanish, Czech, and Russian, making the rare document even more widely known.

Along with these several translations we get a mixed blessing of sorts as the various works present the Bubishi material differently. As I compared the different translations several questions become evident:

1. The separate English translations produced by Patrick McCarthy and Ken Penland seem to be the only ones that present the complete Bubishi text. The French and Japanese translations appear to focus only on the fighting sections of the work.

2. Comparing the translations it often seems as if they are entirely different works altogether.

   a. The text contains different material and in different order.

   b. The 48 two-person drawings are vastly different from that produced in Mabuni Kenwa's 1934 publication, *Seipai no Kenkyu*. The drawings that appear in Ken Penland's work are the closest to Mabuni's version, but are less detailed. The remaining drawings are clearly from different Bubishi texts or are different because of the efforts of the individual preparing them. By different I mean that the anatomical structures being attacked are not the same. This causes some confusion with regards to the original intention of the attack being portrayed.

3. The translations of the medical-related arts is also very different with the two translations, raising questions about how similar or different the original texts used for the translation are, or even the differences between the research methods employed by the authors.

4. Both the McCarthy and Penland translations contain additional

material not in the original Bubishi.

    a. The McCarthy text contains a great amount of historical information as well as additional material on the Chinese meridians and Chi.

    b. The Penland text contains additional material on the Chinese meridians and Chi.

    c. While the actual Bubishi text discusses vital point striking, including the times to strike on a 24-hour cycle, there was no direct material on the meridians in the text.

5. The Habersetzer translation contains an extensive commentary on how he interprets the 48 two-person self-defense techniques. He also presents the Happoren Kata.

6. The Otsuka work I observed compares the 48 two-person drawings with another earlier Chinese work.

For me, differing translations, the lack of original commentary on its actual role in the development of the Okinawan arts, and questions about which were the original drawings, present a conflicting picture. Such mysteries are almost never-ending. Our challenge seems to be as great as those facing the Okinawan instructors who study this work; do we leave it on the shelf because it's too difficult to understand, or do we make an effort to discover its true value.

Tradition tells us that Chinese documents like the Bubishi were handwritten by brush and reproduced in two ways. The most common way was through senior students entrusted to copy the original for themselves. The other way was by engaging a professional copyist to perform the task. I suppose this is the likely source from which some of variations previously mentioned come. The translator also plays a role in this passage of information; it hardly seems possible to translate from one language into another without one's own experience bearing some influence upon the final version of any work.

From the various translations I am familiar with I believe that McCarthy's work best represents the entire Bubishi. He also did a wonderful job in presenting the entire Okinawan context that really helps those of us seeking to better understand the cultural landscape in which it was produced. But what does this picture give us except challenges?

As if looking back through a time portal the Bubishi reveals an earlier fighting art, which placed as much emphasis upon healing as it did developing defensive and destructive capabilities. Did it actually convey the secrets of defending against or applying *kyusho-jutsu,* and which herbal remedies best cured its damage? In turn, do we interpret this text as a call to study the healing arts as part of our own karate?

Do we try and find the self-defense applications within kata and techniques? Do we seek out the older Chinese methods, as some of these researchers have done? Ernest Rothrock, a specialist in Eagle Claw *quanfa* with more than forty years experience, clearly demonstrates that Bubishi-like techniques are, in fact, core techniques in many Chinese Arts. Does this knowledge then enhance our studies, or should we seek out new information?

In addition to borrowing liberally from Bubishi-based philosophical and tactical insights for his early publications, Funakoshi Gichin also reproduced a word-for-word account of no fewer than three articles from this old document; *Eight Important Phrases, The Treatise on Ancient Law of Great Strength,* and *Methods of Escape.* Is this yet another lesson of what we should be doing? The Bubishi material on tactical doctrine is of considerable value and goes far beyond the 48 two-person prescribed self-defense drawings.

It is very possible the Bubishi and its focus on tactical strategy also influenced Okinawan karate pioneer Kyan Chotoku. Published in Miki Nisaburo and Mutsu Mizuho's 1930 book entitled, *Kempo Gaisetsu,* Kyan's advice on the fighting arts rings a bell of Bubishi familiarity. Even more so, is the collection of sayings used by Okinawan fighting arts legend, Motobu Choki, which appear with the English presentation of his book *My Art of Karate.*

While much of Okinawa's karate history remains undocumented, the tactical commentary of these pioneers reveals important information about basic training in the fighting arts of that era. Most importantly, the influence of the Bubishi is clearly obvious through their comments.

Still another example I identified was through the work of the late karate expert, Sherman Harrill of Carson City, Iowa. Harrill studied the Isshin Ryu Karate of Shimabuku Tatsuo for more than forty years of his life, and spent considerable time focusing on unravelling the mysteries of kata through using the Bubishi. His effort resulted in deepening and broadening our understanding of the tactical strategies used in *Isshin Ryu.*

I have only briefly touched on the questions and opportunity the Bubishi presents to us. It's easiest to place it on your bookshelf to show others you posses a copy. It's much more work, however, to dig in, find your own values, participate in the larger discussions and make its existence add texture and depth to your own studies. I hope you will not simply place it on your shelf.

I specifically want to thank Mr. McCarthy for his great efforts to make this work available for our continued studies. The martial arts world has gained considerable resources from his hard work.

⌒◞◟◞◟◞⌒

by Joe Swift
Tokyo, Japan

It is safe to say that there are very few practitioners of the classical Okinawan self-defense traditions that have never at least heard of the Bubishi, even outside of Japan and Okinawa. Private studies and smaller-scale publications notwithstanding, this is due in large part to the efforts of four individuals: Otsuka Tadahiko of Japan; Tokashiki Iken of Okinawa; Roland Habersetzer of France; and the author of the presentation before you, Patrick McCarthy, who was the first to bring the existence of the Bubishi to the attention of the English-speaking karate community. Their analyses and translations of this once obscure document have allowed an entire generation of karate enthusiasts throughout the world reevaluate their understanding of the art.

Its sheer rarity shrouded the document, much like the art of karate itself, in a veil of mystery. Detailing the history, philosophy, and application of the Fujian-based Chinese martial arts that directly influenced the development of Okinawan karate, the Bubishi remains an indispensable tome for the serious karate enthusiast.

Oral tradition tells us that in Okinawa, the *most trusted disciple(s) of the old masters who were in possession of it painstakingly copied the Bubishi by hand*. Of course, one of the reasons for this was the lack of modern photocopying technology, but the act of carefully copying the passages, illustrations, and diagrams by hand brings a deeply personal attachment to the lessons contained therein.

At the time of writing, I am in the process of creating my own handwritten copy of the Bubishi, based on several sources. From this experience, I can personally attest to a somewhat surreal connection to the pioneers who have gone before that comes from throwing oneself selflessly into such a project.

In the decade and a half that I have been residing in Japan, I have had the opportunity to come into contact with senior authorities in the karate world and read the original writings of the early pioneers, all of which have served to greatly enhance my understanding of the Okinawan martial arts. However, time and again, I find myself returning to the wisdom contained in the pages of the Bubishi for personal insight and inspiration.

Living in Japan for this long has also instilled in me an appreciation for the old maxims: *Bunbu Ryodo* (a maxim representing the twin paths of the sword and the pen) and *Onko Chishin* (a saying representing the appreciation of the old in order to understand the new). In an era of no-holds-barred competitions, MMA, and blatant commercialism, the timeless teachings contained in the Bubishi can offer the modern practitioner some sanctuary in the inward journey, the battle with the

Self that the study of traditional martial arts represents.

Or, in the words of Patrick McCarthy: *The path not paved by physical conditioning, moral philosophy and methodical introspection leads nowhere.*

When I heard that Tuttle was planning on publishing a revision of McCarthy *Sensei*'s Bubishi, I was excited. Excited at the prospect that at least one person who has not read this immensely important work may come into contact with this time capsule of martial wisdom. Excited that perhaps it will encourage at least one person who has already read it to reread it, and gain an even deeper insight into the depths of the wonderful tradition of karate-do.

It is my sincere belief that this revised edition of McCarthy *Sensei*'s groundbreaking work will help us all move another step closer to understanding that which the ancient masters had also pursued.

by Li Yiduan
Deputy Secretary General, All-China Athletic Federation,
Fuzhou Branch Vice Chairman, Fuzhou Martial Arts Association

With a breadth of unbelievable proportions and a history of unfathomable depth, the cultural heritage of China had for centuries profoundly influenced those societies with which it once traded. Among those cultures most affected by the "Middle Kingdom" was the Ryukyu archipelago, and in particular, the people of Okinawa.

Based upon the remnants of an ancient grappling discipline cultivated in Okinawa during the time of Tametomo (1139–70), and combined with the principles of Chinese *gongfu,* which had been continuously introduced to the Ryukyu archipelago from before recorded history, a number of indigenous self-defense methods gradually developed. Affected by the foreign cultures it once traded with, political reformation, and military subjugation, Okinawa's self-defense disciplines continued to be fostered in an iron-clad ritual of secrecy up to and during the Meiji era (1868–1912).

With the period of secrecy over, after Japan made the transition from feudalism into democracy, Okinawa's mainstream self-defense traditions were brought together so that they could be modernized and publicly introduced into the school system. As a result, Ryukyu *kempo toudi-jutsu* (as the Chinese and Okinawan self-defense traditions came to be called before the advent of modern karate-do) took on both new characteristics and direction.

Molded by inflexible social ideologies and radically changed for group instruction and the competitive phenomenon in the school system, the original history, philosophy, and application of "karate-do" became overshadowed by commercial exploitation, which resulted in the myriad of eclectic interpretations we find today.

In recognizing the immense value of tracing historical lineages and establishing contact with original sources, foreign enthusiasts of karate-do from all over the world are now appearing in Fuzhou to research, study, and compare their art forms. Gaining new insights while discovering a deeper understanding of Okinawa's civil fighting traditions, karate-do's history, philosophy, and applications are only now being unraveled.

One such man who made the distant journey in order to bridge the gap of obscurity is Mr. Patrick McCarthy. Although not the first, and surely not the last, his intense study and literary contributions are testimony to his dedication toward gaining the deepest understanding of karate-do and its non-utilitarian value. Hopefully, like those who have come before him, Mr. McCarthy's research will serve to bring students closer to finding that which is not always seen by the naked eye. In doing so, enthusiasts may well come to gain more than just a physical understanding of the discipline and its heritage.

Having hosted him in Fuzhou and traveled with him to Shanghai and the legendary Shaolin Temple, I have known Mr. McCarthy for many years and I can say without reservation that it is a pleasure to write this letter of introduction for his edition. The Bubishi is an important cultural discovery and one that highlights the significance of Fuzhou's native fighting traditions. I sincerely hope that others may feel equally impelled to make similar journeys to experience the wonderful cultural heritage that has been preserved in the ancient Chinese fighting traditions.

by Richard Kim
Hanshi, 9th Dan

From an early age, Patrick McCarthy has been a devout student of karate and *kobudo*. Maturing under my direction, he acquired a creative approach to learning, and came to realize the importance of balancing his physical training with metaphysical exploration.

Moreover, through the precepts of karate-do, Mr. McCarthy has learned that empirical research and introspection are absolute necessities for one to discover that which lies beyond the immediate results of physical training.

Formerly one of Canada's most prominent karate teachers, Patrick McCarthy is second to none physically, which made him unparalleled in his reign as a competitive champion. Relocating to Japan where he became my personal representative, Patrick McCarthy's star is now shining on a new horizon. Of all the thousands of students that I have had over the years, Patrick McCarthy is by far the most talented.

The extensive research that he has undertaken over the years while studying the doctrines and history of karate-do makes him uniquely qualified to present this translation. Whatever he does, he does exceedingly well, and this book is a testament to his dedication and understanding of karate-do.

I highly recommend this translation of the Bubishi and hope that it will benefit those who seek the true essence of karate-do.

by Nagamine Shoshin
Hanshi, 10th Dan World Shorin-ryu Karate-do Federation

Brought to Okinawa from Fuzhou long ago, the Bubishi is a secret Chinese book about *kempo (quanfa).* Describing the intricacies of Shaolin Temple Monk Fist Boxing and the principles of Fujian White Crane *gongfu,* the Bubishi is a historically important document whose secrets, until only just recently, have remained closely guarded by karate-do masters in Okinawa.

In addition to the copious amount of intriguing information contained within the pages of this profound document, the Bubishi also reveals the original application of orthodox *kata* and the moral precepts that govern the behavior of those who understand these secrets. Disclosing the principles of *tuidi* and *kyusho-jutsu* (art of attacking vulnerable points on the human body), the reader will come to understand that which has been kept secret for generations.

The Bubishi must be considered mandatory reading for all serious enthusiasts of true karate-do and is therefore an essential addition to one's personal library, a work to be deeply studied by both teacher and student alike. In so doing, the torch of true karate-do will continue to burn long into the future, lighting the arduous path upon which others may follow.

Responsible for the very first English translation of this remarkable text is a Canadian named Patrick McCarthy. A representative of the Kyoto Butokukai, Mr. McCarthy is one of the very few foreign experts of martial arts teaching karate-do here in Japan. A longtime resident of Japan and a regular visitor to Okinawa, Mr. McCarthy's karate research and literary contributions are known worldwide. Having first met him during the mid-1980s, I have come to know Mr. McCarthy as both a friendly and responsible person dedicated to the very principles upon which orthodox karate-do rests.

It was a pleasure to have been of some assistance to Mr. McCarthy during his lengthy research and meticulous analysis of the Bubishi, and I can think of no one better suited to introduce this important work to the Western world.

by Otsuka Tadahiko
Hanshi,
9th Dan Gojukensha Karate-do Renmei

Patrick McCarthy with Otsuka
Tadahiko in his home.

Thanks to my collaborations with Yang Mingshi *Shifu,* Shimizu Mie *Sensei,* and Tokashiki Iken *Sensei,* I was able to research and publish, in Japanese, the Bubishi, a document that has been handed down from master to disciple in Okinawa for generations.

Now, after his own extensive research, Patrick McCarthy has translated the Bubishi into English. Thanks to his efforts, one of karate's most important historical documents is now available to people in English. In this edition, Mr. McCarthy introduces some very provocative historical information, and has also taken the time to fully translate those articles pertaining to herbal remedies, a feat that I was unable to accomplish myself. I am delighted that this knowledge is being introduced, as it is of enormous value.

Originally brushed in classical Chinese, using the Fujian dialect, this document was compiled more than two centuries ago. Passed down from master to disciple, the tradition of copying it by hand has, unfortunately, resulted in grammatical inaccuracies, making its analysis all the more burdensome. As such, the impact of this knowledge will vary depending entirely upon how it is assimilated.

I know exactly how much research went into making this translation possible, and I deeply respect Mr. McCarthy's dedication. I sincerely hope that many people will read and benefit from this publication.

Patrick McCarthy with Konishi Takehiro
in his home.

by Konishi Takehiro
Hanshi,
9th Dan Shindo Jinen-ryu Japan
Karate-do Ryobukai

My father, Konishi Yasuhiro, was the only man to have ever learned from Motobu Choki, Funakoshi Gichin, Mabuni Kenwa, and Miyagi Chojun, the Okinawan masters who first pioneered karate on Japan's mainland during the 1920s and 1930s. He also enjoyed a close friendship with these men and was fortunate enough to receive a number of their original writings.

Lying dormant in my library, many of these original works have remained untouched for more than a half century. However, Mr. Patrick McCarthy, a *Kyoshi* of karate-do from the Dai Nippon Butokukai and a leading martial historian with impeccable credentials, has visited my home on many occasions to translate, analyze, and publish the unknown works of these men.

While translating the 1934 *Outline of Karate-do,* a handwritten manuscript left to my father by Miyagi Chojun, Mr. McCarthy also spent considerable time cross-referencing his analysis of the Fujian Bubishi with the original Okinawan version that was given to my father more than fifty years ago by Mabuni Kenwa, who had himself copied it directly from Itosu Anko's version.

I was delighted to have been able to be of some assistance to Mr. McCarthy's lengthy research. I am deeply impressed by his character and commitment to those values upon which true karate-do rests. I know of no one else who has dedicated as much time and effort to studying the Bubishi as Patrick McCarthy and I hope that his thorough analysis and remark-

Patrick McCarthy with
Konishi Takehiro in Tokyo.

able translation are met with equal enthusiasm. Regarded as the bible of karate-do, Mr. McCarthy's English translation of the Bubishi must be considered essential reading for every serious follower of karate-do.

by Kinjo Hiroshi
Hanshi,
9th Dan Zen Nihon Karate-do Rengokai

Patrick McCarthy with his master Kinjo Hiroshi in Hiratsuka, Japan.

The publication of the Bubishi by the Charles E. Tuttle Company is truly a milestone in the history of modern karate-do. Culminating years of meticulous research, this presentation by Mr. Patrick McCarthy, one of the art's foremost authorities, represents an immeasurable addition towards understanding the magnitude of karate-do.

Mr. McCarthy was the very first person to present an English translation of this once-secret text. Even today, among the most experienced of karate enthusiasts, the Bubishi and its priceless contents remain virtually unknown.

With Mr. McCarthy's hallmark research and publication of the Bubishi, Western enthusiasts of karate-do the world over will finally be able to evaluate the gravity of the Oriental self-defense phenomenon. Methodically guiding its readers through the essential, but all too often unknown, requirements of learning the genuine art form, this text must be considered mandatory reading by all enthusiasts of karate-do. The cultural heritage that this ancient text represents also serves as a unique bridge connecting Oriental thought to the Western mind.

Mr. Patrick McCarthy is one of the very few budo historians who have come to understand the true essence, history, and culture of karate-do. The groundbreaking research of this remarkable man has made him a trailblazer in the annals of modern karate-do. Like the *Kurofune* (black ships) that first introduced genuine Japanese culture to the outside world, so too is Patrick McCarthy the "Black Ship" of karate-do. I look forward to Mr. McCarthy's next publication, his further undertakings, and continued success.

by Hokama Tetsuhiro
PhD, Hanshi, 10th Dan International Karate-do Organization

As a colleague of Mr. Patrick McCarthy, I am delighted to be able to write this letter of congratulations for his splendid translation of the very perplexing and old document, the Bubishi.

There are many theories surrounding the origins of this mysterious but remarkable manual; however, all we can be really sure of is that the Bubishi is a document describing some unique fighting traditions of China and its associated principles. Consisting of thirty-two articles, the contents of the Bubishi are often quite difficult to understand. Until now there have been several people, including myself, who have conducted separate studies into various parts of the Bubishi but, because of its paradoxical nature, the analysis has remained incomplete.

While resolving the mysteries contained within the Bubishi, Mr. McCarthy has frequently visited both Okinawa and China. In addition to spending much time with me at the Okinawa Prefectural Karate-do Historical Material Museum, he vigorously researched a wide variety of plausible sources that brought us both into contact with many of the most respected authorities in karate-do and *kobudo*. Mr. McCarthy is well known in Okinawa, and all those who know him can tell you that his penchant for karate and *kobudo* is far beyond average. As a karateka, I am fascinated by Mr. McCarthy's physical prowess, scholarly pursuits, and friendly character. He is one of Japan's most senior-ranked foreign karate and *kobudo* teachers, and his extensive research has afforded him an international reputation. Mr. McCarthy's analysis of the Bubishi is by far his best work yet, and I hope that everyone will continue to support his ongoing efforts.

❧ Introduction ❧

The work before you is the product of over ten years' research and travel. The arduous journey of investigative research started in my former home in Canada and extended to the outlying islands of the Ryukyu archipelago and mainland Asia. It was a most rewarding venture that brought me in contact with many of karate-do's most eminent authorities, had me exploring the antiquarian book shops in Tokyo's Kanda and Jimbocho districts, allowed me to establish a first-name relationship with the staff at the National Diet library, and even had me listening to the illuminating gossip in Okinawan sake taverns. My exploration included pilgrimages to Taiwan, Shanghai, the legendary Shaolin Temple, and China's southern coastal city of Fuzhou.

It was my honor to introduce the original English translation of the Bubishi to the Western world in 1987. Three years later, in 1990, after considerably more research, although still incomplete, I was able to present an even more comprehensive rendering of this obscure document. This was followed by another printing in 1992, due in large part to a growing interest in what I was researching and revealing.

Since that time, the Bubishi has continued to spark international curiosity and caused many supporters of the orthodox Okinawan fighting traditions to reevaluate their understanding of karate-do. I believe that the Bubishi has become a source of encouragement to the many enthusiasts who otherwise would remain discouraged by the competitive phenomenon and the aberration of commercial exploitation in the art. Looking to get beyond ego-related distractions and transcend the immediate results of physical training, the penetrating wisdom of the Bubishi provides an illuminating alternative point of view as to what the true meaning of karate-do is.

Most importantly, however, the original Bubishi has prompted several other researchers to embark upon independent analyses of their own, some of which have resulted in the publication of complementary works. Providing the entire karate community with an even broader understanding of this profound document, their outstanding efforts are applauded, and their valuable input a welcome contribution. Notwithstanding, the Bubishi remains such a penetrating study that the depth of its wisdom has yet to be fully measured or completely understood. As such, it is my most sincere wish that this edition, the results of my latest research, might subsequently serve to bring the reader that much closer to comprehending the magnificent depth and meaning of this document.

Whereas in previous versions of the text I chose to present the articles in numerical order, I have decided to organize them by subject matter in this book. In this way I hope that the reader will be able to more easily study the various subjects presented.

Any errors that may appear in this translation are mine alone. As such, this translation must be seen as an exposition of my personal research, and in that light, it must still be recognized as a continuing work. I sincerely hope that you will be as fascinated with the Bubishi as I continue to be. The Bubishi is like reading a translation of Musashi's *Book of Five Rings* or Sun Zi's *Art of War*—the more it is read, the more one gets from it.

Patrick McCarthy

The Evolution of Modern Karate and the Bubishi

by Joe Swift
tokyo-mushinkan.com

Until recent years, the unabridged history of karate has been veiled in obscurity. However, a serious reevaluation of the history and anthropology of the Ryukyu Kingdom will reveal even to the most casual of history buffs the cultural landscape that had spawned karate.

Regardless of Okinawan nationalistic sentiments and political maneuvers in recent years, there are indisputable facts in the history and culture of Okinawa that obviously influenced the initial development of karate. One of these aspects would be to look at the clothing and weaponry of the early warriors of Ryukyu. For example, Figure 1 shows a procession of Ryukyuans on a diplomatic visit to Japan in 1701.

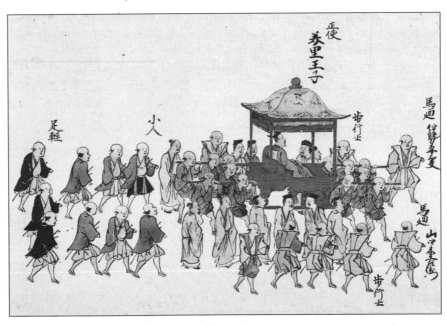

Figure 1

Figure 2

What does this illustration tell us about the Ryukyuan upper classes? Look at the clothing and the swords at their sides. This scroll shows us that the Ryukyuan warriors were dressed and armed much like the Samurai of mainland Japan. If this is true, then we can deduce that since they were armed with Japanese swords, then they would have likely been versed in the use of such blades. Such can be seen in something as simple as the basic stance used in both swordsmanship and the Te of Shuri (see Figure 2, swordsmanship stance and Figure 3, Funakoshi Gichin's front stance).

Figure 3

If this is true, it may then follow that the Chinese boxing forms that were introduced during the time of the Ryukyu Kingdom would have been seen through the eyes of Japanese swordsmanship and subsequently reinterpreted through such principles. This would explain part of the reason that the karate kata passed down mainly in and around the old castle district of Shuri, such as *Naifanchi* and *Kushanku*, do not look much like *gongfu* (see Figure 4, Motobu Choki—*Naifanchi* and Figure 5, Funakoshi Gichin—*Kushanku*). Due to space constraints we can-

Figure 4   Figure 5

not go into detail, so I would like to request that the readers merely ponder this as food for thought.

Fast forward to the Meiji Restoration, a series of events and reforms that restored practical Imperial rule to Japan by 1868. One of these reforms was the abolition of the Samurai class in Japan. This spelled the end of the era of the professional warrior. Military conscription was implemented and drew upon the farming, fishing and merchant populations, people who had never fought, or even run, in their entire lives. Western education, clothing, sport and military exercises replaced the ancient martial bio-mechanics of Japanese swordsmanship.

The Ryukyu Kingdom became Ryukyu Province and then Okinawa Prefecture in a process that can be considered a microcosm of what was happening across the entire nation, meaning that the same repercussions were felt in the former island kingdom. By the early 1900s, an old Okinawan Bushi named Itosu Anko spearheaded a campaign to teach karate in the public school system. Although this campaign was successful in preserving, in part, the ancient Kata, the students that he was teaching were not raised with the ancient warrior ethos and physical disciplines.

Around the same time, a young man named Higaonna Kanryo had traveled to China, where he studied Chinese boxing and which he later introduced back into Okinawa. Several years later, Uechi Kanbun followed in his footsteps. The Chinese-based martial arts that these stalwarts introduced were too late in the history of Okinawa to be completely Okinawanized through the processes described earlier, and retained more of their Fujian origins.

In fact, all one has to do is look at the basic stance of Higaonna's art to see that it is diametrically opposite of the footwork required to wield a Japanese sword (see Figure 6, Mabuni Kenwa's *Sanchin-dachi*). How-

Figure 6   Figure 7

ever, all was not lost to posterity, as we can see from the posture shown by Hanashiro Chomo as he kicks (see Figure 7) and Miyagi Chojun as he oversees *Kumite* training (see Figure 8). Astute readers will be able to see what is being portrayed right away.

The above is merely a snapshot of history, and does not consider the other sources of Chinese and Japanese martial arts influence on karate, such as the legendary shipwrecked Chinese sailors at Tomari, the descendants of the Chinese immigrants in Kume Village and the

Figure 8

military attaches of the *Sappushi*. However, it is from this more recent influx of Chinese martial arts, following the abolition of the warrior class, that comes the modern styles of Goju-ryu and Uechi-ryu. It is the former that was highly influenced by the book that lies in your hands now, the Bubishi.

It is safe to say that there are very few practitioners of the classical Okinawan self-defense traditions that have never at least heard of the Bubishi, even outside of Okinawa and Japan. Private studies and smaller-scale publications notwithstanding, this is due in large part to the efforts of four individuals: the late Otsuka Tadahiko of Tokyo; Tokashiki Iken of Okinawa; Roland Habersetzer of France; and the author of the publication before you, Patrick McCarthy, who was the first to bring the Bubishi to the attention of the English-speaking karate community. Their analyses and translations of this once-obscure tome have allowed entire generations of karate enthusiasts throughout the world to reevaluate their understanding of the art.

The history of the Bubishi itself is also unclear. It has been variously described as a secret crane boxing manual, a personal notebook or even an amalgamation of loosely-related articles that were compiled over a period of years or decades. Indeed, one researcher believes that there are suggestions found within the book itself that hints at a local, as opposed to Chinese, origin (Kinjo Akio, *Karate Den Shinroku*, 1999).

Be that as it may, the Bubishi details the history, philosophy and application of the Fujian-based Chinese martial arts that directly influenced the development of *Goju-ryu* and sister styles, such as *Toon-ryu* and *Shito-ryu*. To that end, the Bubishi remains an indispensable tome for the serious karate enthusiast.

In the twenty-plus years I have lived in Japan, I have mixed with senior authorities in the karate world and read the original writings of the early pioneers. These experiences have instilled in me an appreciation for the old maxims *Bunbu Ryodo* 文武両道 (a maxim representing the twin paths of the sword and the pen) and *Onko Chishin* 温故知新 (a saying representing the appreciation of the old in order to better understand the new). In an era of no-holds-barred competitions, MMA and blatant commercialism, the timeless teachings contained in the Bubishi can offer the modern practitioner some sanctuary on the inward journey, the battle with the Self that the study of traditional martial arts becomes once the physical techniques have been mastered.

Or, in the words of Patrick McCarthy: *The path not paved by physical conditioning, moral philosophy and methodical introspection leads nowhere.*

When McCarthy *Sensei* approached me to write a foreword for a new revision of his translation and commentary on the Bubishi, I was excited. Excited at the prospect that at least one person who has not read this immensely important work may come into contact with this time capsule of martial wisdom. Excited that perhaps it will encourage at least one more person who has already read it to reread it, and gain an even deeper insight into the wonderful tradition of karate-do.

The introduction of the Bubishi-based Chinese martial arts into Okinawa in the late 1800s and early 1900s were an important event in the revitalization of karate for a new era. It is my sincere belief that this revision of McCarthy *Sensei*'s groundbreaking work will help us modern practitioners all move another step closer to understanding that which these ancient masters had also pursued.

Creation and Creator

by Andreas Quast
ryukyu-bugei.com

The Floating Dragon

Today karate has developed on a global scale. With the world karate practicing population estimated to be approximately 50 million across up to 150 countries, karate transcends borders of language, religion, politics, and race. To further develop traditional karate, and in the hope that it contributes to people's well-being and to world peace, in 2005 the Okinawa Prefectural Assembly announced October 25 as the "Day of Karate."[1] Worldwide there are a number of smaller and larger, of better and lesser known schools, and a myriad of associations. For example, currently in Okinawa, the umbrella organization for karate and kobudo is the Okinawa Dento Karate-do Shinkokai, established on February 14, 2008. The respective current Okinawa prefectural governor serves as its president. One of its main purposes is the international spread of Okinawa karate and kobudo and all related matters. Or take the World Karate Federation (WKF), the largest international governing body of competition karate established in 1990, actively supporting and aiming at the inclusion of karate in the Olympic Games. Its individual member associations on the national level are government recognized karate associations, which for the most part are organized under the respective National Sports Committees and the National Olympic Committees. It further splits down to the regional and municipal member organizations. Besides these two examples, there is everything in scope, power, and purposes from large international groups to micro styles consisting of only a handful practitioners.

However, while karate has reached a global scale, various sources in connection with its roots and development are still completely under the radar of the various federations, associations and schools, and for the main part are researched and studied only on individual level. One such source is the Bubishi that has been handed down in Okinawa.

The most complete and authentic Western translation, interpretation, and explanation of the Bubishi, as well as the theories regarding its origins and its impact on karate, are on hand before us. I say this with an absolute conviction, a conviction I obtained by investigating and comparing a large number of handwritten and printed Japanese editions, their lineages, contents, and characteristics up to tiny brush-strokes. As an avid researcher and avowed "bubishician" myself, it is therefore with the greatest pleasure that I follow the call to write a contribution for this new edition of the Bubishi by internationally acclaimed practitioner and researcher Patrick McCarthy (1954), president of the Ryukyu Karate Kokusai Kenkyukai (International Ryukyu Karate Research Society, IRKRS). My contribution attempts to provide the reader with an overview of the various handwritten manuscripts and printed books which partially or completely presents the contents of the Bubishi. At the same time a few details of their emergence and characteristics will be presented. The result of this might allow for a complementary perspective.

Not much is known about the original source manuscript of the Okinawan Bubishi. Handwritten copies are said to have existed in a considerable number. Japanese martial arts historian Fujiwara Ryozo reported that in the early phase, and including those ultimately scattered and lost, a total of about twenty editions of the Bubishi existed. He identified the owners of these handwritten copies as Matsumura Sokon, Asato Anko, Matsumura Kosaku, Itosu Anko, Kojo Taitei, Ko Shoketsu, To Daiki, Go Kenki, Yabu Kentsu, Funakoshi Gichin, Miyagi Chojun, Mabuni Kenwa, Yabiku Moden, Toyama Kanken, Gima Shinkin, Seiko Higa and others. Besides such handwritten manuscripts there are also a number of printed editions. All these handwritten and printed editions together can further be classified into 1) verified editions, 2) indirectly verified editions (e.g., through the existence of verified filial editions), and 3) unverified editions (e.g., only mentioned in stories or in literature). We are talking about more than fifty handwritten and printed editions here, some of which only dealt with fragments of the Bubishi. Besides these, there may still be editions or fragments in existence that have not yet been discovered or considered.

The author, the original scope, the date and place of establishment as well as the whereabouts of the original manuscript of the Bubishi are unknown. The only place name found in the Bubishi that could be verified is Tengshan in Fuzhou, home of then 76-year-old Wang Foudeng. For this reason it had been assumed that the Bubishi was prepared by a Chinese student of Wang's. In addition, as eye-catching portions of the Bubishi deal with the Fujian White Crane Boxing, the Bubishi is also considered to be a martial arts manual of this style. Moreover, the Bubishi reveals a variety of writing styles, showing classical Chinese as well as expressions in colloquial Fuzhou dialect, including the names of Kata and techniques found in Okinawa karate. Hence the Chinese coastal province of Fujian and its capital of Fuzhou are considered to be the main clue to the origin of the Okinawan Bubishi. More discoveries are presented in the following overview about the various editions of the Bubishi and its relation to Okinawa karate.

Lineages

It should first be pointed out that there are reputed editions of the Bubishi which were mentioned in literature but which are otherwise unverifiable. They could also not be detected by the existence of filial editions unique to them. Such unverified editions include those allegedly owned by Matsumora Kosaku, Kojo Taitei, Ko Shoketsu, To Daiki, Yabu Kentsu, Yabiku Moden, Toyama Kanken, Gima Shinkin and others. A first lineage of possible origin is that of famed Chinese tea merchant Go Kenki, which is described below.

Go Kenki Lineage

A Bubishi is ascribed to Go Kenki (1886–1940), a native of Fuzhou and expert of Crane Boxing. Yet, so far no original handwritten manuscript or filial copies of it could be verified.[2] Therefore, the contents and whereabouts of the Go Kenki manuscript are unknown. Occasionally it is mentioned that Go Kenki came to Okinawa in 1912 where he worked at a tea house in Naha Higashi-machi until 1940, but the specific circumstances are unclear.[3] Go Kenki was in friendly relation and exchange with Miyagi Chojun, and is particularly known to have taught *Nepai* to Mabuni Kenwa and Kyoda Juhatsu. This kata is better known under its modern name of *Nipaipo*. In this way Go Kenki not only had a great influence on the karate circles of his time, but still resonates today.[4]

The existence of a Go Kenki manuscript is assumed due to a testimony by his nephew, Yoza Seimi, as reported by Tokashiki Iken in 1995 as follows:

> "One day I was visited by Go Seimi (born 1920, current family name Yoza), who is the son of Go Kenki's older brother, Go Kensei. When shown the Fukuchi Seiko edition of the Bubishi, he said: *When I was 19 years old (1938), according to the instructions by my uncle Go Kenki, I was required to read the Bubishi, which I did several times. It is exactly the same book and contents as that book [you showed me] and I wonder whether it was brought by my uncle from Fuzhou.* With a surprised expression I inquired about the painting of the Busaganashi[5] in the house of the Yoza family. According to Mr. Yoza, this was a colored facsimile made from the Bubishi owned by his uncle Go Kenki. Originally, the picture of the Busaganashi is said to have been colored. Since Mr. Yoza's painting is very similar to the Busaganashi found in the Bubishi, it is presumed that the original was brought to Okinawa together with Go Kenki's edition [of the Bubishi], from which the facsimile was made."[6]

According to the above, Go Kenki owned a picture of the deity commonly referred to as Busaganashi in Okinawa circles. It should be noted that this deity was widespread in both Fujian and Taiwan and is by no means exclusively associated with the Bubishi. In addition, Yoza stated that Go Kenki's manuscript was "exactly the same book and contents" as Fukuchi Seiko's copy of the Bubishi. If correct, this is a very strong validation that Go Kenki actually owned a copy of the Bubishi, which would also suggest that he might have brought it from Fuzhou. Moreover, the era he reached Okinawa matches with the era in which the Bubishi obviously began to spread, i.e., since the Taisho-era (1912–1926).[7]

However, as Yoza's memory related to the year 1938, there are also other options. By that time a number of handwritten copies already existed, owned among others by his friends Miyagi Chojun and Mabuni Kenwa. Eight years prior to Yoza's memoirs the Higa Seiko copy was already in existence, which was the parental edition from which Fukuchi's edition was copied.[8] In addition, no filial copies demonstrably based on a Go Kenki manuscript could be proven so far.

In other words, and while it remains possible, all of the affirmative findings are no proof that allow for the reverse inference that Go Kenki actually brought a Bubishi from Fuzhou in 1912. Certainly he was a person to consult when it came to the Chinese text of the Bubishi and its contents on White Crane, medicine, and others. But it remains unknown whether he brought the Bubishi from Fuzhou, copied it from his friends, or was given a copy of it in return for his help in interpreting and understanding this extravagant manuscript.

Recapitulation

From the above reasons it seems appropriate to use a careful wording when it comes to identifying Go Kenki as the person who brought the Bubishi to Okinawa. Maybe something along the lines of "Go Kenki taught White Crane Boxing, explained the Bubishi, and provided instructions in ancient Chinese medicine."[9]

Matsumura Sokon Lineage

Matsumura Sokon has been variously identified as an owner of an edition of the Bubishi. As reported by Fujiwara in 1990, "the oldest Bubishi edition was copied by Funakoshi Gichin from Matsumura Sokon and Asato Anko, but—together with the Shotokan dojo—burned down during wartime fire."[10] He also reported that "Matsumura Sokon was awarded his edition directly from a military attaché of the Fuzhou government."[11] Since Fujiwara neither specified the origin of his information nor the contents of this Bubishi, details about a Matsumura Sokon edition are unknown, as are its whereabouts.

However, because in Funakoshi's print editions of 1922 and 1925 four articles were included that were subsequently identified as being part of the Bubishi in other lineages, it was naturally assumed that these originated in Asato and Matsumura. In fact, it seems that it was the very existence of exactly these four articles and other writings of Funakoshi that led Fujiwara and others to believe they could only have been handed down from Matsumura via Asato.

Let's look at some of the salient details. According to various sources, Matsumura studied with the military officers Iwa and Waishinzan.[12] This might have been related to the investiture missions (*sapposhi*) of 1838 or 1866. Clues might also be found in the passenger lists of Ryukyuan tribute ships to China and others documents related to the official diplomatic and trade relations between China and Ryukyu, yet so far I am unaware of any findings. Anyway, within these relations, occasions for contacts of Ryukyuan government officials—like Matsumura Sokon—with Chinese military or naval officers were numerous. Besides the obligatory exchange of intelligence and practice between Chinese and Ryukyuan government officials regarding military training, reports on martial arts performances in honor of the Chinese investiture envoys are found for the years 1719, 1756, 1838, and 1867. From this it is at least apparent that martial performing arts were a part of the formal framework of Chinese investiture missions.

For instance, during the celebrations for the Chinese investiture envoys of 1838, we discover the combative demonstration of the "Chinese cudgel" (Tobo/karabo 唐棒) on eight different occasions,[13] while the term "Chinese empty hand skills" (Todi/karate 唐手) is nowhere to be found.[14] On the other hand, the celebrations at the royal tea villa in Sakiyama during the following investiture in 1866 included a large amount of empty handed and armed combative demonstrations, including the term Todi/karate, which is generally understood as an empty-handed form of Ryukyu-ized Kenpo. In the same year, the term Todi is also found in a text about Kumiodori dance from 1867. From this fact it can be assumed that an empty-handed "Ryukyu Kenpo Todi" took a decisive developmental leap between 1838 and 1867. And this could be seen in connection with Matsumura and other Ryukyuan government officials, the Chinese military officials from the Fuzhou government, and the Bubishi.

Similar to Matsumura, Asato Anko (1828–1914) is also considered to have owned a Bubishi.[15] In view of the teacher-student relationship between Matsumura and Asato it is believed to be obvious that Asato made a copy from his teacher. However, so far no proof could be established as regards the existence of such an Asato Anko manuscript. As mentioned earlier, this lineage of a personal tradition of a Bubishi might simply have originated in a reverse inference from the existence of a handful of Bubishi articles found in Funakoshi's books since 1922.

Asato Anko, in addition to his principal teacher Matsumura Sokon, was also in contact with Nagahama of Naha-te, Gusukuma of Tomari-te, as well as with a certain Yabiku. The latter was a person of rank who apparently lived in northern Okinawa before he relocated to the village of Yabiku, probably in today's Nanjo Sashiki in southern Okinawa, hence his name. Yabiku was much older than Matsumura and handed down an old school of martial arts (*koryu bujutsu*). Matsumura, not well versed in this old-style tradition, visited Yabiku and finally received instruction. Through this connection Itosu and Asato also learned of Yabiku, whom they sought out for lessons when he was already a very old man. They performed their karate and Yabiku gave practical commentaries.[16] This way Asato became versed in each of what is referred to today as Shuri-te, Naha-te, and Tomari-te, as well as in Kobudo.[17]

No details are known about scope, contents, or whereabouts of the supposed Asato Anko manuscript. In a three-part article about Anko Asato's narratives on Karate—authored by his student Funakoshi Gichin and published in 1914—no hint is found about the existence, the contents, or the whereabouts of such a manuscript in the possession of Asato, or the Bubishi in general for that matter.[18] Time to move on.

Funakoshi Gichin (1868–1957) is considered the originator of what came to be referred to as Shotokan(-ryu) karate. At the age of six, he received his initiation to karate from his father, who was an expert of Bojutsu (fencing with a wooden pole). At the age of about 12 or 13 years he became a disciple of the Shuri-te masters Asato Anko and Itosu Anko. Furthermore, in November 1922, his book "Ryukyu Kenpo Karate" was published to constitute the first monograph in the history of karate. Moreover, in 1930 he left to posterity the "20 Articles of Karate," intended to improve the concepts of karate among its practitioners.[19]

Funakoshi's "Ryukyu Kenpo Karate" of 1922 is also the first printed book in history that included articles corresponding to what is considered the Bubishi today. Unfortunately it were only four articles and the same were also included in "Rentan Goshin Karatejutsu", published in March 1925.[20] When ten years later Funakoshi's "Karate-do Kyohan" was published in May 1935, we find three new articles added, placed among the previous four articles.[21] These three additional articles are not found in any other Bubishi-related manuscript. Furthermore, the seven articles by Funakoshi 1935 were only partly included in the English translation.[22] It is also significant that nowhere in Funakoshi's books of 1922, 1925, and 1935 is found the title of, or any other reference to, the Bubishi. Only in later editions of "Karate-do Kyohan," published since the late 1950s, was the word Bubishi belatedly added as the source of these articles.[23] No question, this was done because the Bubishi has become quite famous in the meantime.

When comparing the three newly added articles of 1935 with those of 1922 and 1925, an interesting point can be made. The 1922/1925 editions contained a text fragment cited from the *Sunzi Bingfa*. However, the last part of this text is not an original text citation from the *Sunzi Bingfa*. In accordance with this, in 1922 Funakoshi marked only the first part of the text fragment with square brackets (*kagikakko*), thus explicitly identifying it as a citation. The last part of this text fragment was not placed in brackets.

Mabuni Kenwa, on the other hand, who published the exact same text in his 1934 publication, places the complete text fragment within square brackets, thus identifying it all as a quote from the *Sunzi Bingfa*. Furthermore, copies of the Bubishi from the possession of Miyagi Chojun also contain the exact same characters of the text as found in Funakoshi 1922 and Mabuni 1934, however, entirely without brackets.[24] Finally, in his 1935 edition Funakoshi replaced the last part of this text fragment by an actual correct citation from the *Sunzi Bingfa*.[25]

We can extract a few things from the above facts. First of all, as Funakoshi both in 1922 and 1925 used the same unique content, which at the same time is also found in other editions of the Bubishi, his four articles must have originated in an original source of the Bubishi. This is also evident in the other three articles of 1922/1925. And as he used exactly the same return marks (*reten*) as Mabuni, while Miyagi lineage copies do not use return marks at all, it can be said that Funakoshi's and Mabuni's editions came from at least related lineages.

Secondly, the citations from the *Sunzi Bingfa* in different lineages of the Bubishi originally contained the same—partly wrong—quotation. And thirdly, Funakoshi was apparently the only one who realized that the last part of this text fragment was not an original quote. So it was rather logical that he replaced it by an actual entry from the *Sunzi Bingfa*. At the same time, however, in this way he altered this specific original content of the Bubishi.

The most important question in relation to Funakoshi's Bubishi articles that remains unanswered so far is whether he possessed only these fragments or a full copy of the Bubishi. To get closer to the truth, let's return to the second and third articles Funakoshi added in 1935.

The second added article is a citation titled "The *Liu Tao* says..." The *Liu Tao* is a written work created sometime during the Warring States period of China (5th century–221 BCE). It was held in such high esteem that it was subsequently included into the canon of the "Seven Military Classics" of ancient China. The short citation Funakoshi quoted from this work translates as:

> "When a bird of prey is about to attack, it folds in its wings and swoops down. When a ferocious wild cat is about to fight, it flattens its ears and crouches down low. When the Sage is about to move, he will certainly display a stupid countenance."

This article is not found in any of the other editions of the Bubishi. The third article added by Funakoshi in 1935 is called "Lin Hongnian says..." The short citation Funakoshi quoted from this work translates as:

> *"Water does not penetrate the rock—it is hard and unyielding. Water does not leak out of porcelain—it is dense and tight.*
>
> *If a person is externally hard and unyielding (like a rock), and internally dense and tight (like porcelain), then what emotion could penetrate it?*
>
> *However, if an object has a crack, water will immediately penetrate through it. If the object is hollow by the measure of one unit, the measure of one unit of water will immediately enter."*

This article is also not found in any of the other editions of the Bubishi. Lin Hongnian (1805–1885) was born in Fuzhou. In 1836 he passed the civil service exam at the Imperial Hanlin Academy with the best possible result. In 1838 the Chinese Qing court sent him to the Ryukyu Kingdom as the chief envoy of the investiture mission (*sapposhi*), equipped with the authority to appoint Sho Iku as the new king of Ryukyu. Lin's entourage comprised of 417 persons, nearly half of which were government military. They stayed on Okinawa for 160 days and Lin wrote down an official account of their stay entitled "Shi Liuqiu-lu." Later Lin was active as a prefectural magistrate and inspector-general in several Chinese provinces. In 1849 he was instrumental in anti-piracy measures in Guangdong province. Following the outbreak of the Taiping Rebellion (1851–1864) he distinguished himself in the organization of group drills, and in 1864 took part in the military suppression of the Taiping Rebellion, one of the bloodiest conflicts in world history. In 1866, relieved of his military duties, he returned to his home in Fuzhou, where as the master[26] of the Zhengyi Shuyuan academy,[27] he raised a large number of students from 1866 to 1885.

As an interesting note, the statement that Funakoshi attributed to Lin Hongnian was actually only quoted by him from the philosophy work called "Shenyin-yu," written in 1593 by the official, Lü Kun (1536–1618), a man "heretofore neglected in Western and Japanese scholarship, as a leading figure in this turn towards practical action."[28] When it comes to quasi-military arts, this Lü Kun was an interesting character. During his career, he took advantage of the widespread presence of arms in society to implement a local security program that became renowned, with militia training in the use of spears, swords, bow and arrows, short cudgels, rope whips, etc., under the instruction of professional teachers.[29] Studying the old is to understand the new, or so they say. Well, due to the fact that Funakoshi published articles which were later identified as parts of a Bubishi source document, it had been assumed that he owned a handwritten copy of Bubishi manuscripts attributed to Matsumura Sokon and Asato Anko.[30] Yet, hitherto the existence of both of these sources could not be verified. On the contrary, it seems that their supposed existence was a reverse inference based on exactly these articles of Funakoshi. In any case, beyond the four articles published in 1922/1925, and probably the three additional articles of 1935, no details are known about the scope, the contents, or the source of a Bubishi in Funakoshi's possession. In addition, the Funakoshi manuscript itself was destroyed by fire together with the Shotokan-dojo.[31] So there seems to be no chance that the actual contents of his handwritten document can ever be reconstructed.

It is only from Gima Shinkin (1896–1989) that we hear that "Although I was only able to throw a fleeting glimpse at the Bubishi manuscripts of both Funakoshi Gichin and Miyagi Chojun, there seems to be a considerable difference between these two as regards their contents."[32] Therefore a Funakoshi manuscript factually existed, but it was considerably different to that of Miyagi. It should be noted here that the Miyagi Chojun manuscript had at least 29 articles, and there is no doubt that it constituted one of the most complete and original manuscripts of what is considered the Bubishi today. While the Miyagi manuscript had apparently been destroyed, these facts are confirmed in the copy directly prepared from it by Higa Seiko around 1930, which in turn is considered the oldest existing handwritten copy of the Bubishi today. According to this, and reconsidering Gima Shinkin's abovementioned statement, Funakoshi's document might have only included fragmentary parts of the Bubishi.

On the other hand, it should be noted that there might have been a relation between the aforementioned Lin Hongnian as the chief envoy of the 1838 investiture mission, the various military officers and soldiers of its escort, the large number of Ryukyuan officials who came in contact with them, and written documents and records about the martial arts, such as the Bubishi, as well as Bubishi-like manuscripts.

For example, according to the semi-official Ryukyuan history work called "Kyuyo," the senior military officer on the first ship of Lin Hongnian's investiture mission was Chen Xiansheng. The senior military officer on the second ship was Zhou Yanxiang, who was accompanied by the "disturbance quelling official" Yang Shaotang. These were the leading military officers during the 1838 investiture mission.[33] Seen from this perspective, Funakoshi's article called "Lin Hongnian says..." might as well have been a reference to a martial arts tradition of the year 1838. On the other hand, however, Bubishi-like contents appear to have existed in various official and private collections of notes or quotes.

Another perspective opens up when considering the fact that so-called "Crown Ship Commissioners" were dispatched from Satsuma for each of the investiture missions in 1683, 1719, 1756, 1800, 1808, 1838, and finally 1866. Wouldn't it have been in Satsuma's interest to not only gather all sorts of intelligence about Chinese technology, medicine, and the like, but also about Chinese combat methods? Makishi Chocho (1818–62), Asato Anko, and Matsumura Sokon were not the only ones with a background in the Jigen-ryu style of sword fencing originating in Satsuma.[34] External motivation for martial arts studies cannot be limited to an official interest by the Ryukyuan side in the first place. Now let me untie the chronology from the opposite direction.

Since September 1927, Higa Yuchoku (1910–1994) learned karate from Shiroma Jiro, an acquaintance of his father. In 1934 he studied with Shinzato Jin'an of Goju-ryu, and in 1935 he additionally became a disciple of Miyahira Sei'ei, who was known as a versatile martial artist. In this way Higa is said to have explored the ultimate mystery of the martial art in all its profundity. In 1948 he became a disciple of the Shuri-te expert Chibana Choshin, from whom he received a teaching license in January 1951.[35] Besides studying the core secrets of karate in all its depth from numerous masters, he also established the Kyudokan school of Okinawa Shorin-ryu Karate-do, which today is directed by Higa Minoru.

In his congratulatory address for the publication of the "Okinawa-den Bubishi" (1986), Higa Yuchoku noted an interesting thing. I will later refer to this as quote 1:

"20 years ago I too cherished the idea of a translation of the Bubishi that had been handed down in Okinawa. I appealed to a teacher of classical Chinese text of the old middle school system with the request of preparing a translation. However, he was not able to accomplish this. After one week this teacher returned the document to me, saying he wasn't able to translate it because it was an old form of Chinese writing different from regular classical Chinese."[36]

According to the above statement, 20 years prior to Higa's congratulatory address, i.e., in the year 1966, neither Higa Yuchoku nor a Japanese teacher of classical Chinese text were able to translate the Bubishi. By the way, this should give you a decent picture of what Patrick McCarthy has achieved with his English translation. One thing that is noteworthy here is that even a skilled and professionally educated Okinawan teacher of classical Chinese was not able to interpret the document, let alone a regular Japanese person, or Okinawan person, or a karate master, for that matter. Another thing even more noteworthy is that Higa Yuchoku seems to have been in the possession of a Bubishi. In Miyagi Tokumasa's congratulatory address for the publication of Tokashiki Iken's research on the Bubishi (1995), a document referred to as "Book of Martial Arts Characteristic of Okinawa"[37] from the possession of Higa Yuchoku is mentioned as a "variety of the Bubishi." I will later refer to this as quote 2.

> *"Roughly three decades ago [i.e. around 1965], my honored teacher Higa Yuchoku Sensei kindly showed to me his 'Book of Martial Arts Characteristic of Okinawa' (I remember it was a handwritten notebook-like thing). Although I took some brief notes in a big hurry at that time, much later at times I thought how very regrettable it was that in this era there were no such modern conveniences as copy machines. According to the brief notes I took at the time, the book was composed of a part in classical Chinese text and a part in Japanese text. In addition, different genres of illustrations of persons were included, but these were clearly different from the two types described earlier [= the Miyagi und Itosu editions of the Bubishi]. It should further be noted that among those materials was a record by Matsumura Chikudun Pechin from the year Guangxu 8. The Chinese year Guangxu 8 corresponds to the Japanese year Meiji 15 and the Western year 1882. The time of the record is consistent with Matsumura Sokon's (1809–1899) lifetime.*
>
> *By the way, later I wanted to examine the document a little bit more. About ten years after I first saw it, I asked Higa Sensei if he would show me the manuscript one more time. Wondering what his answer might be, Higa Sensei replied, 'That document has been lost and is currently not at hand.' With this reluctant wording at that time I thought that certainly someone must have borrowed the document. In any event, I clearly remember this because it was such an unexpected incident."[38]*

If it is true that this document contained portions which were chronicled in the year Guangxu 8 (i.e., 1882) by Matsumura *Chikudun Pechin*, then Higa's "Book of Martial Arts Characteristic of Okinawa" included contents from the lineage of Matsumura Sokon. No details are known about the contents of the handwriting of Matsumura.

There is an important point to consider here: it is unclear at the time whether the two documents mentioned in above descriptions in quote 1 and quote 2 refer to two different documents, or to one and the same document. While Higa in quote 1 referred to it as "the Bubishi," Miyagi Tokumasa, who is a distinguished expert and who was a student of Higa's, in quote 2 called it "a variety of the Bubishi." Even if it were two different documents it is still possible that Higa assigned the name Bubishi to it retrospectively, although it might not have been labelled as such. Similarly, the designation Bubishi may have been retrospectively assigned to various documents that shared certain character traits of what constitutes a Bubishi in the truest and literal meaning of the word, namely as "Records on Military Preparation" handed down by Okinawan karate practitioners of the past. As a side note, according to Otsuka Tadahiko (1940–2012),[39] around 1982 a handwritten copy of the Bubishi from Ichikawa Sosui was prepared by Otsuka's mother. This manuscript in turn was copied by Higa Yuchoku, who also presented a copy to Otsuka in 1983, as can be seen in the text found on the last page: "For Otsuka Sensei, October 10, 1983: Higa Yuchoku."[40] The original edition prepared by Otsuka's mother further served as the basis for Otsuka Tadahiko's publications "Okinawa-den Bubishi" (1986) and "Chugoku, Ryukyu Bugeishi" (1998), in which he reorganized the 29 articles into a new order.

Here is another extremely interesting citation of Miyagi Tokumasa. I will refer to this as quote 3.

"Speaking of other things I became aware of, on the last page of Shimabukuro Eizo's 'Records of Okinawa Karate-do and the Royal Dynasty'[41] one single sheet of illustrations appeared as a fragment of the Bubishi or otherwise martial arts related materials. On the right-hand side of it is shown one sheet of an illustration. The description says it is one from among a total of sixteen originally bound sheets of atemi and ukemi[42] illustrations that were presented from Todi Sakugawa[43] to Matsumura Sokon (destroyed by fire during the Battle of Okinawa). Although it is still not confirmed whether this is true or not, it is tentatively accepted."[44]

Miyagi Tokumasa saw both the Higa Yuchoku manuscript from quote 2 as well as the illustration as mentioned in quote 3, but distinguished them. Accordingly, these were two different sources. Furthermore, quote 3—if it is authentic—seems to be the only written source so far that can serve as an evidence for a personal teacher-student relationship between Todi Sakugawa and Matsumura Sokon.

Recapitulation

Unfortunately no handwritten copies were detected from the lineage of Matsumura Sokon. As regards the content, only the four articles (or seven, respectively) from the Funakoshi print editions might be said to have originated in this lineage. Further contents are unknown. Let's turn to the next lineage, which is equally intriguing.

Tenson-byo Lineage

TENSON-BYO

The Tenson-byo joss house was dedicated to the supreme deity of Chinese popular Taoism which had been introduced to Okinawa by the 36 families of Kume. This supreme deity refers to Guan Yu (160–219 AD), a general of the kingdom of Shu in ancient China, perceived as a fearless warrior, known for his virtue and loyalty, and who even appeared in the famous historical novel "Romance of the Three Kingdoms." His alias, Kantei O, literally "Monarch of the Frontier Post," points to his role as a protective patron who secured the country's borders. On the name plaques found in the Tenson-byo he is revered as Tenson Kantei, from which the joss house derived its name. He is also considered the "Saint of War" (*wu sheng*), which is complementary to Confucius, the "Saint of Culture" (*wen sheng*). At this point an original concept of Wu-wen (*bunbu*)—i.e. scholarship and military art in unity—can be seen to have existed in Ryukyu since olden times. In addition, Guan Yu was worshiped as the guardian deity of the king of Ryukyu[45] and hence it may be considered no coincidence that the Tenson-byo was situated right beside the Gokokuji, the "Temple for the Protection of the Homeland." Homeland Security, I'd say.

Since institutions such as the Tenson-byo, the Temple of Confucius, the Meirindo and others were an integral part of the cultural sphere of Kume village and simultaneously served as educational facilities, it is easy to imagine that the Bubishi—or the source documents it was compiled from—might have constituted part of a collection used within the Confucian education of the time. As regards such a collection, the emphasis of modern karate on empty-handed martial arts blurs the fact that the use of weaponry was an integral part of martial arts at the time, evidence for which is not limited to the famous martial arts program of 1867. Doesn't this in turn point to the existence of textbooks of a rather integrated form of martial arts?

In addition, the Kume schools not only served the education of Kume people but also for the education of the aristocratic youth of the other urban districts, especially from Shuri. Moreover, since in 1798 the National Academy (*kokugaku*) was established, and subsequently in 1835 the district and village schools of Shuri, Naha, Tomari, and Kume as well as rural village schools, Kume scholars directly or indirectly acted as teachers of these schools. Moreover, besides being educational institutions, the monitoring of law and order in their respective areas was part of the duties of these "schools." Just one thing to note here is that these specific martial arts were therefore by no means a private, but an institutionalized, matter.

The whereabouts and exact contents of the Tenson-byo manuscript are currently unknown. The Tenson-byo joss house was destroyed during WWII so that it seems that the original Tenson-byo manuscript of the Bubishi—and probably other related documents—are lost. However, a few written sources and the existence of filial copies can be regarded proof for the existence of a Tenson-byo Bubishi manuscript.

MIYAGI CHOJUN

The first filial copy of the Tenson-byo manuscript is associated with Miyagi Chojun (1888–1953). Miyagi is known as the creator of Goju-ryu Karate. When in May 1930 Miyagi's student Shinzato Jin'an (1901–1945) took part in the National Budo Congress,[46] Shinzato was asked for the name of the school he was representing. As a makeshift reply, he said that it was Hango-ryu, which means "semi-hard style."[47] Thereafter Miyagi resorted to a verse from the Bubishi when he baptized his style of karate by the name of Goju-ryu.[48]

Well, the above description by no means constitutes proof for the existence of a Miyagi Chojun manuscript of the Bubishi. He might as well have borrowed this verse from a Bubishi in the possession of another person. Therefore, in the following, evidence is sought out for the existence of a Miyagi Chojun manuscript of the Bubishi.

Miyagi Chojun—Inconclusive Provenance

In Goju-ryu circles the existence of a Miyagi Chojun manuscript is sometimes described without establishing a conclusive explanation of its provenance. For example, it is stated:

> *"In May 1915, together with Nakamoto Eisho, for the first time Miyagi Chojun traveled to Fuzhou for the study of Chinese martial arts. There he exchanged ideas with local masters of martial arts from Fuzhou and carried out surveys with respect to Higaonna Kanryo's teacher Ru Ruko. [...] On top of that, he bought the Bubishi and deepened his research on training methods with equipment (hojo undo)."[49]*

It seems the above theory goes back to a statement made by Fukuchi Seiko (1919–1975) already in the 1970s, and most probably dates back earlier.[50] However, this hypothesis is somewhat biased on Miyagi Chojun's travels to China, and above all doesn't consider any other source or possibility. Yet, a compelling solution is readily found in Mabuni Kenwa's 1934 book, which included a large attachment of the Bubishi.[51] In his short introduction Mabuni clearly states that the presented parts of the Bubishi were originally copied by his former teacher Itosu Anko from a book on Kenpo referred to in China as Bubishi. As Itosu Anko died March 11, 1915, it is evident that Itosu owned a copy prior to Miyagi's visit to China in May 1915. Although the Miyagi manuscript was destroyed, the contents of Mabuni 1934 reveal an unequivocal congruence with the Higa Seiko manuscript, which is a filial edition of the Miyagi Chojun manuscript. Therefore, the Bubishi must have existed on Okinawa prior to Miyagi's travels to China in May 1915. This makes it rather untenable that Miyagi "bought the Bubishi" during his 1915 China trip. According to another hypothesis it is also believed that Miyagi's teacher Higaonna Kanryo was once presented with the Bubishi:

"Furthermore, prior to his return (from China) to Okinawa, Higaonna Kanryo is said to have received the Bubishi as a gift, but thereto no details are known."[52]

Unfortunately no sources are provided which would confirm this statement. Again, this theory is found already in the above-mentioned 1970s statement by Fukuchi Seiko. However, the comment that "thereto no details are known" make it obvious that this is a hypothesis. It should also be noted here that Higa Seiko also was a student of Higaonna Kanryo, but Higa's manuscript of the Bubishi is demonstrably a filial copy of the Miyagi Chojun manuscript, and not of a supposed Higaonna edition. In any case, so far no positive evidence was provided for the above theories, which is why they must be considered to be of inconclusive provenance and most probably the result of reverse inference.

Miyagi Chojun—Conclusive Provenance

According to Kuniyoshi Yukei (1905–1987), the former chairman of the Suseikai,[53] the Tenson-byo manuscript of the Bubishi was once copied by his father Kuniyoshi Seiko (?–1917).[54] Judging from his position as the chairman of the Suseikai it may be assumed that he was probably among the most qualified persons who could possibly have made a copy of the Bubishi at that time. This copy passed into the possession of Miyagi Chojun.[55] It is unknown whether Kuniyoshi customized this copy directly for Miyagi, or whether he allocated or sold it to him. It is also unknown when exactly Kuniyoshi prepared this copy. From the year of his death, however, it is evident that the Tenson-byo manuscript as well as the Miyagi Chojun manuscript existed not later than 1917. The very existence of a Tenson-byo Bubishi manuscript can be verified by further written sources. In the preface to the publication of the "Okinawa to Bubishi" by Otsuka Tadahiko (1986), Miyagi Chojun's student Yagi Meitoku specified that the Bubishi was kept together with the official history book, *Rekidai Hoan*, in a bookcase in the Tenson-byo in Kume.[56] In criticism, it might still have been the case that Yagi was referring to the homonymously written *Wubeizhi* (1621) by Mao Yuanyi. However, Tokuda Anshu, nephew of Karate expert Tokuda Anbun, provided a third independent source that verifies the storage of the Bubishi in "the mausoleum of Confucius in the district Kume in Naha" until prior to the war, and that Miyagi Chojun produced himself a copy from this manuscript.[57]

Although the two statements by Kuniyoshi and Tokuda contradict in regard to the person who manufactured the copy as well as the exact place of its storage, both confirm the existence of a Miyagi Chojun manuscript as such, and clearly name a manuscript from the cultural sphere of Kume as its paternal document. Furthermore, the statement by Yagi Meitoku also independently confirms the existence of a Tenson-byo manuscript. Another proof for the existence of the Miyagi Chojun manuscript can be seen in the figurine of the so-called Busaganashi:

> In the years prior to the Pacific War, Miyagi Chojun owned two hanging scrolls with a depiction of the Busaganashi. One of these Miyagi presented to his disciple Madanbashi Keiyo as a gift. While Miyagi's own hanging scroll was destroyed during the Pacific War, in the early postwar period Madanbashi had a wooden statue modeled after his hanging scroll, manufactured by a local wood carver in Saipan. Later Madanbashi presented this wooden statue to Miyagi Chojun, who revered it as the Bujin (Busaganashi)—a deity of the art of war—of Goju-ryu Karate-do ever since.[58]

In 1957 Miyagi Chojun's family presented this wooden Busaganashi sculpture as a gift to Miyazato Ei'ichi. A photograph of it first appeared in 1978 in Miyazato Ei'ichi's book on Goju-ryu[59] and the statue can still be found today in the Jundokan Dojo in Naha Asato. A comparison of the wooden statue of the Busaganashi with the illustrations in the Bubishi shows that "Busaganashi" is nothing but the Okinawan name for the figure shown in the Bubishi called "Jiutian Fenghuo-yuan Santian-du Yuanshai." The fact that Miyagi owned two hanging scrolls of the Busaganashi also shows that the subject was actively studied and that copies were made, although in this case only of one illustration. It should be noted here that the Busaganashi of the Itosu lineage looks a bit different, but the similarity between the Tenson-byo lineage Bubishi and the physical wooden Busaganashi statue leaves no doubt that the latter was produced on the model of the first.

Finally, the existence of the Miyagi Chojun manuscript results from the Higa Seiko manuscript, which is considered the oldest known edition of the Bubishi still extant. It came into being around 1930 as a filial edition from Miyagi's manuscript, which is considered to be lost. Although there is more evidence, the existence of an independent Miyagi Chojun manuscript should be sufficiently confirmed by now. Furthermore, after comparing all the sources and balancing out the evidences, it can—very decidedly—be said that the Miyagi Chojun manuscript with a probability bordering on certainty was a copy of the Tenson-byo manuscript, either copied by Kuniyoshi Seiko and later presented to Miyagi, or copied directly by Miyagi himself.

As regards the whereabouts of the Miyagi Chojun manuscript, hardly any information could be gleaned, but there is also no trace of information whatsoever that it is still existent. As Kai Kuniyuki stated that "Miyagi's own hanging scroll [of the Busaganashi] was destroyed during the Pacific War"[60] it is likely that the Miyagi Chojun manuscript was stored in the same place and was also destroyed by fire. In the tradition of Ichikawa Sosui it also is stated that "Miyagi Chojun said that his edition fell prey to war fire during the Battle of Okinawa in the Second World War."[61]

There are two filial editions which have demonstrably been copied from the Miyagi Chojun manuscript: 1) the Higa Seiko manuscript and 2) the Mabuni Kenwa manuscript; (A) the latter is different to the Mabuni Kenwa manuscript (B), which is of Itosu–Mabuni lineage and will be explained later.

Since the Higa Seiko manuscript consists of 29 articles, it can be assumed that the Miyagi Chojun manuscript also consisted of at least 29 articles.

HIGA SEIKO

At the age of 13 years Higa Sciko (1898–1966) became a student of Higaonna Kanryo. After the death of his master, Higa continued to study under the former's older student Miyagi Chojun, the originator of Goju-ryu.[62] The Higa Seiko manuscript came into existence around 1930, when Higa served at the police station in Itoman, where he copied the Bubishi from the possession of Miyagi Chojun by hand.[63] This Higa Seiko manuscript is currently considered the oldest surviving copy of the Bubishi.[64] Since the whereabouts of the Miyagi Chojun manuscript as the paternal document of the Higa Seiko manuscript is currently unknown, though most probably a loss of war, the probable form of the Miyagi Chojun manuscript—and in consequence the Tenson-byo manuscript—can currently only be reconstructed from the manuscripts in the lineage of Higa Seiko and Mabuni Kenwa (A). For this reason alone the Higa Seiko manuscript is of particular importance.

The binding of the Higa Seiko manuscript bears no title or other sign that says "Bubishi." The complete text consists of a total of about 10,000 characters, subdivided into 29 articles[65] and equipped with 72 illustrations. Within the organization of these 29 articles, one or—since they are not numbered—more pages, including the titles, are missing right before the article "The Eight Precepts of Quanfa." It suggests that one or more articles might have gone missing.

As regards this, there is an important fact to note. Two articles contained in the Mabuni Kenwa print edition of 1934 could not be confirmed in the Higa Seiko manuscript. These two articles are "Hand and Foot, Muscle and Bone Training Postures (of the Shorei-ji-ryu)" and "Delayed Death Touch Twelve-Hour Diagrams." According to this it is possible that they were once a part of the Higa Seiko manuscript and went missing for whatever reason. If so, this would mean that the Miyagi Chojun manuscript and consequently also the Tenson-byo manuscript might have originally also contained these two articles. At the same time it is not imperative and it could also have been some other content.

Filial editions copied directly from the Higa Seiko manuscript include the Izumigawa Kanki manuscript and the Fukuchi Seiko manuscript.

IZUMIGAWA KANKI

Izumigawa Kanki (1908–1967) was born the third son of Izumigawa Kanfu in Naha Makishi. During his primary school he learned the rudiments of karate from Higaonna Kanryo's disciple Kyoda Juhatsu (1887–1968), and since his childhood received lessons from his grandfather Izumigawa Kanchu, who in turn had been a student of the Bushi Matsumura Sokon from Shuri. In addition, he was taught Okinawa Kobudo by his older cousin Izumikawa Kantoku. When at the end of the Taisho era (1912–1926) a friend of his brother began to study karate at his parents' house, Kanki also studied with masters of many different schools. Since around 1929, at the age of 21 years, he was a student of Higa Seiko, from whom he received lessons in Goju-ryu. In 1936 he went to the Mariana Islands of Tinian and Saipan as well as to the Palau Islands, where he ran the training as a deputy teacher (*shihan-dai*) of Higa. In 1937, he copied the Bubishi from Higa and in this way received recognition as a legitimate successor of Goju-ryu.[66]

Two photos of his Bubishi were printed in *The Sun News-Pictorial* of June 14, 1950.[67] One shows the Busaganashi, the other shows No. 47 and No. 48 of the "Forty-Eight Self-defense Diagrams." In 1956 it has been reported again that an illustration of the Busaganashi hung in his dojo.[68] The cover of the Izumigawa Kanki manuscript bears the written title "Bubishi—Izumigawa Kanki, April 1937." In addition, on the inside of the cover is found the handprint of Higa Seiko, accompanied by the date April 28. In other words, the Izumigawa Kanki manuscript has been copied from the Higa Seiko manuscript at the latest on April 28, 1937.[69] According to Matayoshi Seitoku, president of the Goju-ryu Karate-do Kobudo Seigokan Honbu, the Izumigawa Kanki manuscript was prepared by Higa Seiko himself as a handwritten copy of his own manuscript and presented as a gift to Izumigawa Kanki.[70] Since that time, in this karate tradition the Bubishi had been copied by hand and provided with the handprint of the current master to the successor. Like this it is considered a proof of the initiation into the secrets of the art and as a confirmed teaching license (*shihan menkyo*).

Filial editions of the Izumigawa Kanki manuscript include the Ichikawa Sosui manuscript. Second order filial editions of it include the Otsuka Tadahiko manuscript (A) and the Chiba Kenjiro manuscript.

OTSUKA TADAHIKO
Otsuka Tadahiko (1940–2012) was a student of Ichikawa osui. According to Otsuka Tadahiko himself,[71] the Otsuka Tadahiko manuscript (A) was created around 1982 by Otsuka's mother as a copy of the Ichikawa Sosui manuscript. On the cover is written "Book of Teaching License— Bubishi, Otsuka Tadahiko."[72] On the first page follows the handprint of Ichikawa Sosui, accompanied by the text "Handprint of my revered teacher Ichikawa Sosui."[73] Higa Yuchoku prepared a rewritten copy on the basis of the Otsuka Tadahiko manuscript. On the last page is found the text "For Otsuka *Sensei*—October 10, 1983, Higa Yuchoku."

In April 1986, Otsuka Tadahiko (translation) and Yo Meiji (editor) published the *Okinawa-den Bubishi*. According to Otsuka, as well as the description given in the book, this edition was based on the Otsuka Tadahiko manuscript (A). Otsuka here reorganized the 29 articles into a new order, "hoping to make this work easier to understand for many people." He also redrew the figures. As most of those who copied these manuscripts were not artists, quality and details were slowly getting worse, so this was a necessary step. This edition also included the first Japanese translation of the classical Chinese text of the Bubishi.

In July 1998 the *Chugoku, Ryukyu Bugeishi,* by Otsuka Tadahiko, was published, including the same 29 articles as previously. It is an incredible work and there is the following thing to note about it. According to Otsuka's foreword, in 1987, while in Taiwan, he came across the *Jixiao Xinshu* (1561) by Chinese general Qi Jiguang, Chapter 14 of which is called the "Canon of Boxing." In this chapter, the "32 Gestures of Long Boxing of Song Taizu" are found. Otsuka translated and reconstructed their applications and furthermore examined their possible relation to the "Forty-eight Self-defense Diagrams" of the Bubishi, for which—by the way—Patrick McCarthy kindly provided him with own research results. To make a long story short, in the course of the study, Otsuka was able to verify thirteen matches between the boxing techniques from the *Jixiao Xinshu* (1561) and the "Forty-eight Self-defense Diagrams" of the Bubishi. The concordance tables for this study are all found in this work, as well as the reconstructed applications and comparisons with the techniques from the Bubishi.

MABUNI KENWA (A)

Mabuni Kenwa (1889–1952) is well-known as the founder of Shito-ryu Karate who had learned Shuri-te as a disciple of Itosu Anko since 1903. Through introduction by his friend Miyagi Chojun he also studied Naha-te from Higaonna Kanryo from 1908.[74] The Mabuni Kenwa (A) manuscript is a copy of the Miyagi Chojun manuscript. The whereabouts and details of the Mabuni Kenwa (A) manuscript are unknown. However, based on the Higa Seiko manuscript, which used the same parental edition, it can be said that it contained at least 29 articles. The existence of the Mabuni Kenwa (A) manuscript is confirmed by two filial editions, namely the Konishi Yasuhiro manuscript (B) and the Iwata Manzo manuscript.

KONISHI YASUHIRO (B)

Konishi Yasuhiro (1893–1983) was a close friend of Mabuni Kenwa and founder of the Shindo Jinen-ryu Karate. Currently not much is known about this manuscript. It was confirmed though that Konishi owned two versions of the Bubishi by Mabuni Kenwa from two different lineages: one from the Tenson-byo lineage via Miyagi and Mabuni, and one from the Itosu lineage via Mabuni.[75] On the title page of the Konishi Yasuhiro manuscript (B) is written the sentence "Gift for the Honorable Mr. Yasuhiro Konishi."[76] According to this, it seems to have been a present from Mabuni Kenwa. It contains articles such as the "Bronze Man Statue," the "Shaolin Herbal Medicine and Injuries Diagram," and the "Forty-Eight Self-defense Diagrams." These are also found in the Higa Seiko manuscript.[77]

The Konishi Yasuhiro (B) is apparently a filial edition of the Mabuni Kenwa manuscript (A), which in turn originated in the Miyagi Chojun manuscript. Besides other proof, this is also apparent in the fact that two articles only found in the Itosu manuscript lineage are not part of the Konishi Yasuhiro manuscript (B).[78]

IWATA MANZO

During his younger days the late Iwata Manzo (1924–1993) copied the Mabuni Kenwa (A) manuscript by hand. It is now in possession of his son Genzo. This Bubishi of the Iwata family was handed down via the following lineage: Miyagi Chojun → Mabuni Kenwa (A) → Iwata Manzo.[79] Just like the Konishi Yasuhiro (B) manuscript, it is therefore a second order filial document of the Miyagi Chojun manuscript.

Recapitulation

The Tenson-byo lineage editions comprise of 29 articles and numerous handwritten copies, as well as printed editions, demonstrably spread from this lineage. Besides the ones mentioned above, this lineage includes editions such as that of Yun Heui-byeong (1947), Fukuchi Seiko (1958), Tamaki Juei, Ishimine Choshin, Hokama Tetsuhiro, Tokashiki Iken (1995), and the Tokumoto Mitsuru manuscript (around 1978) and print edition (1996).

The Itosu Anko Lineage

The knowledge about the contents of the Itosu Anko manuscript is generally limited to the 11 articles printed in Mabuni 1934. Hitherto no complete handwritten copy from this lineage has been published anywhere.

ITOSU ANKO MANUSCRIPT
Itosu Anko (1831–1915) was born in Shuri Gibo into a Shizoku family. His instructor was the renowned teacher of the martial arts of the royal government in Shuri, Matsumura Sokon.[80] In addition, he invented kata such as Pinan, introduced the formerly carefully preserved karate into school education, and is recognized as a pioneer of the popularization of karate. The whereabouts of the Itosu Anko manuscript are unknown. In the Mabuni Kenwa print edition of 1934, Itosu's student, Mabuni Kenwa, expresses himself in a short introduction about the portions he attached from the Bubishi:

> *"My venerable instructor Itosu Sensei copied a book about Kenpo, which is referred to in China as 'Bubishi.' This I borrowed and copied myself and carefully kept it in secret to this day as a research and reference work. Encouraged by friends, and in the current golden age of Karate Kenpo, one day I could bear no longer to keep it to myself, for which reason I finally chronicled it. If it is of even a little use for zealous researchers, it would mean a great fortune for me."[81]*

From this can be seen that Mabuni Kenwa copied the Itosu Anko manuscript. In other words, while the whereabouts of the Itosu Anko manuscript itself is currently unknown, its existence is confirmed by Mabuni. Only 11 articles were included as the contents of the Itosu Anko manuscript and there are some points which are still unclear.

First of all, it is unknown whether the above-mentioned 11 articles of the Itosu Anko manuscript were copied from one original Bubishi document, and if so, whether it fully reflects the contents of this. Secondly, it is also unclear if Mabuni published all of the contents he copied from the Itosu Anko manuscript. However, as there is no mention of it being an excerpt, both options are possible, i.e., either it consisted only of 11 articles, or it was larger, but Mabuni only published 11 articles from the Itosu Anko manuscript. In the above-mentioned short introduction, Mabuni noted that "Itosu *Sensei* copied a book about Kenpo which is referred to in China as 'Bubishi.'" But there is no mention of exactly which book this was. Because of this, it is unknown whether Itosu Anko himself already used the title "Bubishi" or not.

Although there are a number of theories as regards Itosu's source, the lack of any evidence prohibits their specification within the limited space of this contribution.

MABUNI KENWA MANUSCRIPT (B)

As mentioned above, Mabuni Kenwa copied the Itosu Anko manuscript. This manuscript is referred to here as Mabuni Kenwa manuscript (B). According to the narrative of Mabuni's son Ken'ei, this Mabuni Kenwa manuscript (B) was destroyed during a wartime fire.[82] Fortunately, Konishi Yasuhiro prepared a copy of the Mabuni manuscript (B), which today constitutes the probably oldest Itosu-lineage Bubishi manuscript in existence. The contents of the Mabuni Kenwa manuscript (B) are not unequivocally clear. It might be that they corresponded to the 11 articles included and published in the Mabuni Kenwa print edition of 1934, which is described in the following section. It might also be that it consisted of a larger number of articles. In any case, so far I did not come across evidence that would solve this question once and for all.

Verified direct filial editions of the Mabuni Kenwa manuscript (B) are the Mabuni Kenwa print edition 1934 and the Konishi Yasuhiro manuscript (A).

MABUNI KENWA PRINT EDITION 1934

In October 1934, Mabuni Kenwa published "Kobo Jizai Karate Kenpo—Sepai no Kenkyu." In its appendix 11 articles of the Bubishi were included.[83] This is referred to as the Mabuni Kenwa print edition 1934. It includes the same 11 articles already mentioned in the section about Itosu Anko.

There are the following points to note here.

1. In the text corpus of the Mabuni Kenwa print edition 1934 the same inversions marks[84] are found as are also found in Funakoshi Gichin's works of 1922, 1925, and 1935. On the other hand, no such inversion marks are seen in the Higa Seiko manuscript.

2. Differences in the use of characters between Mabuni and Funakoshi are basically nonexistent. However, when compared to the Higa Seiko manuscript, there are considerable differences. From the above points a similar ancestry can be deduced for the Mabuni Kenwa print edition 1934 (Itosu Anko lineage) and the Funakoshi Gichin print edi-

tions (assumed Matsumura Sokon lineage). At the same time, the Higa Seiko manuscript (Tenson-byo lineage) obviously belongs to a different lineage.

In addition, two articles contained in the Mabuni Kenwa print edition 1934 could not be confirmed in the Higa Seiko manuscript, namely Hand and Foot, Muscle and Bone Training Postures (of the Shorei-ji-ryu) and Delayed Death Touch Twelve-Hour Diagrams. As already mentioned, in the Higa Seiko manuscript, directly before the article The Eight Precepts of Quanfa, one or—since they are not numbered—more pages, including the titles of the articles, are missing. It is therefore possible that the Miyagi Chojun manuscript and consequently also the Tenson-byo manuscript originally also contained these two articles, yet it is not logically imperative. It could have also been something else.

Filial editions of the Mabuni print edition of 1934 include the "Karate-do Taikan (Vol. 2)—Bojutsu Kyohon" (1948) by Yun Heui-byeong, which includes the 34 sheets of "Hand and Foot, Muscle and Bone Training Postures (of the Shorei-ji-ryu)." The fragments published by Yamaguchi Gogen are all without any doubt copies from this lineage and do not contain any content exceeding the Mabuni 1934 print edition.[85] In 1959 a Chinese translation of Mabuni's 1934 print edition was published in Taiwan. The illustrations were reproduced in facsimile, but the text was translated and newly set in traditional Chinese. The translators added their own interpretations into the newly-set print texts. Not only punctuation marks were altered or supplemented, but entire headlines were modified, shortened or completely rewritten. In addition, other characters or completely changed sentences were frequently detected. Moreover, the characters and units of measurement in the articles on herbal medicine were changed to a modern style. This work is therefore only of limited use as regards the original contents of the Bubishi.

KONISHI YASUHIRO MANUSCRIPT (A)

It has previously been pointed out that the whereabouts of the original Itosu Anko manuscript are unknown. It was furthermore shown that the Mabuni Kenwa print edition of 1934 only included 11 articles of the Itosu Anko manuscript, while the Mabuni Kenwa manuscript (B)—which the print edition of 1934 was based upon—had allegedly been destroyed during a wartime fire. In addition, not even the most recent and in-depth research about the Bubishi could bring to light an evidence for the existence of a direct filial copy of the Itosu Anko manuscript. The only document which remains in question as a handwritten, second order filial copy of the Itosu Anko Bubishi is the Konishi Yasuhiro manuscript (A), which has the following lineage:

Itosu Anko → Mabuni Kenwa (B) → Konishi Yasuhiro (A)

Notwithstanding its obvious importance for Okinawa karate, not many details could be found about this Konishi Yasuhiro manuscript (A) in any of the literature about this topic. One related issue is that the Mabuni Kenwa print edition of 1934 only contains 11 articles. In addition, the 1934 edition only comprises Twenty-Eight Self-Defense Diagrams, as opposed to 48 verified in the Tenson-byo-lineage. On the other hand, the two articles Hand and Foot, Muscle and Bone Training Postures (of the Shorei-ji-ryu) as well as the Delayed Death Touch Twelve-Hour Diagrams could so far only be verified in the Mabuni Kenwa print edition of 1934, but not in the Tenson-byo-lineage.[86] The Hand and Foot, Muscle and Bone Training Postures (of the Shorei-ji-ryu) comprise of 34 sheets, each showing a person performing martial movements.[87] The Delayed Death Touch Twelve-Hour Diagrams are 13 sheets with illustrations describing the secret tradition of the Delayed Death Touch, that is, of vulnerable pressure points from which the victim "dies after one day," or "dies after one year." Twelve sheets show the tradition of the double-hours of the day, while sheet 13 shows the 36 vital points of the human body according to this school.[88]

The inscription on the cover of the Konishi Yasuhiro manuscript (A) says "Records for the Study of Karate—From the Bubishi. Copied from the Original Text of Mabuni." Judging from this it can be assumed that it has been copied from the most probably lost Mabuni Kenwa manuscript (B). Because of this the Konishi Yasuhiro manuscript (A) is of extreme importance: it is probably the oldest and sole extant complete handwritten copy of the Itosu-lineage Bubishi. In other words, only by this edition the actual scope and content of the Itosu Bubishi can be reconstructed. Unfortunately, so far, no final evidence could be established that the contents of this edition exceed the 11 articles already found in the Mabuni Kenwa print edition of 1934. In fact, no edition that made use of the Itosu–Mabuni lineage so far showed any contents exceeding the 11 articles of Mabuni 1934. On the other hand, there is also no final evidence that Mabuni 1934 might only have included excerpts and that the Itosu Bubishi included an unknown, larger number of articles. These are the reasons why the Konishi Yasuhiro manuscript (A) is extremely important: it is probably the only manuscript that can confirm the content and scope of the original Itosu edition, as well as the Mabuni filial edition of it, and whether they contain more than just the 11 articles that already have been published in print in Mabuni 1934.

As another interesting note, the Konishi Yasuhiro manuscript (A) is a document collection that does not only include the Bubishi, but also a manuscript entitled "Guidelines for Karate" by Itosu Anko. These are actually "The 10 Maxims of Karate" submitted by Itosu to the Okinawa Prefectural School Affairs Division in 1908 and expressing his intention to firmly incorporate karate within school education. Here, the old characters for karate 唐手 were used. A similar content was verified in the Konishi Yasuhiro manuscript (B), but there it is written with the new notation as 空手. Furthermore, Itosu Anko was here described as the "Founder of Itosu-ryu,"[89] a term that only became widespread after Mabuni Kenwa passed away on May 23, 1952. This can be seen as evidence that the Konishi Yasuhiro manuscript (B) is of a later date than the Konishi Yasuhiro manuscript (A). According to the above, the lineage of the Konishi Yasuhiro manuscript (A) is as follows:

Itosu-Anko-MS → Mabuni Kenwa (B) → Konishi Yasuhiro (A)

Recapitulation

The Itosu-Anko lineage is difficult to analyze from only the written sources in literature. It might have comprised of the 11 articles as printed in Mabuni 1934. It might also have comprised of a larger number of articles. With its two articles from Mabuni 1934 that are not found in the Tenson-byo lineage, it may well have added up to 31 articles, or even more. However, I wasn't able to discover any content from this lineage which exceeds the 11 articles as found in Mabuni 1934. It should be noted that proof may exist for any of the above points which has not yet been published or discovered by the general public. For example, very recently I was provided with two sheets by Patrick McCarthy that indicate that they were from a hitherto unknown and unpublished source document of the Bubishi. They might have come from the source from which the Mabuni Kenwa manuscript (B) was made, that is, the Itosu Anko manuscript. They might have been the source from which the Miyagi Chojun manuscript was made, namely the Tenson-byo manuscript. At the moment this is impossible for me to answer.

Patrick McCarthy

As they will be described in the course of this work, I will not delve into the adventure of the development of the Patrick McCarthy editions. Rather, I would like to point out a few examples of the contents and their characteristics.

First of all, in the article Delayed Death Touch Twelve-Hour Diagrams in Mabuni Kenwa's print edition (1934), the genitals and pubic hair of the person were erased. In the Konishi Yasuhiro manuscript (A) (Itosu lineage), however, these are shown.[90] The drawings of the same part in the McCarthy-Bubishi, and while the hair of head had been omitted here, show the genitals and pubic hair in a hundred percent congruence to the Konishi Yasuhiro manuscript (A).[91]

Next, various slight discrepancies were detected in the article Shaolin Hand and Foot, Muscle and Bone Training Postures as compared between the McCarthy-Bubishi and Mabuni 1934. The exact same discrepancies were found in the Konishi Yasuhiro manuscript (A). Without any doubt the drawings of this article in the McCarthy-Bubishi were from the Konishi Yasuhiro manuscript (A). As a side note, and other than in Mabuni 1934, the illustrations in the Konishi Yasuhiro manuscript (A) are not numbered. This seems to have been the reason why their order in McCarthy differs at times. Third, the Busaganashi appearing in the Bubishi wears an extraordinary kind of attire. When comparing the Busaganashi as shown in the Higa Seiko manuscript (ca. 1930)[92] with the Mabuni 1934 edition,[93] and while these two are the only lineages that show the Busaganashi, it is obvious that they differ considerably in their details. In the Higa Seiko manuscript the iconography of the Busaganashi is drawn rather sketchily. In Mabuni 1934, on the other hand, although the posture of the Busaganashi is basically the same, it is a much more elaborate drawing. In addition, both hands of the Mabuni-Busaganashi are written in Chinese characters: "The name of this is *Xieshou* (Skill of the Fabulous Monster)". Moreover, the Mabuni-Busaganashi is depicted a "Ghost Dog, the Highest General," waving a banner in his right hand. On its back is written the character "bravery" and at its bottom is written "golden lion." Congruency between the illustrations in the two editions can be seen in the position of the left hand pointing downwards and the right hand pointing upwards, both forming a "two-fingers" gesture.

But the most important thing to note here is the following. The figures drawn in the Konishi Yasuhiro manuscript (A) are handmade copies (traces) from the lost Mabuni Kenwa manuscript (B) and show slight variations to Mabuni 1935. But the Busaganashi of Konishi Yasuhiro manuscript (A) is exactly the same as in Mabuni 1934. However, although the same characters were written on both sheets, the writing style is different. In other words, and even though some shades might have been reworked, the image of the Busaganashi in the Konishi Yasuhiro manuscript (A) must have come from the same printing plate as in Mabuni 1934. Mabuni must have had a number of identical sheets showing the Busaganashi. The handwriting was added afterwards, and this was also done in the Konishi Yasuhiro manuscript (A). And without any doubt, the handwriting found at the side of the right and the left hand of McCarthy's Busaganashi was written by the same hand as in the Konishi Yasuhiro manuscript (A).

Well, this Konishi Yasuhiro manuscript (A) was a handwritten copy of the Mabuni Kenwa manuscript (B), which in turn was a handwritten copy of the Itosu Anko Bubishi manuscript. The whereabouts of the Itosu Anko manuscript are unknown. Moreover, according to the talks of his son Mabuni Ken'ei, his father's copy of Itosu's manuscript burned down during wartime fire. According to this, the Konishi Yasuhiro manuscript (A) appears to be the oldest extant handwritten manuscript of the Itosu lineage Bubishi. And as has been shown above, it found its way into the Bubishi researched and published by Patrick McCarthy. This is nothing short of a sensation.

Recapitulation

It has been shown above that the McCarthy-Bubishi, without any doubt, used one or more original manuscripts from the Itosu-lineage Bubishi, namely, at least the handwritten Konishi Yasuhiro manuscript (A). This in turn was copied directly from Mabuni's copy of Itosu's original. For this reason, the Konishi Yasuhiro manuscript (A) is one of the most—if not the most—authentic copies of the Itosu Anko lineage.

Over the years, with the development of the Bubishi, other lineages also entered the McCarthy-Bubishi. This is natural, necessary, and logical in the research process. For example, a comparative analysis of characters and other contents led me to the conclusion that the McCarthy-Bubishi certainly used texts and illustrations from the Konishi Yasuhiro manuscript (B), which was a gift to Konishi by Mabuni Kenwa himself and came from the Tenson-byo lineage via Miyagi Chojun. It should be noted that the lineage of the Tenson-byo manuscript began to accumulate various errors and changes since the Higa Seiko manuscript. For this reason the Konishi Yasuhiro manuscript (B) is one of the most authentic copies of the Tenson-byo lineage. In this sense, its usage in the McCarthy-Bubishi is again nothing short of a sensation.

I hope I am close to the truth. Keep in mind that the above is merely a theoretical analysis, which might be helpful, or not. In the following I would like to address some issues and provide some fresh perspectives that will link the Bubishi more closely with Okinawa karate.

Bubishi—Creation and Creator
The Bubishi as a Single, Self-Contained Work

In the following I would like to refer to the drawings found in one of the original printed editions of the Bubishi. The reason is that the drawings of the McCarthy editions were newly made and artistically implemented, which I think was a good idea. However, some of characteristics I want to refer to here were changed in this process. At the same time I will maintain the titles and numeration of the articles as given in the McCarthy edition for easy reference throughout this paper.

The Forty-Eight Self-Defense Diagrams (Article 29)[94] of the Bubishi contain a total of 96 ink drawings of persons, namely 48 drawings of the victor and 48 drawings of the defeated for each technique described. With the exception of technique No. 16 ("Drunken Arhat") showing the portrait of a close-cropped Buddhist monk, all of the characters exhibit the "Manchu queue" hairstyle compulsory, under threat of punishment, for all males during the Qing Dynasty. Exempted from this hairstyle were Buddhist priests, who shaved their heads, and Taoist priests, who wore a topknot. In this Manchu queue hairstyle, the front hair was shaved while the rest was grown long and often braided into a long ponytail.

Of course, no long ponytail is seen in the illustrations of the Bubishi. This is because during the practice of martial arts the braid was wound up into a spiral form on the back of the head. This was done to prevent the ponytail from entangling or otherwise interfering with the combat movements, and also to prevent it from being used for a technique against its owner. Even among the Chinese community of Kume village there was no such hairdo as a Manchu queue hairstyle on Okinawa. In addition, in the Ryukyu hairstyle of the time hairpins were used to fasten the topknot. Moreover, it should be noted that all the persons depicted here wear typical gauntlets boots and trousers. According to this, the Forty-Eight Self-Defense Diagrams decidedly show Chinese persons from the era of the Qing dynasty (1644–1912).

On the contrary to the above, the 34 illustrations given in Shaolin Hand and Foot, Muscle and Bone Training Postures (Article 32)[95] show very different characteristics. First of all, the hairdo is cut short, but there is neither a sign of shaving, nor of a braid, nor a topknot. In number 27 we even see the hair tied together to the back of the head and fastened by a hairpin or two. What does this say about the person? There are two plausible possibilities: either this is a Taoist priest, who would wear a topknot during the Qing dynasty, or it was a Ryukyuan person. Secondly, all persons here wear shoes, but there seem to be no gauntlets. Finally, the binding of the trousers is reminiscent of the binding of a *hakama*.

According to the above, the persons shown here might have been a Taoist priest with some disciples, or maybe a Ryukyuan leader with some youths. This is just a guess, but it is important to point this out. Similarly, the Delayed Death Touch Twelve-Hour Diagrams (Article 21)[96] all show persons with short hair and without shaved heads or ponytails. The above mentioned articles Shaolin Hand and Foot, Muscle and Bone Training Postures (Article 32) and Delayed Death Touch Twelve-Hour Diagrams (Article 21) were copied by Mabuni from a manuscript in the possession of Itosu Anko. In what is considered the oldest extant handwritten copy of the Bubishi, i.e. the Higa Seiko manuscript, these two articles are not found. Doesn't this point to the possibility of the Bubishi as a selectively-cumulative document, compiled from various sources? According to the above, a generalizing statement that the Bubishi is a single self-contained work based on White Crane and Monk Fist Boxing is probably not explicit enough. Besides the above mentioned differences, how did Sun Zi make it into the Bubishi (see Maxims of Sun Zi, article 15)? How also did White Crane Boxing, and medicine and acupuncture? I tend to believe through a selectively-cumulative adoption of contents into a collected edition. True, flamboyant parts of the content belong to White Crane Boxing. However, more than half of the contents of the Bubishi is about medicine, not directly about combat techniques of a certain style. Wouldn't it be, therefore, logical to call the Bubishi a work based on medicine, with an emphasis on specific martial arts?

In addition, considering the fact that no author nor date of origin is found in the Bubishi, I believe a specific question should be raised. Namely, who were the compilers of the Bubishi? The Chinese military treatise *Wubeizhi* (1621) is a prominent example of selective content accumulated into a new compilation. "Wubeizhi" is pronounced "Bubishi" in Japanese. It is a huge compilation of parts from more than 2,000 Chinese military books from previous epochs. The martial art of the Chinese military officer referred to by the soubriquet of "Kusanku"[97] was described in 1762 as having originated in the *Wubeizhi*. But the only empty-handed martial arts shown in this work were simply borrowed from the earlier work called *Jixiao Xinshu* (1561). These in turn were nothing but the Thirty-two Combat Scenarios of Long Boxing, once developed by Emperor Song Taizu (927–976) as an empty-handed combat system for training the military. Confused?

What if Otsuka Tadahiko, in a highly complex long-term study, compared the above mentioned Thirty-two Combat Scenarios of Long Boxing from the Song dynasty with the The Forty-Eight Self-Defense Diagrams (Article 29) of the Okinawan Bubishi? And what if he identified thirteen matches between these two otherwise completely unrelated systems?

But let's continue. In addition to such subject-specific monographs as noted above, a large amount of encyclopedic compilations made use of the same method of adding individual fragments from any bygone epoch, if the compilers saw fit. This is typical of this kind of Chinese work. Who said that the individual contents of such a compilation had to be directly related to the author? Besides these, there is also a large number of what had been called "Bubishi-like works" by Patrick McCarthy in existence in China. And isn't that exactly what the name "Bubishi" attempts to tell us? Namely, that it is a selective-cumulative compilation of various things from different epochs related by topic?

Assuming for a moment the Bubishi came into existence as a selectively-cumulative compilation, then it is conceivable that individual content was added at different times. This also applies to White Crane Boxing. It is still unclear if White Crane Boxing actually constituted the original contextual premise of the work and its sole reference point. Well, today basically all editions of the Bubishi start with Origins of White Crane Gongfu (Article 1). However, the numbering of the articles is a modern attempt to better organize it and nobody can say for certain at which point White Crane Boxing was originally positioned, or at what time it was added and by whom. This is the reason why the question as regards the time and place of the origin of the Bubishi is problematic: it anticipates the emergence of a self-contained work, at a specific time, by a specific person. Granted, this is a most promising approach, but it isn't the only one. Yet, the Bubishi is a decidedly complex matter which—while being somewhat entertaining—eludes superficial assessment.

According to the above, the original source document of the Bubishi might be seen as a bunch of loose documents which at some point were gathered into a compilation. This in turn was successively enlarged by infrequent, cumulative updates by means of adding documents or citations from other works of varying length—from a few sentences to whole subjects—which matched the broader and related martial arts topics. I want to give two examples: a short citation from a different work would be Maxims of Sun Zi (Article 15). A long citation would be The Forty-Eight Self-Defense Diagrams (Article 29).

At this point, the theory of the emergence of the Bubishi as a single self-contained work at a specific time by a specific author and composed of a fixed number of original articles has to be balanced against the possibility of a work that emerged as a selectively-cumulative compilation.

A Personal Secret Tradition

Another point is the common perception of the Bubishi as a manuscript developed within a private, secret tradition. This perception is due to the prominence of the sections on White Crane Boxing and Monk Fist Boxing, as opposed to a military style of empty-handed combat. According to this hypothesis, while the contents and nature of the original source document are still unverified, the Bubishi is considered a privately made and owned personal martial arts journal. Assuming an opposite perspective, the Bubishi—or the core document it was based upon—might have been a document from the stores of the Ryukyu government. I guess some readers are shaking their heads now. In fact, this point concerns one of the very core premises of the perception of modern karate, namely its perpetual primordial origin as a private, empty-handed self-defense. Anyway, in the preface to the publication of the "Okinawa-den Bubishi" by Otsuka Tadahiko (1986), Miyagi Chojun's student Yagi Meitoku specified that "In a bookcase of a room of the temple in Naha referred to as the Tenson-byo, the official history book *Rekidai Hoan* was kept together with the *Bubishi*."[98] Now, in order to understand the magnitude and implications of this bookcase mentioned in passing by Yagi, I need to give a short explanation of the work, *Rekidai Hoan*.

The *Rekidai Hoan* ("Precious Documents of Successive Generations") is a compilation of documents begun in 1697 on order of the royal government of Ryukyu. Not only documents pertaining to the exchange between Ryukyu and China were included, but also those related to Korea and several Southeast Asian countries (such as Malacca, Java, Sumatra, Annam, etc.). All documents were exclusively written in Chinese, and all dates given according to the Chinese calendar. The oldest document added to this collection dates back to 1424. Two official copies of the *Rekidai Hoan* were stored: One by the government in the capital of Shuri, and the other at the Tenson-byo in Kume village, Naha. The Shuri government copy was snatched by the Japanese following the annexation of Ryukyu in 1879, and taken to Tokyo, where it was lost in the Great Kanto earthquake of 1923. However, the second copy from the Tenson-byo joss house in Kume was kept concealed from the Japanese authorities by the Kume people. In 1933, it was presented and transferred to the Okinawa Prefectural Library. At this time some sheets were already missing, and various characters were no longer recognizable. With the Pacific War finally culminating in the Battle of Okinawa in 1945, the staff of the Okinawa Prefectural Library attempted to save the *Rekidai Hoan* by bringing it to the north of Okinawa Island. However, this edition of the *Rekidai Hoan* was destroyed in its entirety during the war.[99]

Well, first of all, Yagi's statement that the Bubishi was stored in the same bookcase at the Tenson-byo as the official government history book, *Rekidai Hoan*, speaks for its significance. It also suggest that the Bubishi itself might not only have been an official document, but also that two editions of it were stored: one in Shuri, one in Kume. Does that make sense? By the way, the same two-copy method was used with family genealogies, likewise prepared on official order of the royal government of Ryukyu, and not for private consumption. From further sources we glean the information that the Bubishi was not transferred to the Okinawa Prefectural Library in 1933, but remained at the Tenson-byo: According to Tokuda Anshu, the nephew of karate expert Tokuda Anbun, "Until prior to the war, this Bubishi had been stored in the mausoleum of Confucius in the district Kume in Naha."[100] Although slightly contradictory in the mentioned place of storage, the mausoleum of Confucius belongs to the same cultural complex of shrines, temples and schools of Kume village at the time as the Tenson-byo. Today they are all housed in the same compound.

According to the above, the Bubishi was stored in facilities that were closely related to the Ryukyu government, either as administrative or educative institutions. In this connection it should be noted that the overwhelming share of Ryukyuans that went to China did so in their capacity as Ryukyu government officials or staff, such as the resident attaché at the Ryukyukan in Fuzhou, the ship captains, warehouse managers, traders, sailors, various envoys and the like. From this perspective, considering an original source document of the Bubishi exclusively as the result of a private undertaking is problematic. It is a romantic view that veils the obvious and follows the false assumptions of more modern personal studies and private individuals creating and running martial arts schools. But this is simply not consistent with the nature of martial arts during the kingdom period. Furthermore, considering the Bubishi in relation to administrative or educative Ryukyu government institutions opens the possibility of the existence of different copies of the Bubishi—one in Shuri, and one in Kume, as was shown in the example of the *Rekidai Hoan*. This would, in part, also explain the varying contents, as well as other deviations in the various verified lineages and editions of the early Bubishi. Seen from this perspective, and although prominent in scope and characteristics, the contents about White Crane Boxing may have been held at some point in a collection of administrative and educative documents, and further evolved into a "martial compilation" that came to be known as the "Bubishi."

At this point, the theory of a single, private original edition of the Bubishi has to be balanced against the possibility of more than one edition directly or indirectly affiliated to administrative or educative Ryukyu government institutions.

Tradition in Personal Instruction

Now I would like to turn towards the idea of a personal tradition of master to student that has been continued to this day, since the founding days of the Bubishi. The following question comes up: If there has, indeed, been a personal instruction in the techniques contained within the Bubishi during early modern karate tradition, then what happened to the large number of original (Chinese) designations of these techniques?

No modern style goes beyond typical Japanese or Okinawan terminology, most of which are either new developments, or attempts to artificially reconstruct such terms towards a historical Ryukyuan pronunciation. It is not even clear whether the names added to The Forty-Eight Self-Defense Diagrams (Article 29) constitute a single attack-counter scenario, or if they were specific short cuts for more complex scenarios. In the latter case, you might agree that it would be impossible to reconstruct these by just one illustration and a short name. However, the fact that a more elaborated, written description was not added doesn't necessarily mean that they were not complex scenarios. The names of the techniques may simply have been shortcuts to remembering techniques by someone who had practically learned them. Taking this into account, does the Bubishi have to be considered a mere written tradition?

On the other hand, karate, and martial arts in general, are intended to be memorized by the body and it is possible to do so without knowing the names of techniques. Another point is that the names of techniques might have changed over time. In any case, it seems that none of the names of the combat techniques from the Bubishi were handed down into any modern tradition of Okinawa karate. Wait! Did I say none?

One of the very few names of old-style techniques still currently handed down in Okinawa is *koza*, which is interpreted as "chicken beak fist." The original designation *koza* changed over time until it came to be called *shoken-zuki*, or what is otherwise known as *ippon-ken*: that is, a punch with the proximal interphalangeal joint of the index finger. When looking into the etymology of the word *koza*, it might refer to two characters that appear in the Bubishi. In the dialect of Fuzhou they are pronounced *kautso*.[101] This composite word means as much as "knocking (with the) jujube date." As such this designation seems to draw an imaginative analogy of the body part that mainly constitutes the technique—i.e. the proximal interphalangeal joint of the index finger—with the appearance of the jujube stone.[102]

Apart from the above, various kinds of boxing appear in the Bubishi, many of which include numbers in their names. There is Twenty-Eight Strikes found in the article on Nepai Quan (Article 7), which is a method of the Monk Fist Boxing. Twenty-Four Variations is an "iron sand" technique—usually referred to as iron palm, and Twenty-Four Body-Turns is a White Monkey technique. Both of these are found in the article Zheng's Twenty-Four Iron Hand Applications and White Monkey Style (Article 27). And in Article 28 we find the Black Tiger style technique called Fifty-four Steps as well as Eighteen Scholars of White Crane Boxing. Just like in the above examples, there are also many names of Kata in Okinawa that represent numbers. Among these are Nepai, Niseshi, Useshi, or Sepai, to name a few. In light of these names it should be noted that these are all pronunciations using the dialect of Fuzhou.[103] The derivation is as follows.

The characters of Nepai are pronounced in Japanese as *Nijuhachi-ho* (28 Steps). In Chinese standard pronunciation they become *Ershiba-bu*. But pronounced in the dialect of Fuzhou they become *Nisei-pai*, *Nilei-pai*, *Neisei-pai*, *Neilei-pai*, *Nipai*, or *Neipai*.

The characters of Niseshi are pronounced in Japanese as *Nijushiho* (24 Steps). In Chinese standard pronunciation they become *Ershisi-bu*. But pronounced in the dialect of Fuzhou they become *Nileisi*, *Niseisi*, *Nileisei*, *Neiseisei*, *Nisei*, or *Neisei*.

The characters of Useshi are pronounced in Japanese as *Gojushiho* (54 Steps). In Chinese standard pronunciation they become *Wushisi-bu*. But pronounced in the dialect of Fuzhou they become *Uleisei*, *Useisei*, *Ouseisei*, *Usei*, or *Uusi*.

The characters of Sepai are pronounced in Japanese as *Juhachi-ho*. In Chinese standard pronunciation they become *Shiba-bu*. But pronounced in the dialect of Fuzhou they become *Seipai*. As is evident from the above, not only kata names such as *Nepai*, *Niseshi*, *Useshi*, and *Sepai* are all read in an approximation of the Fuzhou dialect, but it can also be seen that the suffix *bu* (step) is omitted in the pronunciation, and only the numbers are read. The same is true for *Sesan* and *Suparinpe*, which had been recorded for the year 1867 as "13 Steps," and "108 Steps," respectively, but here, too, the suffix *bu* (step) is omitted in the pronunciation.

Another example is a kata called *Hofwa* in Okinawan karate, for which the characters of "White Crane" are given, which are read *Baihe* in standard Chinese, and *Hakutsuru* in Japanese. Of course, the meaning of the term *Hofwa* is unknown both in the Japanese language as well as in the Ryukyu dialect. But in the Bubishi, among the sections about White Crane Boxing, the term "Crane Method" is found, which is pronounced *Houhua* in the Fuzhou dialect (read *Hefa* in standard

Chinese, and *Tsuru-ho* in Japanese). Moreover, in the karate style called Ryu'ei-ryu, there is found the kata called *Paiho*. This *Paiho* is an approximation of the Fujian dialect pronunciation of *Pahou*, meaning "White Crane" (*Baihe* in standard Chinese, *Hakutsuru* in Japanese). In other words, the Okinawan Kata called *Hofwa* refers to "Crane Method" in Fuzhou dialect, and not to "White Crane."[104] According to the above a personal tradition of master to student actually took place and even continues to this day, although evidence is quite scant. And the Bubishi was apparently somehow related to it. On the other hand, it is also clear that other things were changed and some things were completely discarded.

Another Perspective

Rin Seiko (1842–1880) from Kume village was an intriguing character. He was scholar, official and diplomat of the Ryukyu Kingdom, as well as a leader of the royalist movement to save the Ryukyu Kingdom from Imperial Japanese annexation by appealing to the Chinese Qing Dynasty government for help. In 1865, at age 25, Rin Seiko passed the Kansho (government sponsored overseas students) examination. Immediately afterwards he enrolled in the National Academy (Kokugaku) in Shuri, where he mastered Chinese poetry and classics and became conversant in Chinese within a few years. In 1868 he was chosen as a member of the twenty-sixth and last group of Kansho and entered the Imperial Academy in Beijing. Among the four students dispatched on this occasion, all others died in Beijing in 1870. Only Rin Seiko survived and returned home after a prolonged stay in 1874. Subsequently he was appointed instructor at the National Academy in Shuri and, at the same time, served as attendant-tutor to the Crown Prince, Sho Ten.[105] It is evident from the above that Rin Seiko was a leading mind at the time of the abolition of the Ryukyu Kingdom. His Ryukyuan official name was Nashiro Satonushi Pechin Shunbo.

During the crucial phase of the Japanese takeover of Ryukyu between 1872 and 1879, the last king Sho Tai secretly dispatched a group of about nineteen loyal royalists to China to request assistance, among which was said Rin Seiko.[106] This mission took up residence at the old Ryukyukan trading facilities in Fuzhou. Here they began their energetic and purposeful activity to win over China to rescue the Ryukyu Kingdom.[107] Over the following years, secret messengers would facilitate communication between King Sho Tai and the royalists in China. As was explained by the royalists to the Chinese authorities: "We will never be subjects controlled by Japan, nor will we assume the Japanese spirit, even when we die."[108]

One member of this group of royalists was Urasoe Uekata Chochu (aka Sho Yutoku), former chief clerk of the Council of State in Ryukyu. Obviously Urasoe had returned to Okinawa, but in 1883 or 1884, in opposition to the abolition of the Ryukyu Kingdom, he exiled himself to China. Again he stayed at the former royal trading station called Ryukyu-kan in Fujian province. In the same year he presented a petition for the restoration of the Ryukyu Kingdom to the Chinese government, and in 1887 he petitioned again.[109] But at some point prior to 1898 he returned to Okinawa again, where we hear about him in connection with a first mention of "karate" in a newspaper.[110]

> *"Urasoe Chochu is a member of an Anji-clan, but had stayed in China for a long time. After he returned home to Okinawa Prefecture in recent years, he was active as a leader of the stubborn party. He invited seven- or eight-year-old school age children to his premises in Shuri Tobaru and taught them various subjects, such as the Four Confucian Classics, arithmetic, calligraphy, and also Karate (a Chinese style of Jujutsu?). He had two or three lecturers of doubtful origin and more than fifty or sixty pupils. No distinctions were being made according to the former classes, but all children obtained admission irrespective of their genealogy."*

A few points should be noted here. Royalists who opposed the Japanese takeover were obviously related to the earliest written notices on karate. At that time the journalists wondered if this karate was "a Chinese style of Jujutsu." In addition, as can be seen in the designation "stubborn party," Urasoe's activities were clearly interpreted from the perspective of contemporary political ideology and considered an oppositional political act. Moreover, the royalists were continuously active for 20 years, with their base in China having been the former royal trading station called Ryukyuan. Wouldn't it make sense that the Bubishi, or parts of it, reached Okinawa by means of these royalists, basically as an empty-handed resistance fighter manual within the ongoing and escalating political disputes? Let's dig for some tangible hints.

In response to the inaction of the Chinese government, the aforementioned royalist Rin Seiko committed suicide in November 1880. Thirty-three years later, on November 18, 1913, a "Memorial Poetry for the Late Rin Seiko" was published in the *Ryukyu Shinpo* newspaper. It was written by a certain Ko Shoketsu (Chinese Gao Xiangjie). Ko Shoketsu is considered one of the persons who might have brought the Bubishi to Okinawa: "[The Bubishi was probably] handed down by Ko Shoketsu from the Chinese coastal province of Fujian, who assiduously operated the Senshunkan teahouse in Naha Higashi-machi."[111] This Ko Shoketsu was also related to other Fujian persons living in Okinawa at the time. One such person was Go Kenki (Chinese Wu Xiangui, 1886–1940), who is said to have reached Okinawa in 1912.

Afterwards he became the head clerk of the tea store called Senshunkai in Naha Higashi-machi. The general manager of this tea house was none other than the above mentioned Ko Shoketsu. Both persons were from Fujian Province.

It is unknown when exactly Ko Shoketsu came to Okinawa, but it can be assumed to have been prior to 1912, as the dates of Go Kenki suggest. Besides running his tea trade, Ko Shoketsu was also a calligrapher and a poet and is "considered one of the few intellectuals in those days." No less a person than Fujiwara Ryozo expressed the theory that Ko Shoketsu was probably somehow related to the Chinese revolutionary and politician Sun Wen (1866–1925, better known as Sun Yat-sen), the first president and founding father of the Republic of China in 1912. In 1900, Qing China was shaken by the xenophobic Boxer Uprising (*Giwadan*). Here we find another newspaper article describing the Boxer fighters' training and techniques, which the article describes as "skill of warding off bullets," as "Tekobushi," and as "Karate," which were all considered as the martial arts of local rebels and bandits.[112] Sun Wen and his group took advantage of this state of affairs and, allied with the secret anti-government societies of the triads and the Gelaohui, tried to procure weapons in the Philippines, Singapore, Hongkong, Taiwan, and Japan. The armed Huizhou Uprising of 1900 initiated by Sun Wen ultimately failed, and many of the members of the uprising party exiled in order to escape prosecution by the Qing Dynasty authorities.

Taking into account this political background as well as the above-cited examples from newspaper articles, it was therefore considered possible that Ko Shoketsu was related to the Chinese rebels, became an exile to Okinawa and might have brought a manuscript of empty-handed martial arts of southern Chinese Kenpo with him.[113]

According to the above, the Bubishi as a manual of Chinese Boxing prepared by a private person and handed down to Okinawa has to be balanced against the option that it was probably a fragmentary part of contemporary Chinese militia-like anti-government rebel groups, as well as a secret martial art of the few remaining Okinawan royalists still active in hope of the return of the kingdom.

Creator and Creation

Everybody knows that the Bubishi does not include martial arts with weaponry. Does that mean that the original martial art of Okinawa was historically an empty-handed martial art? As already mentioned, the Wubeizhi is a massive military treatise, completed in 1621 by Mao Yuanyi (1594–1640). It consists of 240 volumes, covering all aspects from strategy and logistics, engineering, naval warfare, fortifications, vehicles, armor, artillery and bombs, etc. Among the instructions on practice in various weapons and devices was included a chapter with techniques of the classical Japanese sword style of Kage-ryu, which came from a scroll the Chinese defenders took as a trophy from Japanese pirates at the time. Although for some reason in a disorganized order, the *Wubeizhi* also borrowed from the *Jixiao Xinshu* (1561) the "Thirty-two Combat Scenarios of Long Boxing" of Song Taizu, as well as 14 combative scenarios with the naked cudgel (*gun*). Besides, it also features all sorts of polearms used at the time, like the 55 methods of the Shaolin cudgel found in Volume 89, described both in illustration and text. The very title *Wubeizhi* means nothing less than "Records on Military Preparation." It was a complex military treatise meant for the army and navy of the Chinese empire.

Incidentally, in Okinawan karate circles, the designation "Bubishi" was used for quite some time. It is exactly the same designation as the name of the *Wubeizhi* of Mao Yuanyi, just in the Japanese reading of the characters. The reason why Okinawans began to call it "Bubishi" is still unknown. One possible reason might have been that both Mao Yuanyi's *Wubeizhi* as well as the Bubishi of Okinawa included portions with strategies by Sun Zi (*Sunzi Bingfa*), illustrations of Chinese Kenpo, or methods of medical treatment, although the contents itself are different. Another reason might have been that it was considered to be similar in its nature as a selectively-cumulative compilation of an initially official and quasi-military character, and that it borrowed heavily from various other works from history. So when was the name Bubishi first used on Okinawa? In November 1922, Funakoshi Gichin's "Ryukyu Kenpo Karate" was published. It was not only the first monograph about karate, but in its appendix, for the first time parts of the Bubishi were published in a printed matter. However, nowhere in this work the designation Bubishi itself is used. The four articles found here were simply placed under the heading "appendix" and followed without any further identifier after Funakoshi's explanation on "Karate ni sente nashi." Nowhere in the early writings of Okinawa karate is a document named Bubishi mentioned. The first verified occasion of the use of "Bubishi" as a document title took place only in 1934, namely in Mabuni Kenwa's printed edition, and it were printed characters, not handwritten ones by Itosu, from whom Mabuni made his copy. Only 11 articles were included under the title of Bubishi here. From among these 11, three coincide with the four articles of Funakoshi (1922), namely, Grapplings and Escapes, The Principles of the Ancient Law, and Maxims of Sun Zi.

For comparison it should also be noted that in the Higa Seiko manuscript edition of around 1930, no such title as Bubishi is found anywhere. It was only its filial edition of 1937, in the possession of Izumigawa Kanki, that came with the title "Bubishi."

The point here is that it appears to be likely that Mabuni Kenwa chose the title "Bubishi," or at least he was the first who used it in print. If so, isn't it likely that he did so in historical allusion to Mao Yuanyi's 1621 work? At this point, the theory of the existence of an original document titled Bubishi has to be balanced against the possibility that the title was adopted and assigned by Mabuni Kenwa in 1934, and afterwards came to be used retrospectively for all sorts of similar documents. Now, as regards the lack of martial arts with weaponry and the emphasis on empty-handed martial arts in the Bubishi, is this a historical fact, or was it merely the result of the then early modern definition of empty-handed karate? One main reason for the perception of old-style karate as an individual, personal self-defense discipline comes with the classification of the Bubishi as a document revealing the true historical state of karate in the nineteenth century. But that is not the only likely reason.

Since 1905, karate had been introduced into school education as a form of physical education. While a limited number of persons continued to practice karate as a *mongai-fushutsu*—an art carefully preserved and not shown in public, karate began to penetrate the rural areas by way of the former Shuri normal school students. Research activities by karate experts gained momentum since around the early 1920s. The year 1925 saw the establishment of the Okinawa Budo Kyokai, 1930 the founding of the Okinawa Prefecture Athletic Association, 1933 the approval of karate by the Dai Nippon Butokukai, and 1936 saw the clarification of the designation of karate in its new form. This era coincides with the period of initial dissemination of the Bubishi. It therefore seems obvious that our current Bubishi might have been a decidedly selective compilation, along with the development of modern karate. While it is true that the included contents actually constitute authentic historical reference material, these contents were probably selected in the first place on the premise of a) the definitions and ideas of modern twentieth century karate, and b) of the independent existence of historical, empty-handed martial arts indigenous to Okinawa since ancient times. The latter is a theory that has been more or less arbitrarily developed by the Okinawa Prefectural School Affairs Division and karate masters within the procedures towards an affiliation of karate with the Dai Nippon Butokukai in 1933, and has otherwise only romantic historical value. Ever since Itosu's "10 Maxims of Karate" from 1908 and his contradictory historical allusion to Shorin-ryu and Shorei-ryu, which had rather tacitly been discarded rather than explained, karate instructors of Okinawa had been persuaded by government agencies and their affiliates by recommendations along the lines of:

> *"When viewed from the true spirit of Japanese Budo, the designation Karate (Chinese Hand) is not particularly favorable. How about you consider a different designation as a substitute for it?"*[114]

It was from these insinuations that the designations Shuri-te, Naha-te, and Tomari-te were born, and from these finally the whole concept of an empty-handed Ti indigenous to Okinawa since ancient times. It was exactly the opposite to what is commonly believed. In other words, karate's modern premise of an empty-handed martial art may have constituted a formative momentum in the selection of the content of the Bubishi. At the same time, the existence of the Bubishi in return served as a crucial proof for the historical validity of the underlying theory of a historical, empty-handed martial arts indigenous to Okinawa and independent from martial arts with weaponry. The Bubishi might, therefore, be considered both a creation as well as a creator of modern karate. At this point, the possibility of an invention of the title "Bubishi" within the early twentieth century karate movement becomes viable. But most importantly, an interdependence between the Bubishi and karate can be detected, in that the Bubishi was created on the premise of karate's modern theory, and at the same time came to be a creator of exactly that theory.

I would like to finish in summarizing the facts, perspectives, and theories established in the preceding sections. First, the theory of the emergence of the Bubishi as a single, self-contained work at a specific time by a specific author and composed of a fixed number of original articles has to be balanced against the possibility of a work that emerged as a selectively-cumulative compilation.

Second, the theory of one, private, original edition of the Bubishi has to be balanced against the possibility of the existence of more than one edition, directly or indirectly affiliated to administrative or educative Ryukyu government institutions. Specifically, the possibility of the existence of two separate editions, one stored in Shuri, one stored in Kume, as was the case with other important documents. This theory would also explain the various lineages and differences.

Third, the possibility of the invention of the title "Bubishi" within the early twentieth century karate movement becomes plausible. Most importantly, an interdependence between the Bubishi and karate can be detected, in that the Bubishi was created on the premise of karate's modern theory, and at the same time came to be a creator of exactly that theory.

Fourth, the possibility of new developments in society during the labor pains of modern karate and their dependence on the Bubishi, as well as mutual exchange between the two, became recognizable through the issues surrounding the terms and interpretations of Shorin-ryu and Shorei-ryu, as found in the Bubishi and in Itosu 1908.

Fifth, the Bubishi took on the supporting role of an exotic document reminiscent of some crazy sort of martial arts that once reached Ryukyu. At the same time it backed up—by its sheer uniqueness—the new interpretations of karate, i.e., that of an indigenous empty-handed martial arts handed down in Okinawa since ancient times in the forms of Shuri-te, Naha-te, and Tomari-te.

Sixth, a personal tradition of master handing down to student actually occurred, although rare, and continues to this day. And the Bubishi was apparently somehow linked to this. On the other hand, many things and meanings from the Bubishi were simply lost, while others changed. Looking at the Bubishi from simple set theory, it can be said that the intersecting set between Funakoshi 1922 and Mabuni 1934 are three articles.[115] The intersecting set between Funakoshi 1935 and Mabuni 1934 are the same three articles. Nine out of the eleven articles of Mabuni 1934 (including the intersecting set with Funakoshi 1922) are a subset of the 29 articles of Higa 1930, wherein Mabuni's Twenty-Eight Self-Defense Diagrams additionally also constitute a subset of Higa's Forty-Eight Self-Defense Diagrams. The remaining two articles of Mabuni 1934 constitute a surplus set, which, together with the 29 articles of Higa 1930, constitute a new compilation of 31 articles.

Today the Bubishi is considered to comprise the combined set of 32 articles as described in the work before you, researched, translated, and explained by Patrick McCarthy, Hanshi.

NOTES:

1. Okinawa Prefectural Assembly March 29, 2005: Resolution on the Declaration of 'Karate Day.'

2. Ro 2011 (II): 46.

3. Hokama 2001 (II), 48.

4. OKKJ 2008: 429–430. Hokama 2001 (II): 48.

5. That is, the Jiu Tian Feng Huo Yuan San Tian Dou 九天風火院三田都元帥.

6. Tokashiki 1995: 2 (page is not numbered). Furthermore it was said that "Practice began with a bow in formal sitting position in front of the 'Jiu Tian Feng Huo Yuan San Tian Dou' (BusDganashi) enshrined in the central transom of his tea shop." Cf. Ro 2011 (I): 69.

7. Takamiyagi Shigeru, in Uechi 1977: 223.

8. The Bubishi owned by Fukuchi Seiko was a copy from the Higa Seiko manuscript, which in turn had been transcribed from the Bubishi in the possession of Miyagi Chojun (Cf. Uechi 1977: 223; Tokashiki 1995: 1 (unnumbered page); Ro 2011 (II): 147). The match in the illustrations between the Higa Seiko and the Fukuchi Seiko manuscripts is astonishing, so that it seems that they have been photocopied instead of transcribed

by writing brush. However, the accompanying text was clearly written by a different person.

9. Hokama 2001 (II), 48.

10. Fujiwara 1990: 645.

11. Fujiwara 1990: 645.

12. Shoto (=Funakoshi) 1914; Akio 2001: 101, 151.

13. Sakihara 2006: 73. Ikemiya 2001: 2-3, 8. Tsuha Sei, in OKKJ 2008: 60.

14. Iha Fuyu: Ryukyu Gikyoku-shu. "Kansen Odori-gata Nikki." Shunyodo 1929.

15. Fujiwara 1990: 645.

16. Nakayoshi Shinko: Itosu Buyu-den, Part 2. Master of Shorei-ryu. The Lord Yabiku.

17. OKKJ 2008: 373.

18. Shoto (=Funakoshi Gichin): Okinawa no Bugi (Part 1–3). Karate ni tsuite. Asato Anko-uji Dan. Ryukyu Shinpo, January 17–19., 1914.

19. OKKJ 2008: 506-509.

20. Funakoshi 1922: 274–76; Funakoshi 1925: 296–98. The articles are 1. The Eight Precepts of Quanfa, 2. The Principles of Ancient Law, 3. Maxims of Sun Zi, and 3. Grapplings and Escapes.

21. Funakoshi 1935: 301.

22. Neither the 1922 nor the 1925 works of Funakoshi were translated into English. While the 1935 book was, indeed, translated to English by Oshima Tsutomu, only five of the seven Bubishi-related articles were translated here. In doing so, the headings were not marked as such. Cf. Funakoshi/Oshima 1973. The articles were completely translated in Patrick McCarthy's work "Tanpenshu," 2001: 123-29.

23. According to Takamiyagi Shigeru in Uechi 1977: 224.

24. Cf. Tokashiki 1995: 78; Ro 2011 (II): 110; Mabuni 1934: 176.

25. The text in question is from *Sunzi Bingfa*, Chapter 3: Attack by Stratagem, No. 3: "To fight and conquer in all your battles is not supreme excellence; supreme excellence consists in breaking the enemy's resistance without fighting."

26. 山長, literally "mountain elder" or "master," a term in use for academy masters since the Song era.

27. Zhengyi Academy of Classical Learning 正誼書院, also known as the Zhengyi Bookstore, was established in 1866. This kind of "Academies of Classical Learning" existed from the Tang Dynasty to the Qing Dynasty.

28. Brokaw 1986: 375.

29. Robinson 2001: 95.

30. Cf. Fujiwara 1990: 645.

31. Fujiwara 1990: 645.

32. Gima & Fujiwara 1986: 71. See the complete chapter about the Bubishi on pages 70–79.

33. Kyuyo, Article 1770.

34. Cf. OKKJ 2008: 107.

35. OKKJ 2008: 499–500.

36. Otsuka 1986: 1.

37. Okinawa Tokuyu Bujutsu-sho.

38. Tokashiki 1995: 5–6. Pages are not numbered.

39. Telephone interview by Ro Gai in June 2008.

40. 「為 大塚先生昭和五十八年十月十日 比嘉佑直」

41. Miyagi explains: "Although the publication year is not explicitly stated, it must have been approximately 30 years ago from now (i.e. 1965) when I saw it by chance at a book store in Koza City (today's Okinawa City) and bought it."

42. Rather than breakfalls, *ukemi* here has to be understood as "receiving (attacks) with the body."

43. Or copied by Matsumura Sokon from Todi Sakugawa.

44. Tokashiki 1995: 6–7. Pages are not numbered.

45. *Kantei O no Kakejiku ga Satogaeri* (A hanging scroll of Guan Diwang returning home). Ryukyu Shinpo, 1997/6/26.

46. The sources differ. According to Higa Saburo the demonstration took place in the Butokuden in Kyoto (Cf. Kinjo 2001: 330), others name the Meiji-Jingu-Shrine in Tokyo (Cf. OKKJ 2008: 158, 164, 447). Even the date is uncertain and within the OKKJ 2008 two different dates occur: May 1930 (p. 532) and November 1930 (p. 164, 447). Was Shinzato possibly involved in both demonstrations?

47. OKKJ 2008: 532. Kinjo 2001: 330.

48. Miyagi 1968: 15. Kinjo 2001: 330. OKKJ 2008: 532. The verse is "Ho Goju Donto" from the "The Eight Precepts of Quanfa."

49. Higaonna Morio, Kadekawa Tooru, and Takamiyagi Shigeru, in OKKJ 2008: 531.

50. "Since Higaonna Kanryo *Sensei* was unstudied in the reading and writing of characters, Miyagi Chojun acquired it [the Bubishi] probably either in 1915, when he traveled to Fuzhou, or in 1922, when he traveled to Shanghai, and brought it back to Okinawa apparently as an important and valued affair for him." Cf. Uechi 1977: 223.

51. Mabuni 1934: 83–176.

52. Higaonna Morio and Kadekawa Tooru, in OKKJ 2008: 551.

53. Established 1914. Operates the Shiseibyo Shrine complex in Kume, which today includes such shrines and temples as the Temple of Confucius, the Tenson-byo, the Tenpi-gu, as well as the Meirindo and others.

54. Heinze cites Kuniyoshi Seiko as a student of the historically documented Karate experts Arakaki Seisho (1840–1918), cf. Heinze 2009: 20. However, the source of this information is unclear.

55. Interview of Tetsuhiro Hokama with Kuniyoshi Yukei on March 4, 1984. Cf. Hokama 1984: 299–301.

56. Otsuka 1986: 3–4.

57. Tokuda 1956: 43–48. In Kinjo 1997. Although slightly contradictory in the mentioned place of storage, the mausoleum of Confucius belongs to the same cultural complex of shrines, temples and schools of Kume village at the time as the Tenson-byo. Today they are all housed on the same compound.

58. Kai 2004, at the very beginning of the binding, on the back of the photo showing the wooden Busaganashi sculpture from the Jundokan.

59. Miyazato 1978.

60. Kai 2004, at the very front of the inside cover, on the back of the photo of the wooden Busaganashi sculpture from the Jundokan.

61. Ichikawa-ha Goju-ryu Karate-do Shigakukan.

62. OKKJ 2008: 532.

63. Tokashiki 1995: 1.

64. It was also used as a source in the Okinawa Kenshi 1975, see page 622, as was the Fukuchi Seiko copy, a filial edition of the previous.

65. When organized according to the headings.

66. OKKJ 2008: 384.

67. Karate Odori ni takusu Okinawa he no kyoshu. *The Sun Pictorial Daily*. June 14, 1950.

68. Tokuda 1956: 43-48. In Kinjo 1997.

69. *Aikido no Gokui no Himitsu* 2005: 9.

70. Personal interview by Ro Gai in July 2008 in Naha.

71. Telephone interview by Ro Gai in June 2008.

72.「師範免許書　武備志　大塚忠彦」

73.「恩師之手形市川素水師父」

74. OKKJ 2008: 170.

75. The Hiden Koryu bujutsu 1993/07: 78.

76.「呈　敬愛小西康裕氏」

77. Hiden Koryu bujutsu 1993/07: 80.

78. Hiden Koryu bujutsu 1993/07: 78–82.

79. Cf. 「剛柔流い受け継がれる伝書！武備誌の謎に迫れ！！」 "The book with secret traditions inherited in Goju-ryu! Approaching the Mystery of the Bubishi." In *Gekkan Karate-do*, Vol. 381, October 2002, p.4.

80. Tokashiki 1995: 389.

81. Mabuni 1934: 84.

82. Fujiwara 1990: 645.

83. Mabuni 1934: 83-176.

84. Reten レ点, i.e., reading marks for Kanbun texts that instruct the reader in what order to read the characters so they can be understood in Japanese grammar.

85. Yamaguchi (I) (1966) shows only contents from Mabuni 1934, including 4 of the 28 Self-Defense Diagrams. Yamaguchi (II) (1966) also shows only contents from Mabuni 1934, including 24 of the 28 Self-Defense Diagrams.

86. The Hiden Koryubujutsu bimonthly. Vol. 15, 07. July 1993: 80.

87. Mabuni 1934: 94–127.

88. Mabuni 1934: 130–142.

89. *Itosu-ryu ryuso*.

90. Mabuni 1934: 130–142. The Hiden Koryu bujutsu bimonthly. Vol. 15, 07. July 1993: 81.

91. McCarthy 1995: 140ff.

92. Ro 2011 (II): appendix, page 70.

93. Mabuni 1934: 147. The Hiden Koryubujutsu bimonthly. Vol. 15, 07. July 1993: 78.

94. Compare the illustrations in Mabuni 1934: 148–175.

95. Compare the illustrations in Mabuni 1934: 94–127.

96. Compare the illustrations in Mabuni 1934: 130–142.

97. Tobe Yoshihiro: Oshima Hikki, 1762. See also Iha 1938: 313 and Kadekaru 2012: 176.

98. Otsuka 1986: 3–4.

99. Although there is some contradictory information about the Rekidai Hoan having been stored either in the Tenson-byo, the Meirindo, or the Tenpi-gu Shrine, all these belong to the cultural complex of Kume village. In fact, today they are all housed on the same compound and collectively referred to as the Shiseibyo Shrine complex.

100. Tokuda 1956: 43-48. In Kinjo 1997.

101. The characters in question are 扣棗. In standard Chinese they are pronounced as *kouzao*, and in Japanese as *koso*. Tokashiki in 1995 said it is pronounced *kosa* in Fuzhou dialect, but this is not correct.

102. Ro 2001 (II): 149.

103. The modern Latin alphabet used here cannot properly reproduce the original sounds of the Fujan dialect. Therefore the names given here are approximations. The same is true for the Kata names given in Katakana, which also cannot properly reproduce the original sound of the Fujan dialect.

104. Ro 2001 (II): 148–49.

105. Matsuda 1966: 289, 300.

106. *Japan Daily Herald*: 27th August 1879, "China and Japan." In: Beillevaire II, Vol. 2. Kerr 1958: 374. The group was led by Kochi Uekata Chojo (aka Sho Tokuko). Kochi was in Tokyo in 1875 during the negotiations with Japan, together with the envoys Yonabaru Uekata Ryoketsu, Uchima Pechin Chochoku, and Kyan Pechin Chofu. Cf. Chuzan Seifu, Appendix Vol. 7: King Sho Tai, 1875. In: ORJ, Vol. 5. Further members were Ikei Pechin (aka Sai Taitei), Urasoe Uekata (aka Sho Yutoku, chief supervisor of the clerks of the Council of State at the time), Sho Bundo, and Bu Ido (temporary clerk of the Omono-bugyo at the time

107. Chuzan Seifu, Vol. 13: King Sho Tai. In: ORJ, Vol. 5. According to the Chuzan Seifu they were dispatched because in 1876 the Provincial Administration of Fujian inquired for the reasons that in 1875 no tribute ship had come to Fujian.

108. Extracts translated from Li Hung-chang's Letters and Dispatches. No. 12, 1879/05/14.

109. Cf. Kadekaru 2012: 177. Lu 2011: 59.

110. *Ganha no Jido-kyoiku* (Children Education of the Stubborn Faction). In: Ryukyu Shinpo, June 13, 1898.

111. Fujiwara 1990: 645.

112. Giwaken (The Boxer's Boxing). In: Ryukyu Kyoiku, No. 55, July 1900. Shinkoku Giwadan no Doran (The Boxer Rebellion in Qing China). In: Ryukyu Kyoiku, Vol 54, October 9, 1900. pp. 17-18. See also, Kadekaru 2012: 178.

113. Gima & Fujiwara 1986: 72–73.

114. Fujiwara 1990: 641.

115. "The Principles of Ancient Law," "Maxims of Sun Zi," and "Grapplings and Escapes."

PART ONE

HISTORY AND PHILOSOPHY

The Bubishi is both a creator and a product of history. In this section, I will examine the historical origins of this work and show its impact on history. Perhaps we might better understand what the Bubishi represents by breaking down the components of the word itself. The ideogram pronounced *bu* means "military." The ideogram *bi* means "to provide or prepare." The ideogram *shi* means "record." Together, they mean "a manual of military preparation." In the context of karate, the Bubishi represents the patriarchal source of knowledge, a fountain from which flows strength and wisdom for those brave enough to embrace its spirit. Providing disciples with the ancient masters' secrets, the Bubishi has for generations preserved the original precepts upon which the civil fighting traditions rest; teachings now overshadowed by more base pursuits.

Disclosing the original means and methods of orthodox Chinese *gongfu* (also known as *quanfa* or "fist way," which the Japanese call *kempo*), the Bubishi conclusively imparts both the utilitarian and nonutilitarian values of the civil fighting traditions. In so doing, it reveals the magnitude of karate-do, and identifies that which lies beyond the immediate results of physical training. With one's attention turned inward in this way, karate-do becomes a conduit through which a deeper understanding of the self brings one that much closer to realizing one's position in life in general, and the world in which one dwells.

The Impact of the Bubishi on Modern Karate-do

Although the Bubishi is a document peculiar to Monk Fist and White Crane *gongfu,* it achieves an impact of more encompassing proportions. While its exact date of publication and author remain a mystery, it is nevertheless a valuable source of historical information that offers deep insights into karate-do, its history, philosophy, and application. A number of the most recognizable figures in modern karate-do have used it as a reference or plagiarized from it.

Mabuni Kenwa (1889–1952), was a karate genius and *kobu-jutsu* expert who was responsible for bringing together karate-jutsu's two main streams when he created his Shito-ryu tradition more than half a century ago. In 1934 in the book *Kobo Jizai Karate Kempo Seipai no Kenkyu,* he wrote, "Making a copy of a Chinese book on *kempo* that my venerated master, Itosu Anko, had himself duplicated, I have used the Bubishi in my research and secretly treasured it." In that same year, Mabuni *Sensei* was the first to make the Bubishi public. By making the Bubishi available to the public, Mabuni Kenwa introduced a legacy so profound that, even to this day, the depth of its magnitude has yet to be fully measured or completely understood.

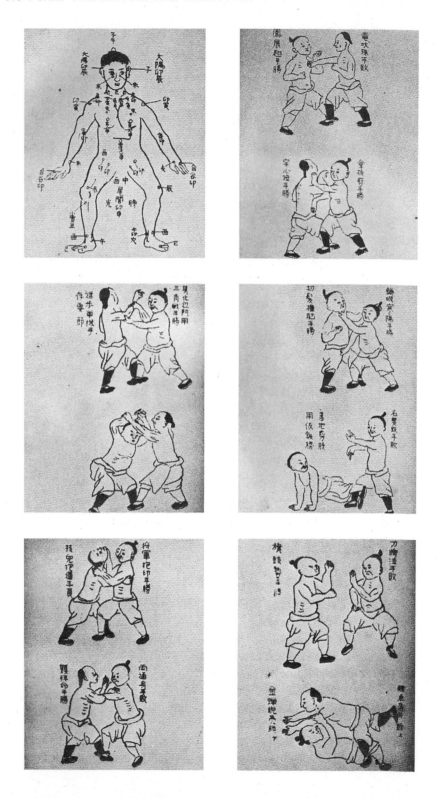

十二時血脈藥方神効　若無青草用此若臣解之

子時用藥　決酒二分冲次音不乳者

丑時用藥　射香不花枝文紅花不乎七五

寅時用藥　射香不次直次滨紅涩予手七不

卯時用藥　真皮一分射者三分毗胆二分方參處分

辰時用藥　紅曲一分白糖一分青桃二分地把把二釘店三

巳時用藥　上步用紅花三分下半用手七三分

午時用藥　酰胆二分虎頭紫二分炖紅玉菜二十

未時用藥　紅仲丁乳者二十丁卷二十内程二十

申西時用藥　參二卜白荣生多配丰熊八分

戌亥時用藥　紅二卜蒲红卜红荣卜方壺虎二十

老酒一杯熬羊杯服下

酒一杯熬羊杯服下

酒一碗熬一一杯服

浮酒服

酒煎服下

冲酒服下

酒三砲熬一砲服

冲酒空心服

空心服

擂末冲酒服下

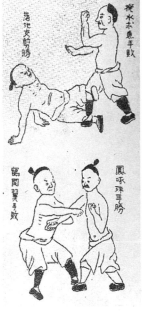

Yamaguchi Bubishi.

A significant portion of *Karate-do Kyohan* by Funakoshi Gichin (1868–1957) is taken directly from the Bubishi.[1] Higashionna Kanryo (1853–1915) revered it; and his principal disciple, Miyagi Chojun (1888–1953), selected the name Goju-ryu from this text (see Article 13, no. 3, p. 261) to represent his unique tradition and considered it

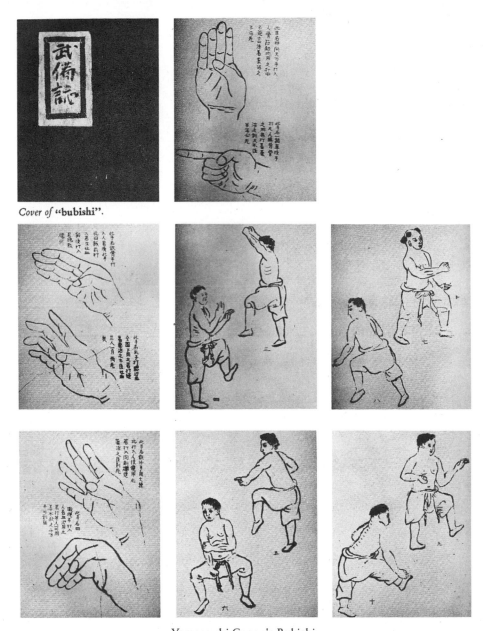

Cover of "bubishi".

Yamaguchi Gogen's Bubishi.

"the bible" of the civil fighting arts. The Bubishi was also used by Shimabukuro Tatsuo (1908–75) when he was establishing his Isshin-ryu karate tradition. The Bubishi had such a profound affect upon Ya-maguchi "the Cat" Gogen (1909–89) that he publicly referred to it as his "most treasured text."

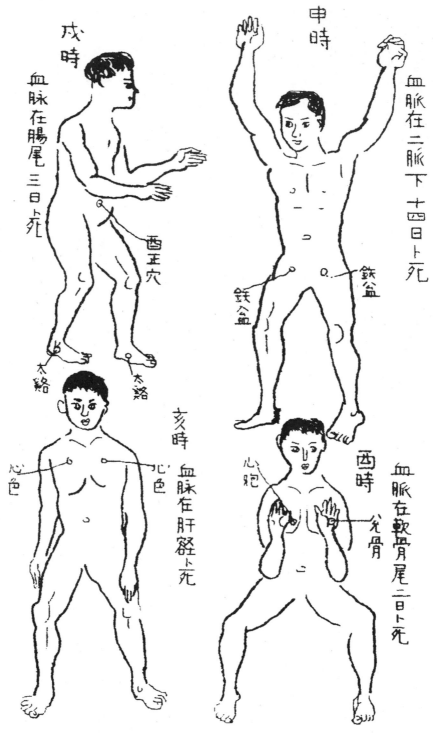

Yamaguchi Gogen's Bubishi.

The profound teachings of this document were no doubt gathered over a period of many hundreds of years. So to begin I think it is important to discuss the theories surrounding the origin of this work.

Possible Origins of the Bubishi in China

The Bubishi bears no author's name, date, or place of publication.

Therefore, accurate details surrounding its origin are unavailable. It is presumed that the Bubishi *was* brought from Fuzhou to Okinawa sometime during the mid-to late-nineteenth century, but by whom

Mabuni Kenwa

remains unknown. There are several hypotheses surrounding the advent of the Bubishi in Okinawa. Unfortunately, none can be corroborated. On the other hand, there is testimony describing the experiences of some well-known *Uchinanchu* (Okinawans) who traveled to the Middle Kingdom for the sole purpose of studying the fighting traditions.

Some insist that the Bubishi appeared in Okinawa by way of their teacher's teacher. Another theory suggests that the Bubishi surfaced independently from within the Chinese settlement in the Kuninda district of Naha. Yet another hypothesis maintains that the Bubishi is a collection of knowledge compiled over many years by *Uchinanchu* who studied in China and belonged to a secret fraternity. All of these assumptions seem perfectly plausible. However, when subjected to critical evaluation and given the lack of data presently available, these theories remain simply speculation.

It is possible that the exact reason for the Bubishi surfacing in Okinawa may be lost to antiquity forever. However, rather than support or oppose conjecture, it might be more fitting to simply appreciate the efforts of those adventurous stalwarts who sailed the turbulent waters between the two cultures to cultivate and perpetuate these ancient traditions. The ancient Chinese combative traditions cultivated by these *Uchinanchu* were the base on which modern karate-do and *kobu-jutsu* were established.

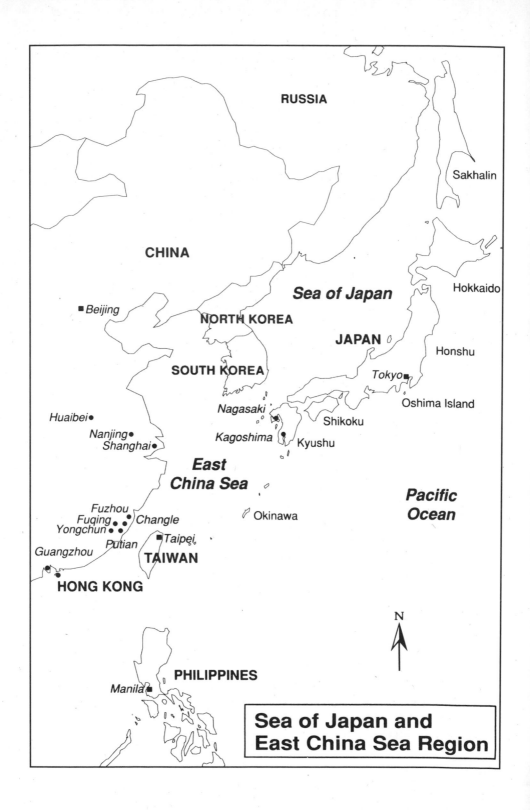

RUSSIA

Sakhalin

CHINA

Sea of Japan

Hokkaido

■Beijing

NORTH KOREA

JAPAN

Honshu

SOUTH KOREA

Tokyo■

Nagasaki

Oshima Island

Huaibei●

Kagoshima

Shikoku

Nanjing●

Kyushu

Shanghai●

East
China Sea

Pacific
Ocean

Okinawa

Fuzhou

Fuqing●● ●Changle

Yongchun● ●

Putian

Taipei■

Guangzhou

TAIWAN

HONG KONG

N

PHILIPPINES

Manila■

Sea of Japan and
East China Sea Region

The Two Bubishi

Actually, there are two Bubishi, both of Chinese origin and from Fuzhou. One is a colossal treatise on the art of war, published in the Ming dynasty (1366–1644); the other, believed to have been produced during the Qing dynasty (1644–1911), is that which surfaced in Okinawa. In its native Mandarin Chinese, the ideograms for Bubishi are read "Wu Bei Zhi," but for the sake of simplicity I shall refer to the text using its Japanese pronunciation instead.

MAO YUANYI'S BUBISHI

This authoritative text on the art of war, not to be confused with Sun Zi's treatise, was published in 1621. The author, Mao Yuanyi, was a man of considerable influence, well versed in military affairs, and was greatly influenced by his grandfather Mao Kun, who was vice-envoy to the Fujian provincial court. Concerned about his government's deteriorating military condition, Mao felt impelled to remedy the situation. Spending more than fifteen years and researching over 2,000 books, he compiled this prodigious document, which consists of 240 chapters in five parts and 91 volumes; today a copy is stored safely within the venerable walls of the Harvard University Library.

Dealing with all military-related subjects, Mao's Bubishi covers everything from strategic warfare, to naval maneuvers and troop deployment, to close-quarter armed and unarmed combat, and includes maps, charts, illustrations, and diagrams. Chapters 1 through 18 concern military decision-making; Chapters 19 through 51 concern tactics; Chapters 52 through 92 concern military training systems; Chapters 93 through 147 concern logistics; and Chapters 148 through 240 deal with military occupations.

In one section there are various illustrations portraying hand-to-hand combat with and without weapons. This part is believed to have been taken from the 18 chapter document *Jixiao Xinshu (Kiko Shinsho* in Japanese), published in 1561 by the great Chinese general, Qi Jiguan (1522–87). There are some similarities between Qi's 32 empty-handed self-defense illustrations and those that appear in the Okinawan Bubishi.

A classified document, it was available only to authorized military personnel, government bureaucrats, and others on a need-to-know basis. During the Qing dynasty, authorities banned it for fear of it falling into rebel hands and being used for anti-government activity.

OKINAWA'S BUBISHI

Okinawa's Bubishi is an anthology of Chinese *gongfu,* its history, philosophy, and application. Focusing on the White Crane style from Yongchun village, Fujian Province, this compilation also addresses Shaolin Monk Fist *gongfu* and reveals its relationship to Okinawa's civil fighting legacy of karate-do.

The contents of this anthology's 32 articles include White Crane *gongfu* history, moral philosophy, advice on etiquette, comparisons of styles, defensive applications, herbal medicines, training mechanics, and Monk Fist Boxing. This may suggest that the Okinawan Bubishi was composed of several smaller books or portions of larger books. While some of this anthology is relatively easy to understand, much of it is not. Written in Classical Chinese, much of the Bubishi is, even at the best of times, perplexing. Many of the terms for the methods date back to a time all but forgotten. Other obstacles include Chinese ideograms that have been either modified since its initial writing or are no longer in use.

In addition, in order to maintain the ironclad ritual of secrecy within the martial art schools of old China, techniques were often described using names that disguised their actual meaning. As such, only those advocates actively pursuing the style were aware of the true meanings and applications of the techniques. A practice once widespread in China, this tradition, for the most part, was not handed down in Okinawa. Hence, these creative names (e.g., Guardian Closes the Gate) made technical explanations difficult to accurately decipher without knowing exactly what physical technique it represented. Contrary to popular belief, the Bubishi is not a manuscript easily understood by most Chinese or Japanese simply because they are able to read the ideograms. For the same reasons mentioned in the preceding paragraphs, most Chinese people, whether directly connected to the native fighting arts or not, would have little or no idea what such abstract descriptions mean. As for the Japanese, and *Uchinanchu* too, without the corresponding *furigana* (phonetic characters) to help clarify the meanings and usage of the Chinese ideograms, the essence of the Bubishi, like its origins, remains unclear.

There is also a surprisingly large portion of the text on the use of Chinese herbs and other medicinal remedies, which provides provocative insights into an aspect of training no longer fashionable in our day and age. Exceedingly brief and hampered by grammatical errors (resulting from being hand-copied down through the ages), Articles 10, 11, 12, 19, 22, 30, and 31 prescribe various concoctions in a way that supposes the reader already understands the principles of herbal medicine. This has proven to be the most difficult section to translate, however, after years of arduous research I am now able to present the first unabridged direct translation of these entries in any language. I should note that another writer attempted to translate this section but in his haste gave up and rewrote it, inserting modern remedies not related to what was in the actual Bubishi.

The Bubishi also includes a rather ambiguous explanation surrounding an even more obscure technique called the "poison-hand" or the "delayed death touch" (dian xue in Mandarin, dim mak in Cantonese). A science understood by very few, mastering dian xue requires remarkable dedication and may very well be the reason the Bubishi has remained such an obscure document for so long, in spite of efforts to publicize it. These articles in the Bubishi do not describe how to render a potentially violent attacker unconscious with carefully pinpointed blows, nor do these articles explain what to do if attacked. Rather, they systematically describe how to extinguish human life in very specific terms, by seizing, pressing, squeezing, or traumatizing specific vital points. These articles are presented here in their entirety.

At first I had some reservations about presenting this information, as I was concerned that it could be misused. However, today, there are a number of books and video tapes on the market that describe the theories and applications of this science. Thus anyone interested in the principles of cavity strikes, artery attacks, blood flow theory, and the death touch, can study the material that is presently available. I trust that this knowledge will not be misused and that those individuals who undertake the time-consuming process of learning this art will be scrupulous and not experiment on unsuspecting victims or use it in anything other than a life-and-death struggle.

Although the exact details surrounding the origin of the Bubishi remain unclear, it is nevertheless a valuable historic treasure. Remaining unanswered, the questions surrounding its advent in Okinawa are not altogether beyond our reach. It is entirely possible to calculate, with some degree of certainty, that which we do not know by more closely analyzing that which we do know.

For example, if, in addition to the historical details previously presented, we were to more closely examine the surviving testimony surrounding karate's early pioneers, we might discover who were most responsible for cultivating China's civil fighting traditions in Okinawa. Even if we are unable to accurately determine the actual source from which the Bubishi materialized, we are at least able to identify the main characters associated with Okinawa's civil fighting traditions. In so doing, we will have isolated the range of analysis through which future study may bring even more profound and enlightening discoveries.

However, those historical discoveries will not come easily. It is the opinion of this writer that much of what was originally brought to Okinawa from the Middle Kingdom either no longer exists, or, like so much of the *gongfu* in China, has been radically changed. In addition to the many major styles of southern *gongfu* that have affected Okinawa's fighting traditions, who is to say how many minor schools have come and gone without a trace? It is virtually impossible to trace the evolution of these styles and schools. On behalf of the Fuzhou Wushu Association's many eminent members, Li Yiduan maintains that an incalculable number of schools and styles (sometimes practiced by as few as a single family or even one person) have either vanished, been exported to a neighboring province, or have been consumed by other styles over the generations. With that in mind, I would now like to conclude my preliminary analysis by exploring the plausible sources from which the Bubishi may have surfaced in Okinawa.

Transmission of the Bubishi

In the following section, I will discuss the various theories explaining how the Bubishi arrived in Okinawa, the personal histories of the masters who may have brought it, and the impact each had on the development of Okinawan karate-do.

In his 1983 book *Hakutsuru Mon: Shokutsuru Ken (White Crane Gate: Feeding Crane Style)*, Master Liu Yinshan wrote that the Shaolin Temple was a sanctuary for resistance fighters during the early Qing dynasty. Seeking to eradicate any pocket of anti-Qing activity, government soldiers burned the monastery down in 1674. Among the monks who fled the monastery in Henan Province was Fang Zhonggong (also known as Fang Huishi), a master of Eighteen Monk Fist Boxing.

There are several accounts of Fang Zhonggong's subsequent travels and activities after his arrival later in Fujian. Notwithstanding, most reports describe him as the father of Fang Qiniang, the girl who grew up in Yongchun village, Fujian, and developed White Crane Boxing. If this history is reliable, then the development of Yongchun White Crane *gongfu* would seem to be somewhere around the early eighteenth century. As we will soon see, a short life history of both Fang and his daughter appear in the Article 1 of the Bubishi (see p. 157). As with Five Ancestors *gongfu*, Monk, Dragon, and Tiger Fist Boxing, Fang's eclectic method has obviously had a profound affect upon the growth and direction of other native boxing styles in and around Fuzhou. Incidentally, many of these *gongfu* styles are believed to have been later introduced to and cultivated in Okinawa. Miyagi Chojun, a direct disciple of Higashionna Kanryo (1853–1917), told us in his 1934 *Outline of Karate-do* that "a style" of *gongfu* was brought from Fuzhou to Okinawa in 1828

East China and environs

☐ areas mentioned in the text

Liu Songshan   Patrick McCarthy with Liu Songshan

and served as the source for Goju-ryu karate *kempo*. After reading Liu Songshan's copy of the *Shaolin Bronze Man Book*[2] and interviewing Xie Wenliang, the great-grandson of Ryuru Ko,[3] the famous *gongfu* master, I believe that this theory is worthy of further exploration. This, then, would seem to indicate that the Bubishi is a book handed down by either Fang's daughter, or disciples of her tradition.[4]

The second theory surrounds Okinawa's oldest surviving testimony regarding the philosophy of the civil fighting traditions. It refers to karate using the Okinawan term *di* (however, for the sake of simplicity I will use the more commonly used Japanese term *te* in the text). Teijunsoku Uekata (1663–1734), a scholar/statesman from Okinawa's Nago district, wrote, "No matter how you may excel in the art of *te* and scholastic endeavors, nothing is more important than your behavior and your humanity as observed in daily life." Whether this statement was influenced by Article 4 of the Bubishi (see p. 163) remains the subject of much speculation. Teijunsoku was a scholar of Chinese classics, and as the previous statement would indicate, a practitioner of the civil fighting traditions. It is possible that he may have possessed a copy of the Bubishi. If so, this would indicate that the Bubishi was extant in Okinawa from at least the eighteenth century onward. By extension this would mean that the book was written either during the lifetime of Fang Qiniang or very soon after her death. It would also indicate a link existed between the practice of *te* and the Bubishi in the eighteenth century, which is more than one hundred years before any of the other Okinawan masters are believed to have come into possession of it.

Xie Wenliang (wearing a Japanese-style uniform) with the author at Tokashiki Iken's *dojo* in Naha.

The third theory concerns the famous karate master Sakugawa *Chikudun Pechin* and the Chinese *gongfu* master Kusankun. In 1762, an Okinawan tribute ship en route to Satsuma was blown off course during a fierce typhoon and drifted to Oshima beach in the jurisdiction of Tosahan (present-day Kochi Prefecture) on Shikoku Island. Petitioned to record the testimony of passengers and crew, Confucian scholar Tobe Ryoen compiled a chronicle entitled the *Oshima Incident (Oshima Hikki)*. In a dialogue with the Okinawan officer in charge, one Shiohira (also pronounced Shionja) *Pechin,* a minister in charge of warehousing the kingdom's rice supply, reference is made to a Chinese named Kusankun—popularly known among karate historians as Kusanku or Koshankun.

Described as an expert in *kempo,* or more specifically *kumiai-jutsu,* it is believed that Kusankun, with "a few" personal disciples, traveled to the Ryukyu Kingdom with the Qing *Sapposhi* Quan Kui in 1756. Shiohira's description of Kusankun's *kumiai-jutsu* demonstration leaves little to question.

Recounting how impressed he was witnessing a person of smaller stature overcome a larger person, Shiohira *Pechin* described what he remembered: "With his lapel being seized, Kusanku applied his *kumiai-jutsu* and overcame the attacker by scissoring his legs." When describing Kusankun's leg maneuver, Shiohira used the term "sasoku," which roughly describes the scissor action

"Toudi" Sakugawa *Chikudun Pechin.*

of a crab's claw. Although Shiohira's description of Kusankun is rather nebulous, it remains the most reliable early chronicle regarding the Chinese civil fighting traditions in Okinawa. Though Shiohira's testimony does not mention the Bubishi, techniques like those described by Shiohira are detailed in the Bubishi.

Oral tradition maintains that Kusankun was one of the teachers of the great Okinawan master Sakugawa *Chikudun Pechin*.[5] Born Teruya Kanga in Shuri's Tori Hori village, Sakugawa rose to prominence due in large part to his heroic exploits on the high seas while in charge of security for a prominent commercial shipping firm. Recognized for his incredible physical prowess and indomitable spirit, folklore says he was elevated to the rank of *Chikudun Pechin* (a warrior rank somewhat similar to the samurai, see p. 142) and assumed the name Sakugawa. He studied the fighting traditions in Fuzhou, Beijing, and Satsuma (present-day Kagoshima Prefecture) and had a profound impact upon the growth and direction of the self-defense disciplines that were fostered in and around Shuri. As such, he is now commonly referred to as "Toudi" Sakugawa, *toudi* being the Okinawan reading of the original Chinese characters for karate (Tang or Chinese hand). It is possible that either he or Kusankun brought the Bubishi from China to Okinawa.[6]

The fourth theory concerns the famous *gongfu* masters Ryuru Ko and Wai Xinxian, and their "student" Higashionna Kanryo. On page 4 of his 1922 publication *Ryukyu Kempo Karate-jutsu,* Funakoshi Gichin describes various Chinese masters who came to Okinawa and taught *gongfu,* presumably during the later part of the nineteenth century. Funakoshi wrote that a Chinese named Ason taught *Zhao Ling Liu* (Shorei-ryu) to Sakiyama, Gushi, Nagahama, and Tomoyori from Naha; Wai Xinxian taught *Zhao Ling Liu* to Higashionna Kanyu and Kanryo, Shimabukuro, and Kuwae; Iwah taught Shaolin Boxing to Matsumura of Shuri, Kogusuku (Kojo), and Maesato of Kuninda. Funakoshi also wrote that an unidentified man from Fuzhou drifted to Okinawa from a place called Annan (if not a district of Fuzhou then perhaps the old name for Vietnam), and taught Gusukuma (Shiroma), Kaneshiro, Matsumora, Yamasato, and Nakasato, all from Tomari. Funakoshi uses generic terms like Shorin (Shaolin) and Shorei *(Zhao Ling)* but did not identify specific schools or traditions. Perhaps the two most talked about figures in the Fuzhou-Okinawan karate connection are Ryuru Ko (1852–1930) and Wai Xinxian. Ryuru Ko (also pronounced Do Ryuko and Ru Ruko in Japanese), and Wai Xinxian are believed to be the principal teachers of the following famous karate masters: Sakiyama Kitoku (1830–1914),[7] Kojo Taitei (1837–1917), Maezato Ranpo (1838–1904), Aragaki Seisho (1840–1920), Higashionna Kanryo (1853–1915), Nakaima Norisato (1850–1927), and Matsuda Tokusaburo (1877–1931).

Ryuru Ko has been variously described as the son of a noble family whose fortune was lost during political unrest, a priest, a former military official in exile, a stonemason, a craftsman, and even a medicine hawker. Perhaps he was all. Until recently little was known about what art Ryuru Ko taught. Some claimed he taught White Crane, others believed it was Five Ancestors Fist, perhaps even Monk Fist Boxing. My research, in accordance with Tokashiki Iken's, indicates his name was Xie Zhongxiang and he was a shoemaker and the founder of Whooping Crane *gongfu*.[8]

Xie Zhongxiang.

Ryuru, which means "to proceed," was a nickname. Ko is a suffix that means "big brother." Ryuru Ko was a student of Pan Yuba, who in turn was taught by Lin Shixian, a master of White Crane *gongfu*.

Similarly, Wai Xinxian's personal history is shrouded in mystery. He has been described as a contemporary of or senior to Ryuru Ko, a master of Xingyi *gongfu,* a teacher of Monk Fist Boxing, and a commissioned officer of the Qing dynasty. Another popular theory is that he was an instructor with Iwah at the Kojo dojo in Fuzhou.

Many believe that Higashionna Kanryo is the most likely source from which the Bubishi first appeared in Okinawa. However, while this theory is prevalent, especially among the followers of the Goju tradition, it is still only conjecture.

Higashionna Kanryo was born in Naha's Nishimura (West Village) on March 10, 1853. He was the fourth son of Higashionna Kanyo, and the tenth-generation descendant of the Higashionna family tree. During his childhood he was called Moshi, and he had a relative named Higashionna Kanyu, who was five years his senior and also enjoyed the fighting traditions. He lived in Naha's Higashimura (East Village) and became known as Higashionna East, while Kanryo was called Higashionna West. First introduced to the fighting traditions in 1867, when he began to study Monk Fist Boxing *(Luohan Quan)* from Aragaki *Tsuji Pechin* Seisho (1840–1918 or 20),[9] Aragaki was a fluent speaker of Chinese and worked as an interpreter for the Ryukyu court. Higashionna spent a little over three years under his tutelage until September 1870, when Aragaki was petitioned to go to Beijing to translate for Okinawan officials. At that time, he introduced Kanryo to another expert of the fighting traditions named Kojo Taitei (1837–1917) who also taught him. It was through Kojo Taitei, and a friend of the family named Yoshimura Udun Chomei (1830–1898), that safe passage to China, accommoda-

Aragaki *Tsuji Pechin* Seisho.

tions (probably in the Kojo dojo in Fuzhou), and instruction for young Kanryo were arranged. Higashionna set sail for Fuzhou in March 1873.

Xie Wenliang (b. 1959), the great-grandson of Ryuru Ko, characterized Kanryo as an enthusiastic youth who had come to Fuzhou from Okinawa to further his studies in Chinese *gongfu*.[10] Kanryo did not start studying with Ryuru Ko until 1877.[11] Yet oral tradition maintains that he set sail for Fuzhou in 1873! Assuming both dates are accurate, a new question arises: what did Higashionna do for the first four years he was in Fuzhou? I believe he spent the time training at the Kojo dojo. It was during this time that he may have studied with *gongfu* Master Wai Xinxian, who is said to have taught at that dojo.[12] Some speculate that he may have even trained with *gongfu* Master Iwah there.

It is not surprising to learn that Kanryo did not become a live-in disciple of a prominent master, as was previously believed. After all, Kanryo was a young non-Chinese who could not speak, read, or write Chinese. Chinese *gongfu* masters rarely, if ever, accepted outsiders as students, let alone foreigners. It was not the way things were done during the Qing dynasty (1644–1911) in China. However, with an introduction from the Kojo family, who were well known in Fuzhou, Kanryo began training with Xie Zhongxiang. The reason why Kanryo studied with Xie remains the subject of much curiosity.

Notwithstanding, Ryuru, who was born a year before Kanryo (in July 1852), was more like a big brother than a teacher to Higashionna. Although just an apprentice shoemaker, evidently his proficiency in *gongfu* was remarkable.

Yoshimura Udun Chomei.

In 1883, the year after Kanryo returned to Okinawa, Ryuru, at age thirty-one, succeeded in opening his own school of *gongfu* in Fuzhou. He went on to become one of Fuzhou's most prominent masters before he died in February 1930 at age seventy-seven. Although the facts surrounding his *Uchinanchu* students have yet to be fully explored, there can be no question that his teachings have profoundly effected the growth and direction of karate-do.

Although it is not presently known what style was taught at the Kojo dojo, we know that Ryuru taught five *quan: Happoren (Baiburen* in Mandarin, also known as *Paipuren* in Japanese), *Nepai (Nipaipo* in Japanese), *Doonquan* (also called *Chukyo* or *Jusanporen), Roujin (Jusen),* and *Qijing (Shichikei),* but is said to have known many more. When we examine the various *quan* that Kanryo *Sensei* taught after returning from China in 1882, we discover that there are *quan* from sources other than Whooping Crane. Furthermore, Higashionna never received a teaching license in Ryuru Ko's art. This would suggest that Kanryo *Sensei* not only learned the principles of other styles, but also blended them into an eclectic hybrid. Otherwise, the discipline Kanryo *Sensei* brought back from Fuzhou would have therefore been Second-generation Whooping Crane *gongfu* or Kojo-ryu. However, such was not the case, and he never used the name Whooping Crane *gongfu* or Kojo-ryu. In fact, the same can be said of Uechi Kanbun, who studied Tiger Fist *gongfu* under Zhou Zihe (1874–1926): why did he not call his style Second-generation Tiger Fist *gongfu?* Cross-checking the Chinese ideograms that represent the *quan* of various other Fujian *gongfu* styles, I believe I may have determined some plausible sources from which Higashionna Kanryo learned his other *quan* if they did not come from the Kojo dojo.

There are four other styles of Crane Boxing, each of which use their own *Saam Chien quan (Sanchin kata),* and one also uses *Sanseiru* and *Niseishi (Nijushiho).* Dragon Boxing uses *Seisan, Peichurrin (Suparinpei), Saam Chien,* and a *quan* called Eighteen Scholar Fists (mentioned in the Bubishi), in addition to other *quan.* Tiger Boxing also uses *Saam Chien, Sanseiru,* and *Peichurrin,* among other *quan.* Dog Boxing, or perhaps better known as Ground Boxing, also uses *Saam Chien* and *Sanseiru,* among others. Arhat Boxing, also known as Monk Fist, uses *Saam Chien, Seisan, Jutte, Seipai, Ueseishi (Gojushiho),* and *Peichurrin* among others. Lion Boxing uses *Saam Chien* and *Seisan* among others.

There can be no question that Higashionna Kanryo had, after living in Fuzhou for nearly a decade, come to learn the central elements of several kinds of Chinese *gongfu.* Remember that Miyagi *Sensei* told us, in his 1934 *Outline of Karate-do* that "the only detail that we can be sure of is that 'a style' from Fuzhou was introduced to Okinawa in 1828, and served as the basis from which Goju-ryu karate *kempo* unfolded."

Itosu Anko.

If we are to consider what Master Miyagi told us, then it would seem that something other than just Ryuru's tradition formed the basis from which Goju-ryu developed. Kyoda Juhatsu, the *senpai* (senior) of Miyagi Chojun while under the tutelage of Kanryo *Sensei,* said that Master Higashionna only ever referred to his discipline as *quanfa (kempo),* and also taught several Chinese weapons, which Miyagi *Sensei* never learned.

The question of whether Higashionna may have obtained a copy of the Bubishi from one of his masters in Fuzhou is the source of much discussion and it remains one of the most popular theories.

The fifth theory claims Itosu Anko (1832–1915) was the source from which the Bubishi appeared in Okinawa. Whereas Higashionna influenced the direction and development of the fighting arts in the Naha area, Itosu was responsible for handing down the other mainstream self-defense tradition, which later became known as Shurite, and possibly the Bubishi as well. His teacher, the legendary "Bushi" Matsumura *Chikudun Pechin* Sokon (1809–1898), had studied *gongfu* in both Fuzhou and Beijing and may very well have been the source from which the Bubishi first appeared in Okinawa. Mabuni Kenwa, the founder of Shito-ryu, wrote in his version of the Bubishi that he had made a copy from the copy his teacher (Itosu) had himself made. We assume that as Matsumura was his teacher, Itosu made his copy from Matsumura's.

A sixth possibility is that the Bubishi was brought to Okinawa by Uechi Kanbun (1877–1948), the founder of Uechi-ryu. The Uechi-ryu karate-do tradition tells us Uechi went to Fuzhou in 1897, where he ultimately studied Guangdong Shaolin Temple Tiger Boxing directly under master Zhou Zihe (Shu Shiwa in Japanese).

One of Uechi Kanbun's students, Tomoyose (Tomoyori) Ryuyu (1897–1970), an accomplished student of the fighting traditions, dedicated most of his life writing an analysis of *kempo,* vital point striking, and the application of Chinese herbal medicine. Entitled *Kempo Karate-jutsu Hiden (Secrets of Kempo Karate-jutsu),* the document, now owned by the Uechi family, addressed a number of articles identical to the Bubishi. Unfortunately Tomoyose died before he was able to complete this analysis. The similarities are too frequent to doubt that the Uechi family once possessed a copy of the Bubishi.

A seventh theory concerns two Chinese tea merchants who moved to Okinawa during the Taisho era (1912–25). Wu Xiangui (1886–1940), who was a White Crane *gongfu* expert, moved from Fuzhou to Okinawa in 1912. Uechi Kanbun wrote that Wu (Go Kenki in Japanese) taught *gongfu* in the evenings in Naha. It is claimed that he had a major influence upon Miyagi Chojun, Mabuni Kenwa, Kyoda Juhatsu,[13] and Matayoshi Shinho, son of Matayoshi Shinko.[14]

The second tea merchant was a friend of Wu's named Tang Daiji (he was called To Daiki in Okinawa). Tang (1887–1937) moved from China to Naha, Okinawa in 1915. In his

Wu Xiangui (Gokenki).

home village, Tiger Fist *gongfu* was very popular and Tang had become well known for his skills. In Okinawa he befriended Miyagi Chojun and other prominent karate enthusiasts, and is said to have had a big impact upon the karate community during that time. It is possible that either of these individuals may have brought copies of the Bubishi that they in turn gave to one or more of these famous Okinawan masters.

The eighth theory concerns Nakaima *Chikudun Pechin* Norisato, founder of the Ryuei-ryu karate tradition. Son of a wealthy family in Naha's Kuninda district, he was required to learn the principles of *Bunbu Ryodo* (the philosophy of the twin paths of brush and sword, symbolizing the importance of balancing physical training with protracted introspection and study) from an early age. He was sent to Fuzhou when he was nineteen years old. Nakaima obtained his formal introduction to Ryuru Ko from a friend of his family, a military attache who had visited the Ryukyu Kingdom in 1866 (from June 22 to November 18) as a subordinate of the Qing *Sapposhi* Zhao Xin. In 1870, Nakaima became an *uchideshi* (live-in disciple) of Ryuru Ko. After six years of sacrifice and diligent training he surfaced in 1876 as a proficient expert. Before departing from Ryuru Ko's, he was required to make copies (by hand) of the many books he had studied. Among the most noted books were: books on etiquette, health, and Chinese medicine, and a book about cultivating a brave spirit through the practice of *quanfa*. Some believe that the present Okinawan Bubishi is a compilation of these documents. Nakaima spent the next year touring Guangdong Province and Beijing to further his understanding of the fighting traditions, and returned to Okinawa with an impressive collection of weapons.

The ninth theory concerns the Kogusuku or Kojo (pronounced Cai in Mandarin) clan (descendants of Naha's Kuninda Thirty-six Families), a family long known for its martial arts heritage in Okinawa. Dating back to 1392, the family has long enjoyed ties with Fuzhou and has been connected with experts like Makabe (Udon) Kyoei, Iwah, and Wai Xinxian.[15] It is said that Kojo Taitei (1837–1917), who had studied *gongfu* in Fuzhou, was a good friend of Higashionna Kanryo. Kojo Kaho (1849–1925) even had his own dojo in Fuzhou, where it is alleged that Wai Xinxian instructed several Okinawans and Uechi Kanbun trained for a short time before becoming Zhou Zihe's disciple.[16] Dr. Hayashi Shingo, the most senior disciple of Kojo-ryu Master Kojo Kafu (grandson of Kojo Kaho), said Kojo Taitei brought back a "secret text" on *gongfu* from Fuzhou upon which much of their style was based.[17] It is entirely possible that this text was the Bubishi.

The tenth theory was brought to my attention by Otsuka Tadahiko,[18] which I shall refer to as the "museum hypothesis." During the Ryukyu Kingdom, an official building called the Tenson, which housed objects of historical, cultural, artistic, and scientific interest, was located next to the *Sanshikan[19]* residence in Naha's Kuninda district. Under this theory, the Bubishi is said to be a compilation of written *gongfu* precepts taught in Naha's Chinese community and several other texts from the Tenson. Folklore says that the book later became a treasure guarded by the masters of the civil fighting traditions in Naha when the kingdom was abolished in 1879; hence, the tradition of it being passed down, copied by hand, unfolded. This theory seems unlikely, however, in light of the existence of Liu Songshan's *Shaolin Bronze Man Book*—a work not associated with Okinawa, yet identical in content to the Bubishi.

It is possible that any one of these theories, or perhaps even several of them, may be true. It appears that many copies of the Bubishi were in circulation in Okinawa by the early twentieth century and not all may have been brought at the same time or in its current complete form. Nonetheless, these theories are worthy of further study and exploration not only for their relevance to the study of the Bubishi in particular but also of the history of the Okinawan civil fighting arts in general.

The History of Karate-do

The evolution of the Okinawan civil fighting arts was shaped by a number of sociological and historical factors. To comprehend how karate became the art that it is today and why the Bubishi had such a strong impact during the latter stages of its development, a knowledge of Okinawan history and society is necessary.

Through presenting karate-do's history, I will describe the Ryukyu Kingdom's connection with China. When exploring this history, China's penetrating effect upon Okinawa's tiny island culture becomes readily apparent, thus establishing the context for the advent of Chinese *gongfu* and arrival of the Bubishi in the Ryukyu Kingdom. This analysis will also illustrate how Chinese *gongfu*, evolving in a foreign culture, was affected by that culture.

Theories on the Development of Karate before the Twentieth Century

There are four common theories explaining the development of karate-do. The first claims that the unarmed fighting traditions were developed by peasants. The second claims the Okinawan fighting arts were primarily influenced by Chinese arts that were taught by the so-called "Thirty-six Families" of Chinese immigrants who settled in Kume village (also known as Kuninda) in the fourteenth century. The third theory concerns the 1507 weapons ban by King Sho Shin, which led to an increased need by wealthy landowners for an effective means of defending themselves and their property. The fourth theory claims that the arts were developed primarily by domestic security and law enforcement personnel who were not allowed to carry weapons after the 1609 invasion of Okinawa by Satsuma.

Folklore would have us believe that Okinawa's civil fighting legacy was developed by the subjugated "pre-Meiji peasant class." Described as tyrannized by their overlords, the peasants, in an effort to break free of the chains of "oppression," had allegedly conceived an omnipotent fighting tradition. Some people have further hypothesized that combative principles had "somehow" been applied to the implements they used in their daily lives.

It has also been postulated that, under cover of total darkness, for fear of reprisal if caught, the peasants not only established this cultural phenomenon but also succeeded in handing it down for generations, unbeknownst to local authorities. Supported by mere threads of historically inaccurate testimony, one discovers that the "pre-Meiji Peasant Class Supposition" is not worthy of serious consideration. Nonetheless, some researchers have erroneously credited the peasant class with the development of both Okinawa's armed and empty-handed combative traditions. However, a further study of the Ryukyu Kingdom reveals findings that suggest a more plausible explanation.

In the following sections I will study the remaining three theories as they relate to Okinawan history and will introduce several new theories, notably, the role of Okinawan *tyugakusei* (exchange students) and *sapposhi* (Chinese envoys) on the development of the Okinawan fighting arts and the influence of Japanese fighting arts.

Indigenous and Japanese Influences Prior to the Fourteenth Century

In 1816, following his expedition to the west coast of Korea and the "Great Loo-Choo" (Okinawa), Basil Chamberlain Hall, in a discussion with exiled Emperor Napoleon, described Okinawa as a defenseless, weapon-less island domain. In fact, the Ryukyu Kingdom had been thoroughly familiar with the ways of war.

From before recorded history, in addition to being versed in the use of the sword, the spear, archery, and horsemanship, Okinawan war-riors had a rudimentary form of unarmed hand-to-hand combat, that included striking, kicking, elementary grappling, and escape maneuvers that allowed them to subdue adversaries even when disarmed.

During the rise of the warrior cliques in tenth-century Japan, wide-scale military power struggles compelled apathetic aristocrats to inter-mittently seek out refuge in more tranquil surroundings. Many solic-ited the protection of more powerful allies, some relocated to bordering provinces, there were even those who journeyed to neighboring islands, including the Ryukyu archipelago.

Militarily dominated by local chieftain warriors *(aji* or *anji),* the *Uchinanchu* had actively engaged in territorial dissension from the sev-enth to the fifteenth centuries, and placed much value upon military knowledge. Arriving with contingents of heavily armed security per-sonnel, Japanese aristocrats were venerated and ultimately retained the services of local soldiers. As a result of this the standard Japanese com-bative methodologies of the Heian Period (794–1185), including grap-pling, archery, halberd, spear, and swordsmanship, were introduced to the *Uchinanchu.*

Perhaps the most profound historical event to effect the evolution of Okinawa's native fighting traditions was the arrival of Tametomo (1139–70). The eighth son of feudal warlord Minamoto Tameyoshi (1096–1156) and a subordinate of Japan's once-powerful Minamoto clan, Tametomo, while still a teenager, is described in the *Tales of the Ho-gen War (Hogen Monogatari),* as a fierce warrior. A remarkably muscular and powerful man, Tametomo is said to have stood over seven feet tall and was a powerful fighter, famous for his remarkable skill in archery.

During a brief military encounter in 1156, the Minamoto clan was defeated by their rivals, the Taira, and several of the leading members of the Minamoto who were not executed were tortured and exiled to Oshima Island near the mountainous Izu Peninsula, in the custody of a minor Taira family, the Hojo. Among the exiled was Minamoto Tame-tomo, who ended up taking control of Izu many years later, and worked his way south to the Ryukyu Archipelago.

Excelling in strategy and the art of striking heavy blows, Tametomo had overrun all of Kyushu within three years. Arriving in Okinawa, at Unten (near Yagajijima Island), he made contact with Ozato *Aji,* lord of Urazoe Castle, and was revered for his military might. Marrying Oza-to's sister, Tametomo became lord of Urazoe and had a son he named

Shunten. In 1186, Shunten defeated Riyu (the last ruler of the Tenson dynasty) and became the island's most powerful *aji*. The Shunten dynasty lasted until 1253 and perpetuated the combative traditions introduced by Tametomo and his *bushi* (warriors).

Notwithstanding, with Okinawa being divided into three tiny kingdoms, territorial dissension continued until one powerful *aji,* Sho Hashi, unified the three rival principalities and formed a centralized government in 1429. Several dynasties later, in 1507, during the thirtieth year of his administration, Sho Shin-O ended feudalism in the Ryukyu Kingdom by ratifying the "Act of Eleven Distinctions," which included a prohibition of private ownership and stockpiling of weapons. This is historically significant for researchers because it explains why the *Uchinanchu* began intensively cultivating an unarmed means of self-defense.

Chinese Influences on the Development of Karate-do

Okinawa's first recorded contact with the Chinese was during the Sui dynasty in 607 A.D. However, unable to understand the Okinawan dialect *(Hogan),* the Chinese envoys returned without establishing substantial commerce. It was not until 1372, some four years after the Mongols fell to the powerful forces of the Ming dynasty (1368–1644), that Emperor Hong Wu sent his special representative, Yang Zai, to Chuzan, the most powerful of Okinawa's three rival kingdoms, to establish a tributary alliance.

Landing at Maki-minato (Port Maki) during the reign of Satto (1350–95), the imperial envoy outlined China's unification and omnipotence. The Ming representative advised Chuzan to become a tributary colony and make plans to accommodate the Chinese.

Having previously enjoyed limited, but unsanctioned, commerce with Fujian Province, Satto recognized this opportunity and ultimately welcomed the petition. Taiki, the king's brother and special emissary, took tribute to China, where the liaison was ratified.

THE THIRTY-SIX FAMILIES
By 1393, a Chinese mission was established in Naha's Kuninda, which is now referred to as the "Thirty-six Families." This is important because it shows how the Chinese fighting traditions were first systematically transmitted in Okinawa.

Douglas Haring's translation of the 1896 *Takanoya Account* provides an illuminating description of this arrangement.

> The leading city and capital of Okinawa, Naha has absorbed various nearby villages as well as the one-time royal capital of Shuri. Kume village has played a unique role in Okinawa's history. It was settled in 1393

by immigrants of China and provided a place where Chinese diplomats resided and where Okinawan nobles could learn the language and manners of China. Formal relations with China dated from 1372 until Japan annexed Ryukyu in the 1870s; the last Okinawan tribute mission was sent to China in 1873. For five centuries Kume served as a center of diffusion of Chinese culture in Ryukyu. Young Okinawans learned to speak and write Chinese in Kume; those who did well were accepted for study at China's capital and received scholarships from the government of China. The enrichment of Okinawan culture via Kume was incalculable. Here men not only learned how to write Chinese and acquire literary arts, but on occasion technicians also taught ship-building, various crafts and the practicing arts, making of paper and books, lacquer ware, building and architecture, divination and festivals, Confucian morals, and Chinese music.[20]

The settlement at Kume has been referred to as Okinawa's "window to Chinese culture." It is highly likely that along with the aforementioned crafts, the Chinese martial arts were also introduced to Okinawa by the "Thirty-six Families."

THE RYUGAKUSEI

During Okinawa's tributary alliance with the Middle Kingdom, contingents of *Uchinanchu ryugakusei* (exchange students) made extended pilgrimages to various parts of China to receive an education. In many ways, the *Uchinanchu ryugakusei* were not unlike Japan's *kentoshi*. Special envoys of the emperor, the *kentoshi* sought out cultural knowledge in exchange for special tribute. Between 630 and 894, the *kentoshi,* along with sizable entourages, made sixteen excursions to China seeking knowledge and technology to enhance their own society. Studying in Beijing, Nanjing, Shanghai, and Fuzhou, the *ryugakusei,* like the *kentoshi,* also brought valuable learning back to their homeland. It is likely that these *ryugakusei* learned the Chinese fighting arts and brought these back to their homeland as well.

THE SAPPOSHI

The most profound cultural influence from China came by way of the *sapposhi* (also pronounced *sappushi* or *sakuhoshi),* who were special envoys of the Chinese emperor. The *sapposhi* traveled to the outermost reaches of the emperor's domain carrying important dispatches and returning with situation reports.

Requested by the Okinawan king, the *sapposhi* were sent to the Ryukyu Kingdom more than twenty times over a 500 year period, approximately once for every new king that came into power from the time of Bunei in 1404. Rarely staying longer than four to six months, the *sapposhi* were usually accompanied by an entourage of 400–500 people that included occupational specialists, tradesmen, and security experts.

These specialists could have introduced their arts while in Okinawa and as I had noted earlier, in Nakaima *Chikudun Pechin* Norisato's case (see pages 135–136), assisted Okinawans studying the Chinese fighting arts in China.

Individual preoccupation with the civil fighting traditions gradually escalated, as did domestic power struggles. Ultimately, political reform prompted the adoption of Chinese *gongfu* for domestic law enforcement. As a result of the official Japanese injunction prohibiting the ownership and stockpiling of weapons, government personnel were also disarmed. After the Japanese invasion, Okinawan Chinese-based civil self-defense methods became shrouded in an ironclad ritual of secrecy but continued to be vigorously cultivated by its *pechin*-class officials.

The Pechin in Okinawan Society

The *Takanoya Account* delineates the Ryukyu Kingdom's class and rank structure.

> The people are divided into eleven classes: princes, *aji, oyakata, pechin, satunushi-pechin, chikudun pechin, satunushi, saka satunushi, chikudun, chikudun zashiki,* and *niya.* Princes are the king's brothers and uncles. *Aji* are (but not always) sons of the king's uncles and brothers and are generally district chieftains; hence, during the Satsuma period, *aji* are not included in the *shizoku* (military, i.e., samurai). The Japanese have compared the *aji* to *daimyo* (feudal lords). *Oyakata* are upper samurai, *pechin* and *satunushi pechin* are middle samurai. The other classes were sons and brothers of upper and middle *shizoku (keimochi).* The *niya* were commoners.

> There are nine ranks *of shizoku.* Each has its distinctive apparel and accessories. Sometimes, however, lower samurai have been selected for promotion, even to the Three Ministers. Outstanding ministers were awarded full first-rank or semi-first-rank. All other ranks are determined according to circumstances. A commoner who had served as *jito* (administrator of a fief) for a number of years, or who had served with a consistently good record in the office of a *magiri* (also written *majiri;* originally the territory or village controlled by an *aji*) could be appointed to *chikudun* status. If exceptionally competent, he might be elevated to *chikudun pechin* rank, although he could not become a samurai or wear a *haori* coat or *tabi* (split-toed socks).[21]

The *pechin* served from 1509 to 1879, starting from when Sho Shin imposed a class structure upon the gentry, until the dynasty was abolished. The *pechin* officials were largely responsible for, but not limited to, civil administration, law enforcement, and related matters. The *pechin* class was divided into *satunushi* and *chikudun.* The *satunushi* were from gentry while the *chikudun* were commoners. These two divisions were even further divided into ten subcategories based upon seniority.

Administrative aspects of law and order were governed by senior officials at the *okumiza* bureau, which incorporated a police department, prosecutors, and a court system. The *hirasho* (also *hirajo),* that era's version of a city hall, which was located within Shuri castle, had two specific functions: maintaining the family register system that kept the records of all births and deaths, and investigating peasant criminal activities. Outlying districts had smaller bureaus, called *kogumiza,* and often served as territorial or self-governing *hirajo.*

The Ryukyu Kingdom's judiciary system engaged the services of bailiffs who served writs and summonses, made arrests, took custody of prisoners, and ensured that court sentences were carried out. These *chikusaji pechin,* or "street-cops" so to speak, enforced the law while the *hiki* (garrison guard), provided military defense, guarded the castle, and protected the king. It was these officers who were responsible for cultivating and perpetuating the development of unarmed self-defense disciplines.

In 1507, nearly 100 years before the private ownership and stockpiling of swords and other weapons of war was ever contemplated on Japan's mainland, Sho Shin, in the thirtieth year of his reign, enacted such a decree in the Ryukyu Kingdom. One hundred and fifty years before Tokugawa Ieyasu (the first shogun of the Edo *bakufu*) ever compelled his own *daimyo* to come to Edo (Tokyo), Sho Shin commanded his *aji* to withdraw from their fortresses and reside at his side in the castle district of Shuri, hence strengthening his control over them. Nearly a century before the Edo *keisatsu* (policemen of the Tokugawa period, 1603–1868) ever established the civil restraint techniques using the *rokushaku bo* and the *jutte* (iron truncheon), the Ryukyu *pechin*-class officials had already cultivated a self-defense method based upon the principles of Chinese *gongfu.*

The Satsuma Invasion

Having supported Toyotomi Hideyoshi's failed campaigns on the Korean peninsula and then later being defeated at Sekigahara by Tokugawa Ieyasu's forces, Shimazu Yoshihisa (the sixteenth-generation leader of the Kyushu-based Satsuma clan) had drawn heavily upon his subordinates, but without reward. With financial resources unstable and his warriors' morale sinking, invading the prosperous Ryukyu Kingdom began to look like a sure way for Shimazu to resolve his financial difficulties and appease the Tokugawa Shogun.

In February 1609, the Satsuma clan began its campaign against the Ryukyu Kingdom. In May, Shuri castle was captured and King Sho Nei surrendered. Satsuma control lasted nearly three centuries until 1879,

"Bushi" Matsumura *Chikudun Pechin* Sokon.

when King Sho Tai abdicated and the island officially became part of the Japanese empire.

During Okinawa's 270-year military occupation, eclectic fighting traditions haphazardly evolved, some of which applied the principles of self-defense to a myriad of domestic implements. It was largely because of this phenomenon that *kobudo* evolved. During the occupation, there were some *pechin* who traveled up to Satsuma. Evidently while there, some of these stalwarts were schooled in Jigen-ryu *ken-jutsu* (the combative methodology of the Satsuma samurai), and, in so doing, affected the evolution of Okinawa's "indigenous" fighting methods upon returning to their homeland.

In Okinawa, this theory is rarely addressed, and yet, *kobudo* tradition maintains that the *rokushaku bo-jutsu* (the art of using a six-foot staff) of "Toudi" Sakugawa *Chikudun Pechin* Kanga and Tsuken *Chikudun Pechin* Koura (1776–1882) did not surface until after they returned to Okinawa from studying in Satsuma. To corroborate this important historical hypothesis, I would like to draw the reader's attention to two other independent sources.

Among the many *pechin* to make the journey from the Ryukyu Kingdom to Satsuma during the later part of the nineteenth century was Matsumura *Chikudun Pechin* Sokon. Perhaps better known as "Bushi" Matsumura, he came to be known as the Miyamoto Musashi of the Ryukyu Kingdom. In many ways, Matsumura is considered the "great-grandfather" of the karate movement that surfaced in and around Shuri. Matsumura first learned the native Okinawan fighting traditions under the watchful eye of "Toudi" Sakugawa and later, while serving as a security agent for three consecutive Ryukyuan kings, studied in both Fujian and Satsuma. Also as I noted earlier (see p. 130), he studied under the *gongfu* Master Iwah.

Receiving his *menkyo* (teaching certificate) in Jigen-ryu *ken-jutsu* from Ijuin Yashichiro, Matsumura was responsible for synthesizing the unique teaching principles of Jigen-ryu to the Chinese and native Okinawan fighting traditions he had also studied. By doing so, Matsumura established the cornerstone upon which an eclectic self-defense tradition surfaced in and around the castle district, which in 1927 became known as Shuri-te (Shuri hand).

After retiring from public service, Matsumura was one of the very first to begin teaching his self-defense principles in Shuri's Sakiyama village. His principal disciples included Azato Anko (1827–1906), Itosu Anko (1832–1915), "Bushi" Ishimine (1835–89), Kiyuna *Pechin* (1845–1920), Sakihara *Pechin* (1833–1918), Matsumura Nabe (1850–1930), Tawada *Pechin* (1851–1907), Kuwae Ryosei (1858–1939), Yabu Kentsu (1866–1937), Funakoshi Gichin, Hanashiro Chomo (186–1945), and Kyan Chotoku (1870–1945).

In Volume Eight of the Japanese encyclopedia *Nihon Budo Taikei* there is a provocative passage on page 51 that provides an interesting explanation of the origins of the Ryukyu Kingdom's fighting traditions. The passage notes that Lord Shimizu instructed second-generation Jigen-ryu headmaster Togo Bizen no Kami Shigekata (1602–59) to teach self-defense tactics to farmers and peasants in Satsuma. This was done so that in case of an invasion, these farmers could act as a clandestine line of defense for their homeland. This non-warrior tradition was disguised in a folk dance called the Jigen-ryu *Bo Odori,* and incorporated the *jo* (three-foot staff) against the sword; the *rokushaku bo* against the spear; and separate disciplines employing an *eiku* (boat oar), the *kama* (sickles), *shakuhachi* (flute), and other implements.

This phenomenon clearly illustrates how the principles of combat were ingeniously applied to occupationally related implements and then unfolded into a folk tradition, not unlike that of Okinawa's civil combative heritage nearly a century before. When I asked the eleventh-generation Jigen-ryu headmaster Togo Shigemasa about this potential link, he said, "There can be no question that Jigenryu is connected to Okinawa's domestic fighting traditions; however, the question remains, which influenced which!"[22]

The Satsuma period was one of great growth and development for both Okinawan karate-do and *kobudo.* However, the fundamental character and form of these fighting traditions were to undergo an even more radical change after Okinawa became a part of Japan and its proud warrior heritage.

History of Karate-do from the Meiji Era

After the abolition of the Tokugawa Shogunate in 1868, the Meiji Restoration delivered Japan from feudalism into "democracy." Hence, the class structure and the samurai practice of wearing of swords, samurai yearly stipends, and the *chonmage* (top-knot hair-style), faded into the annals of history, as did many of the other social phenomena that symbolized feudalism's authoritarian forces. However, unable to abruptly escape the powerful strain of machismo under which Japan had evolved and fearful of losing its homogeneous identity in the wake of foreign influence, many of modern Japan's fundamental elements still reflected its feudal-based ideologies. Perpetuating old traditions while encouraging the development of many new social pastimes and cultural recreations, *bugei* (martial arts) became an instrumental force in shaping modern Japanese history.

Based upon ancient customs, inflexible ideologies, and profound spiritual convictions, Japan's modern budo (martial ways) phenomenon was more than just a cultural recreation. In its new sociocultural setting, budo served, in many ways, as yet another channel through which the ruling elite could funnel *kokutai* (national polity), introduce the precepts of *shushin* (morality), and perpetuate *Nihonjinron* (Japaneseness). Based upon sport and recreation, the modern budo phenomena fostered a deep respect for those virtues, values, and principles revered in feudal bushido (the way of the warrior), which fostered the willingness to fight to the death or even to kill oneself if necessary. Both kendo and judo encouraged *shugyo* (austerity) and won widespread popularity during this age of escalating militarism.

Supported by the Monbusho (Ministry of Education), modern budo flourished in Japan's prewar school system. Embraced by an aggressive campaign of militarism, modern budo was often glamorized as the way in which "common men built uncommon bravery." Be that as it may, judo, kendo, and other forms of modern Japanese budo during the post-Edo, pre-World War II interval, served well to produce strong, able bodies and dauntless fighting spirits for Japan's growing war machine.

Ryukyu Kempo Karate-jutsu

With the draft invoked and Okinawa an official Japanese prefecture, the military vigorously campaigned for local recruits there. In 1891, during their army enlistment medical examination, Hanashiro Chomo (1869–1945) and Yabu Kentsu (1866–1937) were two of the first young experts recognized for their exemplary physical conditioning due to training in Ryukyu *kempo toudi-jutsu* (karate-jutsu).

Hence, the mere possibility that this little-known plebeian Okinawan fighting art might further enhance Japanese military effectiveness, as

Yabu Kentsu.

kendo and judo had, a closer study into the potential value of Ryukyu *kempo* karate-jutsu was initiated. However, the military ultimately abandoned this idea due to a lack of organization, impractical training methods, and the great length of time it took to gain proficiency. Although there is little testimony to support (or deny) allegations that it was developed to better prepare draftees for military service, karate-jutsu was introduced into Okinawa's school system (around the turn of the twentieth century) under the pretense that young men with a healthy body and moral character were more productive in Japanese society.

Around the turn of the twentieth century, a small group of local Okinawan karate enthusiasts led by Itosu Anko established a campaign to introduce the discipline into the island's school system as a form of physical exercise. Itosu's crusade to modernize karate-jutsu led to a radical revision of its practice.

Removing much of what was then considered too dangerous for school children, the emphasis shifted from self-defense to physical fitness through group *kata* practice, but neglected its *bunkai* (application). By not teaching the hidden self-defense moves, the actual intentions of the *kata* (e.g., to disable, maim, and or even kill by traumatizing anatomically vulnerable areas if necessary) became so obscured that a new tradition developed.

This radical period of transition represented the termination of a secret self-defense art that embraced spiritualism and the birth of a unique recreational phenomenon. This creation was introduced to mainland Japan, where it ultimately conformed to the forces of Japanese society and evolved in a completely new direction.

Japanization of Karate

Konishi Yasuhiro (1893–1983), a ju-jutsu expert and prominent kendo teacher, had studied Ryukyu *kempo* karate-jutsu before it was formerly introduced to mainland Japan. Later, he studied directly under Funakoshi Gichin, Motobu Choki (1871–1944), Mabuni Kenwa, and Miyagi Chojun. When comparing it to judo and kendo, Konishi described karate-jutsu as an incomplete discipline. With Otsuka Hironori (1892–1982), the founder of Wado-ryu ju-jutsu *kempo* karate-do, Konishi was largely responsible for initiating the modernization movement that revolutionized Ryukyu *kempo* karate-jutsu on Japan's mainland.

Konishi quite frankly said that modern karate was forged in the exact image of kendo and judo. The ancient samurai warrior's combative ethos, which was based on the various schools of ken-jutsu (swordsmanship) and ju-jutsu (grappling), provided the very infrastructure upon which the modern budo phenomenon evolved. Using the fundamental concepts of ken-jutsu's most eminent schools, kendo was established; ju-jutsu's central principles served as the basis upon which judo unfolded.

The Japanese proverb *deru kugi wa utareru* (a protruding nail gets ham-mered down) aptly describes how things or people that are "different" (i.e., not in balance with the *wa*[23] or harmony principle) ultimately con-form or are methodically thwarted in Japanese society. As a result karate was not able to escape Japan's omnipotent cultural forces. In contrast to kendo and judo, the karate-jutsu movement lacked a formal practice uniform and had no competitive format. Its teaching curricula varied greatly from teacher to teacher and there was no organized standard for accurately evaluating the varying grades of proficiency. When compared to kendo and judo, the humble discipline of Ryukyu *kempo* karate-jutsu remained, by Japanese standards, uncultivated and without suitable or-ganization or "oneness." In short, it was not Japanese. Ryukyu *kempo* karate-jutsu was thus subject to the criticism of rival and xenophobic op-position during that early and unsettled time of transition when it was being introduced to the Japanese mainland during the 1920s and 1930s.

The period of transition was not immediate nor was it without op-position. It included a justification phase, a time when animosities were vented and the winds of dissension carried the seeds of reorganization. It was a time in which foreign customs were methodically rooted out (*Uchinanchu* were openly discriminated against and anti-Chinese senti-ment was rampant) and more homogeneous concepts introduced.

The Dai Nippon Butokukai

Representing centuries of illustrious cultural heritage, the Butokukai's (Japan's national governing body for the combative traditions) ultra-traditional *bugei* and budo cliques were deeply concerned about the hos-tilities being openly vented between rival karate leaders. This, coupled with the disorganized teaching curricula, lack of social decorum, and absence of formal practice apparel, compelled the Butokukai to regard the escalating situation as detrimental to karate-jutsu's growth and di-rection on the mainland and set forth to resolve it.

The principal concern focused not only upon ensuring that karate teachers were fully qualified to teach, but also that the teachers actually understood what they were teaching. For karate-jutsu to be accepted in mainland Japan, the Butokukai called for the development and imple-mentation of a unified teaching curriculum, the adoption of a standard practice uniform, a consistent standard for accurately evaluating the various grades of proficiency, the implementation of Kano Jigoro's *dan-kyu* system, and the development of a safe competitive format through which participants could test their skills and spirits. Just as 12 inches always equals one foot, the plan was to establish a universal set of standards, as judo and kendo had done.

The Kara of Karate-do

No less demanding were the powerful forces of nationalism combined with anti-Chinese sentiment. Together, they propelled the karate-jutsu movement to reconsider a more appropriate ideogram to represent their discipline rather than the one that symbolized China. In making the transition, the Ryukyu *kempo* karate-jutsu movement would also abandon the "-jutsu" suffix and replace it with the modern term "do," as in judo and kendo.

The original ideograms for karate meant "China Hand." The initial ideogram, which can be pronounced either "tou" or "kara," stood for China's Tang dynasty (618–907), and later came to represent China itself. The second ideogram, meaning "hand," can be pronounced either "te" or "di." Master Kinjo Hiroshi[24] assured us that, until World War II, the *Uchinan* karate masters generally referred to karate as "toudi."

Kinjo's teacher, Hanashiro Chomo, a direct disciple of "Bushi" Matsumura, made the first recorded use of an ideogram to replace the "China" ideogram in his 1905 publication *Karate Kumite*. This unique ideogram characterized a self-defense art using only one's "empty" hands to subjugate an adversary. The new character for *kara* meant "empty" and can also be pronounced "ku" (void) and "sora" (sky). As such, *kara* not only represented the physical but also embraced the metaphysical; the deeper plane of an ancient Mahayana Buddhist doctrine surrounding detachment, spiritual emancipation, and the world within (inner void). During the pursuit of inner discovery, *kara* represents the transcending of worldly desire, delusion, and attachment.

The suffix "-do," which is found in kendo, judo, and budo, means "way," "path," or "road." The same character is also pronounced "dao" in Mandarin and is most notably used for the Daoist philosophy of Lao Zi, the reputed author of the *Dao De Jing*. In the philosophical context adopted by the self-defense traditions, the *do* became a "way" of life, a "path" one travels while pursuing karate's goal of perfection. The ideogram "jutsu" in karate-jutsu meant "art" or "science."

As such, the new ideograms proclaimed that Okinawa's plebeian discipline of karate-jutsu had transcended the physical boundaries of combat and had become a modern budo after embracing that which was Japanese. Like other Japanese cultural disciplines, karate-do became another vehicle through which the Japanese principle of *wa* (harmony) was funneled. Thus, the innovative term "karate-do" (the way of karate) succeeded the terms *toudi-jutsu* and karate-jutsu.

While the new term "karate-do," using the two new ideograms *(kara* and *do)*, was not officially recognized in Okinawa until 1936, it was ratified by the Dai Nippon Butokukai in December 1933, finally signaling karate-do's recognition as a modern Japanese budo.

Today, most historians conclude that Ryukyu *kempo* karate-jutsu, as introduced to the mainland in those early days, was at best an effective but unorganized plebeian self-defense method. The Butokukai concluded that the improvements it called for would bring about a single coalition under their auspices, like that of judo and kendo. However, karate-do development was overshadowed by the destruction of World War II, so much so that a universal set of standards failed to materialize.

Many believe that when the Butokukai and other organizations considered contributors to the roots of militarism were dissolved in 1945 after Japan unconditionally surrendered to the Allied forces, karate-do development as a unified discipline was abandoned. However, like judo and kendo, karate-do did come to enjoy an untold popularity through the sport format that was born in the school system.

In spite of karate-do's popularity, differences of opinion, personal animosities, and fierce rivalries clearly showed that karate-do was destined to maintain its divided individuality. While a myriad of eclectic interpretations unfolded—many of which shared similarities—karate-do styles were never really brought together to form a single tradition. This is a phenomenon that, for better or worse, continues to this day.

Okinawan Dynasties

Island folklore maintains that the Tensonshi (lit. "the grandchildren from heaven") governed the Ryukyu archipelago for twenty-five generations before Shunten.

Tametomo (1139–70), the eighth son of Tameyoshi and a subordinate of Japan's once powerful Minamoto clan, was exiled to Oshima Island but escaped and ultimately made his way to the Ryukyu Islands. There he married and had a son, Shunten. Shunten defeated Riyu (the last ruler of the Tenson) and became the island's first king in 1186.

The Shunten dynasty (1186–1253)	Shunten (1186–1237)
	Shumma-junki (1238–48)
	Gihon (1249–59)
Eiso dynasty (1260–1349)	Eiso (1260–99)
	Taisei (1300–8)
	Eiji (1309–13)
	Tamagusuku (1314–36)
	Seiji (1337–49)

Satto dynasty (1349–1407)

First Sho dynasty (1407–69)

The Second Sho dynasty (1470–1879)

Satto (1350–95)
Bunei (1396–1405)
Sho Shiso (1406–21)
Sho Hashi (1422–39)
Sho Chu (1440–44)
Sho Shitatsu (1445–49)
Sho Kinfuku (1450–53)
ShoTaikyu (1454–60)
ShoToku (1461–68)
Sho En (1470–76)
Sho Seni (1477)
Sho Shin (1477–1526)
Sho Sei(1527–55)
Sho Gen (1556–72)
Sho Ei (1573–88)
Sho Nei (1589–1620)
Sho IIo (1621–40)
Sho Ken (1641–47)
Sho Shitsu (1648–68)
Sho Tei (1669–1709)
Sho Eki (1710–12)
Sho Kei (1713–51)
Sho Boku (1752–94)
Sho On (1795–1802)
Sho Sei (1803)
ShoKo (1804–34)
Sho Iku (1835–47)
Sho Tai (1848–79)

NOTES:

1. In the English translation, Funakoshi's Chapter Six "Vital Points of the Human Anatomy" is quite clearly based on the data presented in the Bubishi. The "Eight Important Phases of Karate" and the five sentences that follow them are taken word-for-word from the Bubishi's "Eight Precepts of *Quanfa*" (Article 13) and "Maxims of Sun Zi" (Article 15). Similarly the mislabeled "Chinese *kambum*" that appear on the next page (which were left untranslated) are none other than "The Principles of the Ancient Law" (Article 14) and "Grappling and Escapes" (Article 16), as they appear in Chinese in the Bubishi.

2. Having met Liu Yinshan's brother, Liu Songshan, in Fuzhou, I came to learn of a "secret book" on *gongfu* that had been in the Liu family for the last seven decades. After meeting him in Fuzhou, hosting him at my home in Japan, and visiting him in Taiwan, I have become familiar with that book, entitled the *Secret Shaolin Bronze Man Book,* and can testify that it is, in almost every way, identical to the Bubishi. Master Liu's Bubishi is divided into seventeen articles in three sections, whereas the Okinawan Bubishi contains 32 articles; however, the same data is covered in both works though it is categorized differently.

3. In an interview at Tokashiki Iken's dojo in Naha in August 1994.

4. British karate historian Harry Cook noted that Robert W. Smith, in his book *Chinese Boxing: Masters and Methods* (Kodansha International, Tokyo, 1974), refers to a "secret book" that was made and given to the twenty-eight students of Zheng Lishu. Zheng (also spelt Chen) is described as the servant and disciple of Fang Qiniang by Robert W. Smith, but is described as a third-generation master in Liu Yinshan's book, after Zeng Cishu. Notwithstanding, I was able to confirm that a disciple of Zheng's named P'eng passed on a copy of the book to Zhang Argo who along with three other White Crane *gongfu* experts— Lin Yigao, Ah Fungshiu, and Lin Deshun—immigrated to Taiwan in 1922. While Zhang Argo's copy was passed on to his son Zhang Yide (spelled Chang I-Te in R.W. Smith's book), Master Lin Deshun, one of the four original Fujian *gongfu* experts, passed his copy of that secret book down to his disciple Liu Gou, the father of Liu Songshan. It has remained a treasure of the Liu family for the seven decades that have passed since then.

5. Another theory suggests that Sakugawa did not study directly with Kusankun but rather learned the principles of that system from Yara Guwa (AKA Chatan Yara). There are three birth and death dates for Sakugawa: 1733–1815, 1762–1843, and 1774–1838. The first date is used in most texts as it makes possible the pervading theory of Sakugawa's direct study with Kusankun. The second date was suggested by Nakamoto Masahiro, a student of Choshin Chibana and Taira Shinken, and founder of the Bunbukan Shuri-te School. The third date was given by Sakugawa Tomoaki (Sakugawa's seventh-generation descendant) in the *Nihon Budo Taikei*, Volume Eight. One other fact supporting this theory concerns the *kata Kusanku*. "Bushi" Matsumura *Chikudun Pechin* Sokon taught only one *Kusanku kata, Yara Kusanku*. This title would seem to indicate a link with Yara Guwa.

6. As we know, from Mabuni Kenwa's testimony, that Itosu Anko possessed a copy of the *Bubishi*, we can only speculate whether it was his teacher "Bushi" Matsumura *Chikudun Pechin* Sokon, or his teacher's teacher, "Toudi" Sakugawa, who introduced this text to the Shuri-te lineage.

7. The Nakaima family tells an interesting story about Ryuru Ko's visit to Okinawa in 1914. Apparently on the day he arrived, one of his former students, Sakiyama Kitoku from Naha's Wakuta village (a man renowned for his remarkable leg maneuvers, who had traveled to Fuzhou and trained under Ryuru with Norisato), was on his deathbed. Upon being informed of Kitoku's grave condition, Ryuru demanded to be taken to his home immediately. Arriving too late, Ryuru said, "If he had had a pulse remaining, I would have been able to save him."

8. In an article in the 1993 special commemorative publication for the tenth anniversary festival for the Fuzhou Wushu Association, I discovered a biography of the White Crane Master Xie Zhongxiang (1852–1930). I had come across Xie's name during my earlier interviews with Master Liu Songshan and Master Kanzaki Shigekazu (second-generation master of To-on-ryu and a respected karate historian). Upon more closely examining the biography of Xie Zhongxiang (provided by Wu Bin, the director of the Wushu Institute of China), I discovered that Xie was a shoemaker from Fuzhou's Changle district, and the founder of the Whooping Crane style *of gongfu*. In examining the five *quan (kata)* of Whooping Crane *gongfu*, I discovered that two of them were among the six *quan* described in the *Bubishi; Happoren* and *Nepai*. I also discovered, in a newsletter from Tokashiki Iken, that Xie's nickname was Ryuru, a fact corroborated by Master Kanzaki.

9. A student of Aragaki Seisho (from Kuninda) named Tomura *Pechin* demonstrated *Pechurrin (Suparinpei)*, on March 24, 1867 during a celebration commemorating the March 1866 visit of the *Sapposhi* Xhao Xin at Ochayagoten, which is Shuri Castle's east garden. We know that *Suparinpei, Seisan*, and *Sanchin kata* had been handed down in Kuninda long before Higashionna went to China. As the *Seisan* and *Peichurrin* are not practiced in the system Ryuru Ko taught, it would seem that Higashionna learned them from Aragaki Seisho. Other *kata* not taught in Ryuru Ko's system include *Sanseiryu, Saifua, Kururunfa*, and *Sepai*, which he may have learned from one of the Kojos, Wai Xinxian, or even Iwah.

10. In an interview at Tokashiki Iken's dojo in Naha in August 1994.

11. Not all researchers are of the opinion that Xie Zhongxiang is the man who taught

Higashionna Kanryo. Okinawan karate historian Kinjo Akio and Li Yiduan believe that a different man with the same nickname was Higashionna's teacher. They claim that Xie and Kanryo were too close in age; that Higashionna referred to Ryuru Ko as an "old man." Based on Higashionna's statement that Ryuru Ko was a bamboo craftsman who lived in a two-story house, they said that Xie, a shoemaker, must be a different person.

I disagree with these points for several reasons. In light of existing evidence, the age gap argument does not hold water. There is no evidence to show that Higashionna ever said that Ryuru Ko was an old man. Though Xie Zhongxiang was a shoemaker, his father was a bamboo craftsman who lived in a two-story house. I think the facts became confused over the years but remain convinced that Xie Zhongxiang taught Higashionna Kanryo.

12. The fact that Iwah definitely taught Matsumura and Higashionna's teacher Kojo, indicated a link between the traditions that evolved in Naha and Shuri. If Higashionna also studied with Iwah, then the link would be that much closer.

13. An interesting point brought to my attention by Master Kanzaki Shigekazu. He said that the *Nepai quan* (see Article 7, p. 260) descended directly from Fang Qiniang, and was taught to his teacher, Master Kyoda Juhatsu, by Go Kenki. Given the time frames surrounding the advent of the Bubishi in Okinawa we must not overlook Go Kenki as a plausible source from which the secret text may have appeared.

14. While most *Uchinanchu* are remembered for their prowess in the fighting traditions traveled to Fuzhou, Matayoshi Shinko (1888–1947) enjoyed a pilgrimage of broader proportions. Matayoshi traveled to China more than once and spent considerable time and effort studying a myriad of Chinese fighting disciplines. With Funakoshi, Matayoshi demonstrated at the Butokuden in 1917 and was among those who enjoyed the privilege of performing before the Japanese Crown Prince Hirohito in 1921 at Shuri castle.

Matayoshi had a profound affect upon the growth and direction of Okinawa's civil fighting traditions. Son of a *keimochi* family, he learned *kobudo* from an early age. At age twenty-three he ventured north to Hokkaido and first entered the Middle Kingdom by way of Sakhalin Island in 1911. In Manchuria, he befriended a tribe of mountain bandits and learned many of their ways. In Shanghai, Matayoshi augmented his studies by briefly training at the legendary Jing Wu (also known as the Qing Mo) Athletic Association, the same school where Miyagi Chojun studied for several months in 1936.

Matayoshi Shinko also ventured to Fuzhou, where he diligently continued his pursuit of the fighting traditions and related interests. Returning to Okinawa in 1934, he is remembered for his skill in White Crane Boxing, acupuncture, herbal medicine, and a myriad of Chinese weapons.

15. Wai Xinxian also taught Aragaki Seisho, who in turn taught Higashionna before he went to China. However, Gichin Funakoshi, in his 1922 *Ryukyu Kempo Toudi-jutsu,* wrote that Higashionna studied directly under Wai Xinxian. It is possible that Higashionna spent the first few years of his stay in China studying under Wai at the Kojo dojo.

Funakoshi also wrote that Iwah taught Shaolin *gongfu* to Kojo. Hence, the relationship between Aragaki, Kojo, Higashionna, Wai Xinxian, and Iwah would suggest that the fighting traditions that developed in Shuri and Naha were connected.

16. The Kojo dojo in Fuzhou was relatively large, taking up a space of fifty *tsubo* (one *tsubo* equalling the size of two tatami mats). As it was located very near the Ryukyukan dormitory, the dojo often served a gathering place for *Uchinanchu* living in Fuzhou.

17. In an interview in Tokyo, December 9, 1994.

18. Otsuka Tadahiko is the chief director of the Goju Kensha Karate-do Federation and author of the Japanese translation of the Bubishi.

19. The *Sanshikan* were the top three ministers under the Okinawan king.

20. Douglas Haring (Trans.), *Okinawan Customs: Yesterday and Today,* Charles E. Tuttle Publishing Company, Tokyo, 1969, pp. 38-39.

21. Ibid., pp. 42-44.

22. At the International Seminar of Budo Culture, International Budo University, March 1993.

23. *Wa* is a truly pervasive concept in Japanese society. It embodies a number of attributes including order, calmness, peace, unity, conformity, and group-consciousness. It has been claimed by intellectuals and politicians that *wa* is the central pillar supporting Japanese society and the reason for its growth and success.

24. Kinjo Hiroshi started his study of karate in 1926 under Hanashiro Chomo (1869–1945) and Oshiro Chojo (1888–1935), both of whom in turn were students of Itosu Anko. Described by Master Richard Kim as a "walking encyclopedia of karate history" and "a master's master," Kinjo *Sensei* is one of Japan's most respected karate masters.

The Chinese characters for *mushin* (no mind) as
brushed by Nagamine Shoshin.

"Itosu's Ten Articles"

Karate did not descend from Buddhism or Confucianism. In the olden days two schools of *karate,* namely the *Shorin* and *Shorei* style, were introduced from China. Both support sound principles and it is vital that they be preserved and not altered. Therefore, I will mention here what one must know about *karate.*

1. *Karate* does not only endeavor to discipline one's physique. If and when the necessity occurs to fight for just cause *karate* provides the fortitude in which to risk one's life in support of that campaign. It is not meant to be employed against a single adversary but rather as a means of avoiding the use of one's hands and feet in the event of a potentially dangerous encounter with a ruffian or a villain.

2. The primary purpose of *karate* training is to strengthen the human muscles making the physique strong, like iron and stone; so that one can use the hands and feet like weapons such as a spear or halberd. In doing so *karate* training cultivates bravery and valor in children and it should be encouraged in our elementary schools. Don't forget what the Duke of Wellington said after defeating Emperor Napoleon: *Today's victory was first achieved from the discipline attained on the play-grounds of our elementary schools.*

3. *Karate* cannot be adequately learned in a short space of time. Like a torpid bull, regardless of how slowly it moves, it will eventually cover a thousand miles. So, too, for one who resolves to study diligently two or three hours every day. After three or four years of unremitting effort one's body will undergo a great transformation, revealing the very essence of *karate.*

4. One of the most important issues in *karate* is the training of the hands and the feet. Therefore one must always make use of the *makiwara* in order to develop them thoroughly. In order to do this effectively lower the shoulders, open the lungs, focus your energy, firmly grip the ground to root your posture and sink your *qi* (commonly referred to as one's life force or intrinsic force) into your *tanden* (just below the navel). Following this procedure perform one to two hundred *tsuki* (thrusts) with each hand every day.

5. One must maintain an upright position in the training postures of *karate.* The back should be straight, loins pointing upward with the shoulders down, while maintaining a pliable power in your legs. Relax and bring together the upper and lower parts of the body with the *qi* force focused in your *tanden.*

6. Handed down by word of mouth, *karate* comprises a myriad of techniques and corresponding meanings. Resolve to independently explore the context of these techniques, observing the principles of *Tuidi* (theory of usage), and the practical applications will be more easily understood.

7. In *karate* training one must determine whether the specific application is suitable for defense or for cultivating the body.

8. Intensity is an important issue for *karate* training. To visualize that one is actually engaged on the battlefield during training does much to enhance progression. Therefore, the eyes should dispatch fierceness while lowering the shoulders and contracting the body when blocking a blow. Training in this spirit prepares one for actual combat.

9. The amount of training must be in proportion to one's physical reservoir of strength and condition. Excessive practice is harmful to one's body and can be recognized when the face and eyes become red.

10. Participants of *karate* usually enjoy a long and healthy life thanks

to the benefits of unremitting training. Practice strengthens muscle and bone, improves the digestive organs and regulates blood circulation. Therefore, if the study of *karate* were introduced into our (athletic) curricula from elementary school and practiced extensively we could more easily produce men of immeasurable defense capabilities.

With these teachings in mind, it is my conviction that if the students at the *Shihan Chugakko* (old name of Okinawa's teachers college) practice *(karate)* they could, after graduation, introduce *karate* at the local levels; namely elementary schools. In this way *karate* could be disseminated throughout the entire nation and not only benefit people in general but also serve as an enormous asset to our military forces.

Articles on History and Philosophy

Article 1: Origins of White Crane Gongfu

In spite of his fighting skills in Monk Fist Boxing, Fang Zhonggong was no match for the scoundrels from a neighboring village who deceived and then viciously beat him while vying for control of his village. The injuries Fang sustained during the altercation were so severe that he was unable to fully recuperate, and fell gravely ill. Attended to by his loving daughter and personal disciple, Fang Qiniang, his condition gradually deteriorated. No longer even able to eat, he finally died.

Deeply troubled by the loathsome circumstances of her beloved father's death, Fang Qiniang vowed to take revenge. Although just a country girl from the rural village of Yongchun, Fang Qiniang was nevertheless a promising and spirited young woman. She longed to vindicate her family name, but she had not yet mastered the fighting skills her father was teaching her. She deeply pondered upon how she might find the power and strength to overcome such adversaries.

One day, not long after the tragedy, Fang was sobbing over the memory of her loss when suddenly she heard some strange noises coming from the bamboo grove just outside her home. Looking out the window to see what was making such a racket, she saw two beautiful cranes fighting. She noticed how the magnificent creatures strategically maneuvered themselves away from each other's fierce attacks with remarkable precision. In the midst of piercing screams, the vigorous jumping, and deceptive wing flapping, the barrage of vicious clawing and lethal pecking was well concealed.

Deciding to frighten off the creatures, Fang went outside and grabbed the long bamboo pole she used for hanging clothes to dry. As she approached the cranes, Fang swung the pole but was unable to get close. Each time she attempted to swing or poke with the pole, they sensed her proximity, and, before the pole could reach its intended target, the birds instinctively evaded her every effort and finally just flew off.

Reflecting deeply upon this incident, Fang concluded that it was a revelation and soon set about evaluating the white cranes' instinctive combative methods. If someone could fight the way the white cranes had, that person would be unbeatable. After considerable time and study, Fang finally came to understand the central principles of hard and soft, and yielding to power. Fusing the central elements of Monk Fist *gongfu* with her own interpretation of the birds' innate defensive movements, she created a new style.

After three years of relentless training, Fang developed into an unusually skillful fighter. Capable of remarkable feats of strength and power, Fang Qiniang was no longer the weak and frail girl she had once been. Her skill and determination finally gained her a notable reputation. Undefeated in those three years, Fang's innovative style ultimately became one of the most popular civil self-defense traditions in and around Fujian Province, and became known as Yongchun White Crane Boxing *(Yongchun He Quan)*.

In an effort to govern the behavior of those who studied her tradition, Fang cautioned her followers to only use their skills in self-defense. She maintained that great bodily harm, including death, could easily result from excessive force. Imparting her late father's wisdom, Fang maintained that without first finding inner peace and harmony, one could never truly master the fighting traditions, and hence never master their own lives. Master Fang asserted that it is only through discovering and then mastering the world within that the power of positive human force can be developed in harmony with nature and used to defeat any adversary.

Fang said that the principles upon which her tradition was established (i.e., correct breathing, moral precepts, inner-discovery, etc.) had been handed down from ancient times and were not native to the district of Fuzhou.

Fang's Test

Fang's reputation attracted many challengers wanting to test their skill against that of a woman. However, none were successful. Zeng Cishu was one of the men who dared to test Fang's ability.

Described as invincible, Zeng was a hard-style boxing expert with fingers like iron and a body as hard as a rock. Demanding to do battle with the girl, Fang promptly agreed and Zeng prepared to meet his opponent. Without even being hit once, Fang swiftly dispatched the challenger. So taken by her remarkable skill and gracious character, the fallen warrior immediately petitioned her to accept him as her student. As her personal disciple, Zeng Cishu went on to become Fang's most prized student and eventually became the second-generation master of White Crane *gongfu*.

In describing his bout with Master Fang, Zeng announced that he had mistakenly relied too much upon physical strength. Fang only had to use her evasive style and inner force to subjugate him. Zeng Cishu said she was truly a master and worthy of her reputation. Because Zeng was regarded as such a powerhouse, their bout served to greatly enhance Master Fang's reputation and brought much more recognition to her unique boxing method.

From that time on, Master Fang maintained that anyone learning the fighting tradition must always make sure not to place too much emphasis upon just physical training. True power and wisdom come from within and are reflected without. Introspection and philosophical assimilation must balance strict, hard physical conditioning. This is the way to transcend ego-related distractions and get beyond the immediate results of physical training. People who truly understand the fighting traditions are never arrogant or unscrupulous, and never use their skill unjustly.

In the White Crane fighting tradition an instructor must teach according to the student's own individual ability. Learning the *quan,* one can progress at one's own pace. Subsequently, the more earnestly one trains, the more swiftly inner strength develops. As in the case of Zeng Cishu, who through the relentless practice of the form *Happoren* developed his inner strength so that it ultimately manifested itself and flowed inward and outward through his 36 Vital Points, invigorating his body so that he could, at will, summon his *qi* (life energy; *ki* in Japanese) to any of his vital points. Zeng Cishu made this *quan* a popular tradition, which was perpetuated and handed down.

Developing Inner Strength Through the Quan (kata)

1. Eliminate external distractions and concentrate only upon intention.
2. Coordinate breathing and synchronize it with the muscular activity. When you extend your arm, exhale and strike but conserve 50% of your air. Be sure never to expel all of your air at one time. When you inhale, your body becomes light. When you exhale, your body becomes rooted.
3. Listen to your breathing and become aware of every part of your body.
4. There must be a constant but pliable muscular contraction in the deltoid, trapezius, latissimus dorsi, serratus, and pectoral muscle groups.
5. To encourage perfect diaphragm breathing, the spine must be parallel to the stomach.
6. Techniques are executed forward and back from where the elbows meet the waist.

Understanding the physical and metaphysical precepts of hard and soft *(gangrou* in Mandarin, *goju* in Japanese), one must learn that it is the even balance between the two that enables one to overcome the greatest adversary of all: oneself. Hardness represents both the material force of the human body and one's fierceness. Softness represents the gentleness of one's character and the resiliency to yield in the face of adversity. Together, these are attributes that unfold through continual analysis and genuine commitment.

One must counter force with pliability, and vice versa. All body movement, including stealthy and evasive maneuvering, must be governed by correct breathing. The body must be resilient like a willow branch being blown in a fierce gale; it gives with the force of the wind, but when the strength of the wind vanishes, the bough spontaneously resumes its posture. When the body stretches up and inhales, it resembles a giant ocean wave, knowing no resistance. However, when a stable posture is assumed and the air is forced out from the lungs while contracting the muscles, one becomes immovable, like a majestic mountain.

Principles of Movement

1. Foot movement must be similar to walking. One initiates the step naturally and concludes it with firmness.
2. Smoothly make each step identical to the last, with the big toe of the rear foot aligned with the heel of the other (shoulder width apart).
3. Foot movement, both in a forward and backward direction, should correspond to the crescent shape of a quarter moon, with the knees slightly bent, moving quietly.
4. Leg muscles must be firm but flexible to engender mobility.

Immeasurable self-conquests are made possible through a peaceful mind and inner harmony. The strength and resiliency gained from *quanfa* training fosters an inner force with which one can overcome any opponent and conquer worldly delusion and misery. Even when just walking, you should always be conscious of combining your breathing with your movement. In this way, should you be attacked, you will not lose your balance. The relationship between your legs and body is similar to that of the wheels of a wagon. Of what good is a sturdy buggy without wheels to move it? Hand techniques must be supported by the legs to foster both stability and mobility.

Advice for Engagement

1. The mind must be calm but alert.
2. Look for that which is not easily seen.
3. Use your peripheral vision.
4. Remain calm when facing your opponent.
5. Have confident body language and facial expression.
6. Use a posture that will support mobility.

Using Your Hands

Hand techniques require the use of the body. The body generates the power and the hands serve as the instruments of contact. Like a cat catching a rat, a tiger pulls down a wild boar with its body; the claws serve as the means of contact.

It takes great courage and skill to take out an adversary with a calm mind. True masters establish a balance between their lives and their art to a degree that their lives become as much a product of the art as is the art a product of their lives.

When thrusting with the tips of the fingers, maximum force is achieved only when the four fingers are squeezed tightly together and supported by the thumb. Cultivating this special technique, one can generate remarkable force.

Balance

Perfect balance is a reflection of what is within. It is also a prerequisite for combative proficiency. It is by mastering balance that one is able to easily take advantage of, or deliberately create, a weakness in an opponent's posture. Such weaknesses must be attacked without hesitation.

If someone attempts to seize you by surprise, you might be better off to escape, reestablish your balance, and then engage the opponent. However, the circumstances dictate the means. It is good to employ evasive tactics when forcefully attacked. It is a good time to launch a counteroffensive upon perceiving that the opponent's energy is exhausted.

Like the sun's strength, your energy must radiate outward, your eyes should be as clear as the moon, and your legs should be like the rolling wheels of a cart. Your posture, too, from head to toe, must be evenly balanced so that footwork and hand techniques support each other. If everything is in balance, no one will be able to defeat you.

Be sure to practice according to your teacher's advice and always be open to learn the ways of others. It takes a long time to achieve perfection based upon our experience. Do not be in a hurry; patience is a virtue. Above all, be honest with yourself, do not deceive others, and live a modest life. If you do not follow these rules, you will never realize the Way.

Passing on Fang's tradition to the families in Yongchun village, Zeng Cishu came to have many students, one of whom became the second successor. His name was "Teng Shan" Wang Foudeng and he was responsible for perpetuating Fang's tradition in the years that followed.

In his 1983 book *Hakutsuru Mon: Shokutsuru Ken,* Liu Yinshan describes Fang Zhonggong (he refers to him as Fang Huishi) as a Shaolin recluse and a master of Eighteen Monk Fist boxing *(Shiba Luohan Quanfa).* While waiting for the overthrow of the Qing dynasty, Fang sought refuge at the Shalian Temple (Shoren-ji in Japanese) in Putian, Fujian.

Although it is not in the text, according to Master Liu Songshan, Fang Qiniang transcended any desire to violently revenge her father's death upon having mastered her art of self-defense. The *kata* referred to in this article is *Happoren.* (TR)

⌒⌒⊙⌒⌒

Article 2: Master Wang Reveals His Secrets

True mastery can only result after years of uncompromising training. Austere conditioning must be evenly balanced with philosophical assimilation and protracted introspection. Wisdom is putting knowledge into action.

Laws of Wisdom

1. Let anger be your enemy.
2. Remember, an empty vessel makes the most noise.
3. Patience is the foundation upon which security and long life rest.
4. Know well your station in life.
5. Trustworthy reputations are only gained from virtuous merit.
6. Success is the fruit of the strong and wise.
7. Delay is the best remedy for anger.
8. Those who will be enlightened are the ones who live moderate lives, have simple tastes, consume natural foods, and pursue the wisdom of the sages.
9. Remain honest in your heart, true to your discipline, and refrain from overindulgence, and you will enjoy great rewards in life.
10. Mind your manners and your own business.
11. Discretion is the better part of valor.
12. The barriers of human achievement lie only in the mind.
13. An idle mind is a demon's workshop.
14. Justice exists for those who live according to the Way, as these are one in the same.
15. Be happy without cause and make the best of what you have.
16. True friendship knows no boundaries.
17. It is a humble virtue to be wealthy and not affected by it.
18. Cause and effect are mutually consistent.
19. Despair is the conclusion of fools. Tomorrow's success is built upon yesterday's failures. Live in the here and now. Do not seek more but learn to enjoy less.

Article 3: Advice on Correct Etiquette

We are all responsible for our own health and behavior. Our physical health and mental well-being must always be the highest priorities in our lives. Hence, training in *quanfa* must be an even balance of physical conditioning and metaphysical study to foster both vitality and virtue.

Regardless of whether people study *quanfa* for health, recreation, or self-defense, everyone must understand that it is not to be misused. Therefore, teachers should have their disciples swear an oath. In this oath, disciples must pledge to never intentionally hurt anyone or do anything unjust.

For disciples whose progress remains hampered, more emphasis should be placed upon metaphysical study. In so doing, the value of patience and diligence will make itself apparent.

If one is moody and has irresistible urges to behave violently and disturb the tranquillity of heaven or nature, they are sure to meet with extremely prejudicial circumstances.

This advice holds an extra special importance for the education of young men who study the fighting traditions. Young men are often known to fly off the handle without reason. A lack of confidence and ego-related distractions are the source of unwarranted aggression. Like animals, they often run in packs, making trouble. Misusing their *quanfa* skills, they develop reputations worthy of criminals and the outcasts of society. As a teacher, it is critically important to recognize such character weaknesses early if one is to prevent such disgrace from occurring.

Do not deceive your fellow man. If the moral precepts of *quanfa* are disregarded, by teacher or disciple, one's life will be doomed to failure. Deceiving people is the most serious of all crimes, as there is no defense against it. Should someone take it upon themselves to deceive another, the gods will protect the good and judge the evil. Those who use deceit and violence will never know peace or enjoy a long life.

One must always respect the rights of others and exercise humanity in daily life. Those who abide by the natural laws of heaven and earth will prosper and their descendants will continue on forever.

An old proverb says: "Look at a crab with cold eyes; ignore the wicked as, sooner or later, they will meet their own fate."

This proverb indicates that one should view immoral or evil individuals dispassionately. (TR)

Article 4: Philosophy

The true meaning of *wu* (martial [way], *bu* in Japanese) lies not in victory or defeat, but rather, in patience, sincerity, honesty, and benevolence. In spite of developing only mediocre skills, one can still enjoy immeasurable rewards and find direction through helping their fellow man. Austere conditioning and balanced nutrition are the cornerstones of mental stability. Together, this combination will foster and support vigorous *qi* energy. The innermost secrets of *quanfa* emerge when a vigorous *qi* is developed through dedicated training.

Understanding how personal achievements are made possible through diligent daily training, *quanfa* must be recognized as a lifelong pursuit. Without warning, almost as if by magic, one's *qi* will surface, compelling one to stay in touch with nature.

There are many signs and lessons that must not be overlooked along the unyielding path of *quanfa*. Most make themselves known within the first few years of training. Patience and perseverance are seen as two of the biggest stumbling blocks for most disciples.

Lacking confidence about self-protection is the mind's subliminal message to the body that more training is necessary to overcome fear. Indomitable fortitude illuminates the darkness of fear. At a glance, others will recognize this inner strength. Regardless of one's punching power or the stability of their posture, *quanfa* can be an effective deterrent against unwarranted aggression.

One can overcome an opponent's dominance and thwart others' oppressive behavior through *quanfa* training. Be a person of dignified behavior, recognized for kindness and consideration of others less fortunate. Managing animosity calmly and impartially will establish a reputation with which a peaceful and happy life will be enjoyed.

However, beware, as the same laws, both good and bad, apply to all. If the power of *quanfa* is misused, misfortune is sure to occur. Enemies will be quick to target those who are easily lured by the wrath of others. Their slander can ruin a reputation and result in having one's station in life lowered. Do not forget the old saying, "Enemies are easily made and often decide the fate of wrong-doers who take pleasure in impertinence."

The following philosophy has also been handed down by the ancient masters and should be considered carefully. Nothing is more important than one's patience and consideration as practiced in daily life. Live in the "here and now," and do not be distracted by the ways of the world. If you rush, your path will be narrow, but by keeping one step back, the way will be wide. Simplicity is more desirable in the end. Write down what you have learned and study the wisdom of those who have come before you.

Article 5: Master Wang's Observations on Monk Fist Boxing

Containing an infinite variety of outstanding skills, Monk Fist Boxing shares many similarities with the White Crane tradition. As it has no weak points, I cannot help but remain deeply impressed by this elusive but superb method. There can be no question that Monk Fist Boxing has either been the forerunner, or served to influence the development of many other civil fighting disciplines.

By using simple, but clever, geometrical principles of movement, Monk Fist Boxing leaves no weaknesses in its defensive application. Its formidable arsenal of defensive and offensive techniques can be easily used in both linear and circular patterns in a wide range of directions and elevations.

Enhancing its application, Monk Fist Boxing also employs the principles of hard and soft. Evasive and resilient, the defensive applications of Monk Fist Boxing are complemented by its remarkably aggressive offense.

Monk Fist Boxing's elusiveness embodies all the deception of a desert mirage, while its jumping maneuvers are meant to be performed with the quickness of a bolt of lightning flashing out from a cloud. To that end, Monk Fist Boxing remains an omnipotent system of self-defense.

Studying the hand and foot principles of Monk Fist Boxing will serve to enhance one's own ability. The harder one trains, the more proficient one becomes.

Advice

If you should be attacked by a powerful force, be sure never to become desperate. Diligent training cultivates an inner calm that enhances one's instinctive ability to counter any offensive. Linear attacks are neutralized from an angle while angular attacks are repelled in a straight line. This is a fundamental practice used by Monk Fist Boxers and a practice we must all master.

Etiquette

It is said that a person who truly knows himself will never harm another human being, even under provocation. True *quanfa* disciples are never haughty or proud, but are honest and simple folk.

Conclusion

Be careful never to demand more than that which is considered reasonable from people in any situation. Exercise modesty at all times. Feel comfortable to discuss the secrets of *quanfa* with those with whom you are close. However, stay clear of unscrupulous and spiteful people. One must be especially careful of the "wolves in sheep's clothing."

Article 26: The Guardian Deity Jiu Tian Feng Huo Yuan San Tian Dou

Otsuka Tadahiko *Sensei* described this deity as the third son of an all-powerful Chinese god of war. Holding the position of Feng Huo Yuan, he is the guardian of Zheng Li (old name for Fujian). Young, handsome, and virtuous, he is also an aspiring disciple of the combative disciplines.

Representing virtue, propriety, and perseverance, he was once revered by ardent disciples of *gongfu* in Fuzhou. The same Chinese characters describing this god appear in the Liu family's *Shaolin Bronze Man Book*. Xie Wenliang, master of Whooping Crane Boxing, also has an illustration of this deity in the altar in his home. According to Liu Yinshan, Fang Zhonggong worshipped this deity while at the Shalian [sic] monastery. After her father's tragic death, Fang Qiniang adopted the god as a symbol of justice and propriety for her tradition. He appears in Mabuni Kenwa's Bubishi and poorly reproduced likenesses of this deity also appear in other versions of the Bubishi as well. The deity in the illustration (*above*), owned by Matayoshi Shinho, was brought from Fuzhou back to Okinawa by his father, Matayoshi Shinko, after his first trip to China, and also appears in his secret book on White Crane. (TR)

PART TWO

CHINESE MEDICINE AND HERBAL PHARMACOLOGY

Folk medicine maintains that herbs and exercise are man's only natural protection against illness. Herbs can and do provide energy and promote smooth blood circulation, allowing the human body to eliminate the accumulation of toxins and the congestion that cause disease. In addition, herbs aid digestion, assimilation, and elimination. Moreover, herbs can be used to treat minor aliments as well as acute chronic conditions. Herbs have a remarkable history of healing the human body and maintaining good health when properly used. Unlike modern chemical medicines, natural herbs are much safer and do not leave residue in the body that produces side effects.

Of all countries in the world, China has the longest unbroken tradition of herbal medicine. In China, medicinal herbs have played an inseparable role in the civil fighting traditions for centuries. For masters of traditional *gongfu,* the principles of herbal medicine, acupuncture, massage, and other related forms of trauma management were an integral part of training; a speedy recovery was always necessary during a period void of social security. However, that knowledge, like the moral precepts upon which the fighting traditions rest, have been overshadowed in the modern era with its myriad of eclectic traditions, commercial exploitation, and the competitive phenomenon.

Articles 10, 11, 12, 19, 30, and 31 appear in the Bubishi with neither detailed explanation nor direction, and, like the other articles in this old text, are plagued by grammatical errors. The absence of any detailed information led this writer to believe that the prescriptions illustrated in the Bubishi were originally recorded by, and for, those who had previous knowledge of their application. However, after being copied by hand for generations, much has been lost because of miscomprehension and mistranslation. Mr. Li Yiduan said that orthodox Chinese herbal medicines, their names, and prescriptions are standardized throughout the country. However, in the case of local folk remedies, the names of prescriptions and ingredients are not standardized and vary from district to district. After consulting several local experts in Fuzhou, Mr. Li also said, "the information that appears in the Bubishi, especially the herbal prescriptions and vital point sections, is filled with numerous grammatical inaccuracies. In some parts of the Bubishi, whole sections have been omitted, while other parts have been recorded incorrectly, leaving the remaining information unintelligible." Mr. Li concluded by saying that "there can be no question that these problems have occurred during the process of copying the text by hand over the generations."

I have grouped the aforementioned six articles together, along with some preliminary research, to help explain the history and significance of Chinese herbal therapy or *zhong yao,* its related practices, and its relationship to the fighting traditions.

According to Chinese folklore, many centuries ago, a farmer found a snake in his garden and tried to beat it to death with a hoe. A few days later he discovered the same snake slithering around in his backyard, and he tried to kill it again. When the seemingly indestructible serpent appeared again a few days later, the farmer gave it another beating, only to see the bleeding viper squirm into a patch of weeds, where it commenced eating them.

Upon observing the reptile the following day, the farmer was astonished to find it invigorated with its badly beaten body rapidly healing. Such was the discovery, as legend has it, of *san qi (Panax Notoginseng)*, a powerful healing herb, now used in a variety of herbal medicines.

Like so many other aspects of Chinese culture, herbal medicine has also had a host of heavenly deities or semi-divine idols representing it. The "Three August Ones," Fu Xi, Shen Nong, and Yao Wang, once depicted the divine accuracy and propriety of this science. In Chinese history, the legendary emperor and last of the "Three August Ones," Shen Nong (3494 B.C.) is regarded as the creator of medicine. Yao Wang, the second of the "Three August Ones," is known as the "King of Medicinal Herbs." Fu Xi, the first of the "Three August Ones," reputed to have lived about 4,000 years ago, is generally credited with having invented just about everything else.

The tradition of using Chinese herbs for medicinal applications predates Christianity by more than three millennium. Shrouded in a veil of myth and mysticism, the history of herbal concoctions have been associated with such rituals as Shamanism and the forces of the supernatural. Although used more often to create an appropriate ritualistic atmosphere rather than strictly for their medicinal properties, ancient religious sects customarily used herbal concoctions in ceremonial rites. These shamans paved the way for the Daoist recluses who later chose to leave their communities to live in wild mountainous areas and lengthen their lives by using herbs, training in the civil fighting arts, and doing breathing exercises.

Confucian, Daoist, and Buddhist philosophy have also had a profound effect upon the development of herbal medicine. Confucius (551-479 B.C.) developed a moral and social philosophy based on the premise that the balance of yin and yang creates a correct order and harmony in the universe. He claimed that man must be moral and study and act in accordance with the Five Virtues (e.g., benevolence, justice, propriety, wisdom, and sincerity) in order to bring harmony to the world. In contrast Lao Zi taught that nature was harmonious when left alone and that man could have no positive impact on it. He claimed that one had to learn to stop resisting nature and that it was only through passivity, the following of the path of least resistance, and embracing nature in all its glory that positive results could be attained. Later Daoists invented a path to salvation and a spiritual destination, a mythical "Island in the Eastern Sea" where there was a herb that had the power to bestow immortality.

By the first century B.C., Dong Zhongshu had applied the yin-yang theory to internal medicine and nutrition. During the tumultuous Zhou dynasty *(ca.* 1000–221 B.C.) many scholars, like their forebearers the mountain recluses, sought out sanctuary deep in the mountains, and became known as the "Immortals of the Mountains." Continuing the tradition of medical analysis, their research ultimately became the principal force behind the development of herbal medicine.

The first records of Chinese herbal concoctions, after graduating from sorcery to sophistication, are discovered in the classic discourse on internal medicine written by Huang Di (2698–2587 B.C.), the legendary "Yellow Emperor." However, it was not until the Han dynasty (206 B.C.–A.D. 220) that Zhang Zhongjing *(ca.* A.D. 160–200) developed the practice of herbal medicine as a science. Considered the great codifier of medicine, Zhang's unique application of the yin-yang and five-element theories helped establish a basis from which to more accurately diagnose and treat illness with herbal medicines. As such, sicknesses could be associated with specific organ dysfunctions and herbal remedies prescribed accordingly.

Many herbal formulae have been handed down from the Han dynasty. They have been refined, tested, verified, and experimented on by a hundred generations of herbalists, and in each generation their findings have been recorded and preserved.

It was during the Han dynasty that herbal formulae were notated and began to be used as an anesthetic in surgery. The eminent physician Hua Tuo (A.D. 141–208) used herbal soups to anesthetize patients in the surgical treatment of superficial diseases and wounds, and also experimented with hydro-therapy and the use of herbal baths.

Profoundly influenced by the mountain ascetics, Hua Tuo was also an ardent disciple of the fighting traditions. Concluding that balanced exercise and intelligent eating habits were instrumental in the cultivation of "a healthy life," Hua developed a therapeutic *gongfu* tradition based upon the movements of five animals: the deer, tiger, monkey, crane, and bear. Through invigorating the vital organs, Hua's therapeutic practice improved one's circulation, respiration, digestion, and elimination. It also helped to improve physical strength while eliminating fatigue and depression. As such, the importance and relationship between physical exercise and herbal medicine was established over 1700 years ago.

Meridian Channels in Chinese Medicine

Over the course of centuries, an unending line of devout and observant physicians detected the existence of internal energy passageways and recorded their relationship to a number of physiological functions. Physicians came to observe specific hypersensitive skin areas that corresponded to certain illnesses. This ultimately led to the recognition of a series of recurring points that could be linked to organ dysfunction. By following these fixed paths, the points came to be used to diagnose organ dysfunction. The route linking these series of points to a specific organ became known as a meridian.

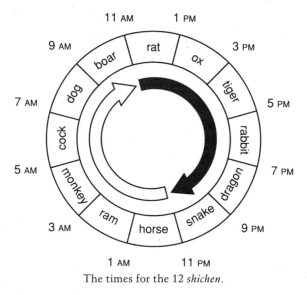

The times for the 12 *shichen*.

The idea for attacking the 12 bi-hourly vital points surfaced from research surrounding the polarity or "Meridian Flow theory" of acupuncture. By the Song dynasty, Xu Wenbo, an eminent acupuncturist and the official doctor for the Imperial family, developed this theory into a science. Concluding that the breath (respiratory system) and blood (circulatory system) behaved within the body in the same way as the earth rotated in the sky, he discovered how the vital point locations changed with time. He found that the human body's 12 meridians correspond to the 12 bi-hourly time divisions of the day. There are twelve *shichen* to a day and each *shichen* is equivalent to two hours. The *shichen* are named after the 12 animals of the Chinese zodiac: therefore, the period between 11 p.m. and 1 a.m. is the Time of the Rat, 1 a.m. to 3 a.m. is the Time of the Ox, and so on. It is through this method that a certain vital point could be most fatally traumatized during a corresponding *shichen* interval. Meticulously recording his research, he documented more than 350 vital points. His analysis identified how the respiratory and circulatory systems correspond to a given meridian or vital point, and which vital point opened and closed at what time.

Responsible for remarkable advances in medical science, Xi Yuan, an eminent thirteenth-century Chinese physician, standardized the methods of how to improve a sick patient's prognosis by stimulating the points of a corresponding meridian. Xi Yuan was also among those who furthered the research into the influence of solar and lunar cycles on the circulatory system and organs.

Xi Yuan determined precisely at what time of each day the 12 regular meridians exhibited two-hour periods of maximum and minimum energy by comparing his findings to the *shichen*. To demonstrate his analysis, Xi Yuan drew charts and diagrams illustrating the central principles of this complex theory.

In time, ways of utilizing herbs to cure dysfunctioning organs and correct the flow of energy in the body were developed. Some herbs were used for a specific meridian and would not be mixed, for they could cause disease instead of curing it when combined.

With the advent of Buddhism, a growing intercourse between India and China gradually affected the growth and direction of herbal medicine and the fighting traditions. From the first to the ninth centuries A.D., pilgrims, sages, translators, teachers, trade delegates, ambassadors, etc. crossed and recrossed the mountains between the two cultures. Part of that intercourse was directly concerned with healing.

India has long had a profound tradition of herbal medicine. By the start of the Tang dynasty (618–907 A.D.), all serious Chinese physicians and doctors were familiar with both the Chinese and Buddhist texts of healing. This cross-fertilization of knowledge advanced Chinese medicine considerably.

By the Ming dynasty, the principles of acupuncture and herbal medicine had spread widely and a great number of books had been written on all aspects of them. Every physician in China, from Imperial Court doctor to village medicine man, vigorously employed the principles of herbal medicine and acupuncture to help sick people.

One of the most important documents on herbal medicine of that time was the *Ben Cao Gang Mu* (General Outline and Division of Herbal Medicine), by Dr. Li Shizhen (1517–93). Considered one of Ming China's most eminent medical scholars, his classic encyclopedia of herbal medicine listed 1892 different herbal medicines, in 52 volumes (scrolls), and took 27 years to research and compile. Translated into Vietnamese, Japanese, Russian, French, German, Korean, and English, it has even been claimed that Li's prodigious treatise even influenced the research of Charles Darwin.

Following the Qing dynasty, China's Imperial Medical College established a national standard for the healing sciences of acupuncture, herbal medicines, *qigong,* moxibustion, and massage therapy.

However, Western medical standards have, until only quite recently, always considered these ancient natural principles of medicine a kind of "backwoods" tradition. It has only been after lengthy analysis and astonishing results that these concepts have been widely accepted in the Western world and are now often used side by side with modern technology.

In the *Shaolin Bronze Man Book,* there is an article that describes the important connection between medicine and the civil fighting traditions, "a person who studies *quanfa* should by all means also understand the principles of medicine. Those who do not understand these principles and practice *quanfa* must be considered imprudent."

In his 1926 publication *Okinawa Kempo Karate-jutsu Kumite,* Motobu Choki (1871-1944), unlike his contemporary Funakoshi Gichin, described revival techniques, the treatment of broken bones, dislocated joints, contusions, and the vomiting of blood caused by internal injury, and explained the value of knowing medical principles. Much like the Bubishi, Motobu refers to various herbal concoctions and how they are able to remedy numerous ailments, be they external or internal. Motobu's book lists many of the same herbs noted in both the Bubishi and the *Shaolin Bronze Man Book* (see Article 31, p. 191).

Examples of Herbal Medicine

Chinese herbal medicine employs a myriad of ingredients from the undersea and animal kingdoms, the world of plants, fruits, and vegetables, along with minerals and a select number of exotic elements. While there are virtually hundreds of kinds of products that are extracted from mother nature, the following list represents the principal sources from which most are derived: roots, fungi, shrubs, sap and nectar, grass, wood and bark, floral buds, petals, leaves, moss, plant stems and branches; fruits, nuts, seeds, berries, and various vegetables; various insects, reptiles, pearls, sea life, and ground minerals; deer antlers and the bones of certain animals. Unusual elements include the internal organs of various animals and fish, scorpion tails, wasp or hornet nests, leeches, moles, praying mantis chrysalis, tortoise shell, bat guano, dried toad venom, male sea lion genitalia, urine of prepubescent boys, domestic fowl gastric tissue, the dried white precipitate found in urinary pots, powdered licorice that has been enclosed in a bamboo case and buried in a cesspool for one winter (the case being hung to dry thoroughly and licorice extracted), dried human placenta, and human hair.

Generally speaking, prescriptions are drunken as tea or soups; made into hot and cold compresses, poultices, powders, ointments, liniments, and oils for massaging directly into wounds or sore areas; refined into paste for plasters; or put in pills or gum to be taken orally. Herbs are usually prescribed together to enhance their effectiveness, with the exception of ginseng, which is usually taken by itself. Described as the "master/servant" principle, herbs of similar properties and effects are used together.

Following serious injury or sickness, it is essential to reestablish homeostasis within the glandular, circulatory, and nervous systems to ensure a healthy recovery. Sharing corresponding principles, herbal medicines, acupuncture, moxibustion, and massage have, and continue to be, effective practices in trauma management and the curing of disease.

Nowadays, with the growing concern over the side-effects of prescription drugs, an understanding of ecology, and people's desire to take greater responsibility for their own health, the use of medicinal herbs is experiencing a remarkable revival.

Effects of Herbal Medicine

The following terms meticulously describe the effects of herbal medicines:

analgesic: eliminates pain while allowing the maintenance of consciousness and other senses
anesthetic: eliminates pain and causes unconsciousness
anthelmintic: kills or removes worms and parasites from the intestines
antidote: counteracts poisons
antiphlogistic: reduces inflammation
antipyretic: reduces fever
antiseptic: kills microorganisms
antispasmodic: reduces or stops spasms
antitussive: suppresses coughing
aphrodisiac: increases sexual desire
astringent, styptic: reduces blood flow by contracting body tissues and blood vessels
carminative: assists in the release of flatulence
cathartic: assists the movement of the bowels
demulcent: soothes infected mucous membranes
diaphoretic: assists perspiration
digestive: assists digestion
diuretic: assists urination
emetic: causes vomiting
emmenagogue: assists menstruation
emollient: softens, soothes
expectorant: assists in expulsion of phlegm
hemostatic: stops blood flow

laxative: assists bowel movements gently
purgative: assists bowel movements strongly
refrigerant: cooling, relieves fever
sedative: reduces anxiety, excitement
stimulant: increases sensitivity and activity
stomachic: tonifies the stomach tonic: restores or repairs tone of tissues

---

Through meticulous research, unending cross-referencing, and the untiring assistance of the Fujian *gongfu* masters and herbalists associated with Mr. Li Yiduan, Mr. and Mrs. Okamoto of the Tokiwa Herb Emporium, botanist Suganuma Shin, my friend Mitchell Ninomiya, and my wife Yuriko, I am able to present the translation of the following articles.

For the sake of easy future reference, the botanical lerms of these plants and elements of nature have been transcribed. Over the years, in the various old reproductions of the Bubishi I have come across, rarely did I find precise weight measures or accurate preparations for the herbal prescriptions detailed. Furthermore, in at least one notable case, the prescription had been completely rewritten (no doubt by a modern herbalist). Nonetheless, I did learn that the precise weights and preparations for all the legible prescriptions in the Bubishi could be accurately determined by any Chinese herbalist, especially after diagnosing a sick patient's condition.

However, the following prescriptions are presented here as informative matter only, and are not intended to be construed by the reader as reliable or in some instances safe treatments for the corresponding maladies. (TR)

This calligraphy by Grandmaster Yagi Meitoku means "Inhaling represents softness while exhaling characterizes hardness." This quote was taken from Article 13 (p. 261) of the Bubishi and inspired Grandmaster Miyagi Chojun to name his style Goju-ryu.

Articles on Chinese Medicine and Herbal Pharmacology

Article 10: Prescriptions and Medicinal Poems

1. *Dipsacus asper* Wall. (Dipsacaceae): used as a tonic for bones and tendons
2. *Achyranthes bidentata* Blume. (Amaranthaceae): for sprains or fractures to the hip and leg
3. *Chaenomeles sinensis* Koch. (Rosaceae): used for convulsions, spasms, and as an antispasmodic
4. *Acanthopanax spinosum* Miq. (Anacardiaceae): prescribed as an analgesic for rheumatic pain, spasms, colic, gastralgia, and impotency
5. *Pistacia lentiscus* L. (Anacardiaceae): also known as mastic, employed as analgesic and sedative for gastralgia, cardiodynia, mastitis, peptic ulcers, boils, and carbuncles; also as an antitussive and expectorant
6. *Salvia miltiorhiza* Bunge. (Labiatae) and *Rehmannia glutinosa* Lib. (Scrophulariaceae): prescribed to improve circulation and for production of new blood
7. *Angelica sinensis* (Umbelliferae) and *Carthamus tinctorius* L. (Compositae): used to cure congestion, improve poor circulation, and clear extravasted blood
8. *Arethusa japonica* A. Gr. (Compositae) or (Labiatae): used to promote blood circulation and smooth monthly menstruation
9. *Scirpus yagara* (Cyperaceae) and *Curcuma zedoaria* Roc. (Zingiberaceae): helps remedy old injuries or chronic pain
10. *Akebia quinata* Decne. (Lardizabalaceae): prescribed as a diuretic and antiphlogistic; in particular for bladder infections and intestinal problems
11. Rice Brew: when mixed with wine, good for gastric disorders, diarrhea, and fever
12. *Typha latifolia* L. (Typhaceae) and *Semen sinapis* Albae. (Cruciferae), or *Schizonepeta tenuifolia* Briq. (Labiatae): astringent, styptic
13. *Caesalpinia sappan* L. (Leguminosae) and *Curcuma longa* L. (Zingiberaceae) or *Curcuma aromatica* Salisb. (Zingiberaceae): used to clear extravested blood; used externally for bruises and orchitis
14. *Drynaria fortunei* (Kze.) J. Sm. (Polypodiaceae): used for bone fractures
15. *Bletilla hyacinthina* R. Br. (Orchidaceae): used externally as emol-

lient for burns and skin disorders when the pseudobulbs are powdered and mixed with sesame oil; also an effective agent when used with other herbs for fractured bones

16. Copper, native: analgesic, decongestant for bruises, contusions, fractures, and dislocations
17. *Allium sinensis* G. Don. (Liliaceae): effective in eliminating intestinal blockage in both the small and large intestines
18. *Imperata cylindrica* Beauv. (Graminae) and *Nelumbo nucifera* Gaertn. (Nymphaceae): prescribed together with a pint of lotus roots for hemostasis
19. *Nelumbo nucifera* Gaertn. (Nymphaceae), and *Biota orientalis* Endl. (Cupressanceae): used to treat the vomiting of blood
20. *Corydalis bulbosa* DC. or *Corydalis ambigua* Cham. (Papaveraceae): improves blood circulation and dissipates bruises
21. *Gynura pinnatifida* Vanniot. (Compositae): prescribed as a hemostatic or used externally as a styptic drug
22. *Curcuma longa* L. (Zingiberaceae): when thinly sliced, effective in suppressing pain in arm injuries
23. The clear urine of boys under age 12 is an effective pain killer when used on incised wounds
24. *Achyranthes bidentata* Blume. (Amaranthaceae): used to stop profuse bleeding
25. *Imperata cylindrica* Beauv. (Gramineae) and *Senecio palmatus* Pall. Moore (Compositae): for hemostasis
26. *Leonurus heterophyllus* Sweet (Labiatae): an effective pain killer used for serious injuries
27. *Allium tubersum* Roxb. (Liliaceae): used for hemoptysis (coughing up blood)
28. *Ampelopsis japonica* (Vitaceae): used against tetanus after being wounded by a metal weapon
29. *Morus alba* L. (Moraceae): used for lung-related disorders—asthma, bronchitis, coughing, etc.
30. Malted rice and vinegar are used together to reduce swelling
31. *Daemonorops draco* Blume. (Palmae): used to clear internal extravasted blood, improve circulation, and promote the production of new blood
32. Minium (red lead oxide): combats poison, congestion, and improves the condition of blood; used externally as a disinfectant

Article 11: Twelve-Hour Theory Recuperative Herbal Prescriptions

MERIDIAN   *SHICHEN*
Gall Bladder   *Rat (11 p.m.-1 a.m.)*
1. *Bupleurum falcatum* L. (Umbelliferae) 3.75 grams
2. *Platycodon grandiflorum* DC. (Campanulaceae) 3.75 grams
3. *Ophiopogon japonicus* Wall. (Liliaceae) 3.75 grams
4. *Pinellia ternata* (Thunb.) Breit. (Araceae) 3.75 grams
5. *Rehmannia glutinosa* (Gaertn.) 7.5 grams
6. *Ziziphus sativa* Hu (Rhamnaceae) 3.75 grams
7. *Semen persicae* (L.) Batsch. (Rosaceae) 7.5 grams

Liver   *Ox (1-3 a.m.)*
1. *Dipsacus asper* Wall. (Ditsacaceae) 3.75 grams
2. *Achyranthes bidentata* Blume. (Amaranthaceae) 3.75 grams
3. *Ligusticum wallichii* Franch. (Umbelliferae) 3.75 grams fried
4. *Angelica sinensis* (Umbelliferace) 7.5 grams
5. *Rehmannia glutinosa* (Gaertn.) 7.5 grams
6. High quality *Allium tuberosum* Roxb. (Liliaceae) 3.75 grams
7. *Berberis lycium* (Solanaceae) 7.5 grams

Lungs   *Tiger (3-5 a.m.)*
1. *Schizonepeta tenuifolia* Briq. (Labiatae) 3.75 grams
2. Glue prepared from the hide of a black ass 3.75 grams
3. *Dioscorea japonica* Thunb. (Dioscoreaceae) 7.5 grams
4. Limonite 7.5 grams
5. *Morus alba* L. (Moraceae) 3.75 grams
6. *Xanthoxylum piperitum* DC (Rutaceae) 3.75 grams

Large Intestine   *Rabbit (5-7 a.m.)*
1. *Morus alba* L. (Moraceae) 7.5 grams
2. *Allium sinensis* G. Don. (Liliaceae) 3.75 grams
3. *Salvia miltiorhiza* (Labiatae) 7.5 grams
4. *Caesalpinia sappan* L. (Leguminosae) 3.75 grams
5. *Corydalis bulbosa* DC. or *Corydalis ambigua* Cham. (Papaveraceae) 3.75 grams
6. *Anemone cernua* Thumb. (Ranunculaceae) 3.75 grams
7. *Curcuma longa* L. (Zingiberaceae) 3.75 grams

Stomach   *Dragon (7-9 a.m.)*
1. *Aegle sepiaria* DC. 3.75 grams
2. *Saussurea lappa* Clarke (Composite) 3.75 grams

3. *Ophiopogon japonicus* Wall. (Liliaceae) 3.75 grams
4. *Pheretima asiatica* Michelsen (Lumbricidae) 7.5 grams grilled and powdered
5. Rice Brew 3.75 grams
6. *Angelica sinensis* (Oliv.) Diels (Umbelliferae) 3.75 grams
7. *Davillia mariessi* (Polypodiaceae) 7.5 grams

Spleen/Pancreas   Snake (9-11 a.m.)

1. *Amomum cardamomum* L. (Zingiberaceae) 6.24 grams
2. *Poria cocos* (Schw.) Wolf. (Polyporaceae) 6.24 grams
3. *Atractylodes lancea* (Thunb.) DC. (Compositae) 3.75 grams fried
4. *Dioscorea japonica* Thunb. (Dioscoreaceae) 3.75 grams
5. *Paeonia albiflora* Pall. (Ranunculaceae), or *Anemone raddiana* Regel (Ranunculaceae) 6.24 grams charred
6. *Ligusticum wallichii* Franch. (Umbelliferae) 6.24 grams

Heart   Horse (11 a.m.-1 p.m.)

1. *Clansena lansium* (Lour.) Skeels (Rutaceae) 6.24 grams
2. *Magnolia officinalis* Reh. et Wils. (Magnoliaceae), or *Angelica sinensis* (Oliv.) Diels (Umbelliferae) 3.75 grams
3. *Drynaria fortunei* (Kze.) J. Sm. (Polypodiaceae) 6.24 grams
4. *Semen persicae* (L.) Batsch. (Rosaceae) 6.24 grams

Small Intestine   Ram (1-3 p.m.)

1. *Allium macrostemon* Bge. (Liliaceae) 6.24 grams
2. *Akebia quinata* (Thunb.) Decne. (Lardizabalaceae), or *Arctium lappa* L. (Compositae) no weight listed
3. *Juncus decipiens* (Buch.) Nakai (Juncaceae) or *Imperata cylindrica* Var. Major (Nees) Hubb. (Gramineae) 6.24 grams
4. *Caesalpinia sappan* L. (Leguminosae) 6.24 grams
5. *Rehmannia glutinosa* Libosch. (Gaertn.) (Scrophulariaceae) 6.24 grams

Bladder   Monkey (3-5 p.m.)

1. *Akebia quinata* Decne. (Lardizabalaceae) 3.75 grams
2. *Alisma plantago* L. (Alismaceae) 6.24 grams
3. *Poria cocos* Wolf. (Polyporaceae) 3.12 grams
4. *Rehmannia glutinosa* Libosch. (Gaertn.) (Scrophulariaceae) 6.24 grams
5. *Spirodela polyrhiza* Schleid. (Lemnaceae) 3.75 grams
6. Rice Brew (no weight listed)
7. *Carthamus tinctorius* L. (Compositae) 3.75 grams

Kidneys   Cock (5-7 p.m.)

1. *Achyranthes bidentata* Blume. (Amaranthaceae) 3.75 grams
2. *Rehmannia glutinosa* Libosch. (Gaertn.) (Scrophulariaceae) 3.75 grams

3. *Baiji* 3.75 grams
4. *Fructus foeniculi* (Umbelliferae) 3.75 grams
5. *Vitex trifolia* L. (Verbenaceae) 3.75 grams
6. *Davillia mariesii* (Polypodiaceae) 3.75 grams
7. *Lonicera japonica* Thumb. (Loniceraceae) 3.75 grams

Pericardium   Dog (7-9 p.m.)
1. *Rheum oficinale* Baill. (Polygonaceae) 3.75 grams
2. *Ophiopogon japonicus* (Thunb.) Ker-Gaw. (Liliaceae) 6.24 grams
3. *Salvia Miltiorhiza* Bunge. (Labiatae) 3.75 grams
4. *Rehmannia glutinosa* Libosch. (Gaertn.) (Scrophulariaceae) 6.24 grams
5. *Typha latifolia* L. (Typhaceae) 3.75 grams

Three Heater   Boar (9-11 p.m.)
1. *Gardenia floridah.* (Rubiaceae) 3.75 grams
2. *Eucommia ulmoides* Oliv. (Euconmiaceae) 6.24 grams
3. *Lycium chinense* Mill. (Solanaceae) 6.24 grams
4. *Prunuspersica* (L.) Batsch. (Rosaceae) 3.75 grams
5. *Caesalpinia sappan* L. (Leguminosae) 3.75 grams
6. Native copper 6.24 grams

The Bubishi does not say exactly how to utilize these prescriptions (i.e., to drink them or use them externally).   (TR)

Article 12: A Physician's Treatment for Twelve-Hour Injuries

For Complications Arising from an Injury to the Kidneys or Carotid Artery
1. *Imperata cylindrica* Var. Major (Nees) Hubb. (Gramineae) 6.24 grams
2. *Rehmannia glutinosa* (Gaertn.) Libosch. (Scrophulariaceae) 6.24 grams
3. *Scrophularia ningpoensis* Hemsl. (Scrophulariaceae) 6.24 grams
4. *Platycodon grandiflorum* (Jacqu.) A. DC. (Campanulaceaea) 3.75 grams
5. *Colocana antiquem* Schott. 6.24 grams
6. *Angelica sinensis* (Oliv.) Diels (Umbelliferae) 3.75 grams
7. *Curcuma longa* L. (Zingiberaceae) 3.75 grams

Treating Muscle Injuries
1. *Chaenomeles sinensis* Koeh. (Rosaceae) 3.75 grams
2. *Acanthopanax gracilistylus* W. W. Smith. (Araliaceae) or *Dipsacus asper* Wall. (Dipiscaceae) 6.24 grams

3. *Achyranthes bidentata* Blume. (Amaranthaceae) 6.24 grams
4. *Paeonia lactiflora* Pall. (Ranunculaceae) 6.24 grams fried
5. *Rehmannia glutinosa* (Gaertn.) Libosch. (Scrophulariaceae) 6.24 grams

Treating Burns

1. *Scirpus yagara* Ohwi. (Cyperaceae) 4.68 grams
2. *Curcuma zedoaria* Roc. (Zingiberaceae) 4.68 grams
3. *Gynura pinnatifida* Vanniot (Compositea) 21.84 grams
4. *Prunus persica* (L.) Batsch. (Rutaceae) 6.24 grams
5. *Angelica sinensis* (Oliv.) Diels (Umbelliferae) 6.24 grams

Treating Back Injuries

1. *Curcuma longa* L. (Zingiberaceae) 3.75 grams
2. Native Copper 3.75 grams
3. *Arenthusa japonica* A. Gr. (Compositae) 3.75 grams
4. *Dipsacus asper* Wall. (Dipsacaceae) 3.75 grams
5. *Anemone cernua* Thumb. (Ranunculaceae) 3.75 grams
6. Urine of healthy boys under age 12

Head Injuries

1. *Schizonepeta tenuifolia* Briq. (Labiatae) 3.75 grams
2. *Siler divaricatum* Benth. et Hook. (Umbelliferae) 3.75 grams
3. *Anemone raddiana* Regel (Ranunculaceae) 6.24 grams
4. *Pueraria pseudo-hirsuta* Tang et Wang (Leguminosae) 3.75 grams
5. *Vitex rotundifolia* L. (Vervenaceae) 6.24 grams

Loss of Consciousness

1. *Poria cocos* (Schw.) Wolf. (Polyporaceae) 6.24 grams
2. *Polygala tenuifolia* Willd. (Polygalaceae) 3.75 grams
3. *Moschus moschiferus* L. (Cervidae) 0.15 grams
4. *Panax ginseng* C.A. Mey (Araliaceae) 6.24 grams

To Stop Bleeding

1. *Coptis chinensis* Franch. (Ranunculaceae) 3.75 grams powdered
2. *Elephas maximus* L. or *Elephas africanus* Blum. (Elephantidae) 3.75 grams
3. *Artemisia argyi* Levl. et Vant. (Compositae) 0.31 grams
4. *Calamina* (Smithsonitum) 3.75 grams powdered

Treating Head Injuries Resulting from Being Traumatized by Iron Objects

1. *Carthamus tinctorius* L. (Compositae) 6.24 grams
2. *Angelica sinensis* (Oliv.) Diels (Umbelliferae) 6.24 grams
3. *Rehmannia glutinosa* (Gaertn.) Libosch. (Scrophulariaceae) 6.24 grams

4. *Boswellia carterii* Birdwood (Burseraceae) 6.24 grams
5. *Commiphora myrrha* Engler. (C. molmol Engler.) (Burseraceae) 6.24 grams
6. *Prunus persica* (L.) Batsch. (Rosaceae) 6.24 grams

Extraction of Internal Injuries

1. White malted rice, 1 small scoop
2. *Eugenia caryophyllata* Thunb. (Myrtaceae), 7 small scoops
3. *Schizonepeta tenuifolia* Briq. (Labiatae) 6.24 grams
4. *Mentha arvensis* L. (Labiatae) 3.75 grams
5. *Carthamus tinctorius* L. (Compositae) 6.24 grams
6. *Angelica sinensis* (Oliv.) (Umbelliferae) 6.24 grams

Treating Back Pain

1. *Saussurea lappa* Clarke (Compositae) 3.75 grams
2. *Paeonia lactiflora* Pall. (Paeoniaceae) 3.75 grams roasted
3. *Boswellia carterii* Birdwood (Burseraceae) 6.24 grams
4. *Commiphora myrrha* Engler. (Burseraceae) 6.24 grams
5. Urine from a healthy boy under age 12, 1 cup

Pain Killer

1. *Dipsacus* asper Wall. (Dipiscaceae) 6.24 grams
2. *Paeonia lactiflora* Pall. (Paeoniaceae) 3.75 grams fried
3. *Paeonia lactiflora* Pall. (Paeoniaceae) soaked in rice wine and fried
4. *Allium tuberosum* Roxb. (Liliaceae) 3.75 grams of bulb only
5. *Lycium chinense* Mill. (Solanaceae) 6.24 grams
6. *Rehmannia glutinosa* (Gaertn.) Liboch. (Scrophulariaceae) 3.75 grams
7. *Angelica sinensis* (Oliv.) Diels (Umbelliferae) 6.24 grams
8. *Carthamus tinctorius* L. (Compositae) 3.75 grams
9. *Boswellia carterii* Birdwood (Burseraceae) 3.75 grams
Soak in one bottle of aged wine and cook slowly over a low flame to prepare prescription.

Remedy for Malaria

1. *Aconitum carmichaeli* Debx. (Ranunculaceae) 6.24 grams
2. *Cyperus rotundus* L. (Cyperaceae) 6.24 grams
3. *Dichroa febrifuga* Lour. (Saxifragaceae) 12.48 grams
4. *Areca catechu* L. (Palmae) 1.24 grams
5. *Morus alba* L. (Moraceae) 3.75 grams
6. *Anemarrhena asphodeloides* Bunge. (Liliaceae) 3.75 grams
7. *Ophiopogon japonicus* Ker-Gaw. (Liliaceae) 6.24 grams and a pinch
Ferment for one day in aged wine and then decoct over a low flame to prepare prescription, which can be used immediately.

Remedy for Lower Back and Hip Pain

1. *Panax Ginseng* C.A. May (Araliaceae) 6.24 grams
2. *Chaeomeles lagenaria* Koidz. (Rosaceae) 3.75 grams
3. *Achyranthes bidentata* Blume. (Amaranthaceae) 6.24 grams
4. *Melia toosendan* Sieb. et Zucc. (Meliaceae) 3.75 grams even weight
5. *Paeonia lactiflora* Pall. (Paeoniaceae) 3.75 grams
6. *Angelica sinensis* (Oliv.) Diels (Umbelliferae) 3.75 grams
7. *Rehmannia glutinosa* Libosch. F. Hueichingensis (Chao et Schih) Hsiao (Scrophulariaceae) 6.24 grams
8. *Lycium chinense* Mill. (Solanacheae) 3.75 grams even weight
9. *Ligusticum wallichii* Franch. (Umbelliferae) 3.75 grams

Ferment in one bottle of aged wine and cook over a low flame to prepare prescription.

Treating Open Wounds

Take an ant's nest that was built on a longan tree and roast it on a new tile. Ground the remains into a powder, mix with water, and steam it until it is thick. Apply directly to open wounds.

Article 18: Four Incurable Diseases

People not recovering from serious sword or spear wounds, even after medical treatment is rendered, usually die. Characteristics of the illness causing this are difficulties in breathing and the inability to keep the mouth shut.

If a wound becomes complicated by infection and the patient begins getting cold, with signs of stiffening, fever, and shaking violently, departure from this world is certain.

When the eyeballs are locked in place without moving, a person's spirit has withdrawn, which means he is no longer in charge of his mental faculties.

Any deep wound that causes an organ to dysfunction, impairing the circulatory system, usually results in death.

In addition to *quanfa,* a disciple must be patient and endeavor to acquire the medical knowledge to treat and cure the injured and sick. True *quanfa* disciples never seek to harm anyone, but are virtuous, kind, and responsible human beings.

This knowledge has been compiled and handed down from the Shaolin recluses from long ago. Never deviating, it remains constant.

Article 19: Effective "Twelve-Hour Herbal" Prescriptions to Improve Blood Circulation for *Shichen*-Related Injuries

Rat Time *(11 p.m.-1 a.m.) Medicine*

1. *Lycopus lucidus* Turcz. (Labiatae) 5-10 grams
2. *Aquilaria sinensis* (Lour.) Gilg. (Thymelaeaceae) 1-3 grams
3. *Boswellia carterii* Birdwood (Burseraceae) 3-9 grams

Decoct in one cup of old wine. Strain and drink a half cup.

Ox Time *(1-3 a.m.) Medicine*

1. *Moschus moschiferus* L. (Cervidae) 3.75 grams
2. *Aquilaria sinensis* (Lour.) Gilg. (Thymelaeaceae) 3.75 grams
3. *Lycopus lucidus* Turcz. (Labiatae) 6.24 grams
4. *Cinnamomum cassia* Bl. (Lauraceae) 9.36 grams
5. *Achyranthes bidentata* Blume. (Amaranthaceae) 6.24 grams

Decoct in one cup of rice wine. Strain and drink a half cup.

Tiger Time *(3-5 a.m.) Medicine*

1. *Moschus moschiferus* L. (Cervidae) 3.75 grams
2. *Aquilaria sinensis* (Lour.) Gilg.(Thymelaeaceae) 3.75 grams
3. *Lycopus lucidus* Turcz. (Labiatae) 6.24 grams
4. *Cinnamomum cassia* Bl. (Lauraceae) 6.24 grams
5. *Achyranthes bidentata* Blume. (Amaranthaceae) 6.24 grams

Decoct in one bowl of rice wine. Strain and drink one cup.

Rabbit Time *(5-7 a.m.) Medicine*

1. *Pictata martensii* (L.) (Pteriidae) 3.75 grams
2. *Moschus moschiferus* L.(Cervidae) 6.24 grams
3. Python *Molurus bivittatus* Schlegel (Boidae) 3.75 grams
4. *Wu du hu* 6.24 grams

Soak them in rice wine, strain and drink.

Dragon Time *(7-9 a.m.) Medicine*

1. Malted nonglutinous rice, 1 scoop
2. Malted rice, 1 scoop
3. Young *Prunus persica* (L.) Batsch. (Rosaceae) 15.60 grams
4. *Eriobotrya japonica* Lindl. (Rosaceae) 6.24 grams
5. *Carthamus tinctorius* L. (Compositae) 6.24 grams

Decoct in rice wine, strain, and drink.

Snake Time *(9-11 a.m.) Medicine*

1. *Carthamus tinctorius* L. (Compositae) for upper torso-related injuries 6.24 grams
2. *Achyranthes bidentata* Blume. (Amaranthaceae) for lower body injuries

Decoct in rice wine, strain, and drink.

Horse Time *(11a.m.-1 p.m.) Medicine*

1. Python *Molurus bivittatus* Schlegel (Boidae) 6.24 grams
2. *Shizophragma integrifolium* (Franch.) Olive. (Saxifragaceae) 6.24 grams
3. *Cyperus rotundus* L. (Cyperaceae) 21.84 grams
4. *Rubia cordifolia* L. (Rubiaceae) 6.24 grams

Decoct in three cups of rice wine, strain, and drink one cup.

Ram Time *(1-3 p.m.) Medicine*

1. *Eucommia ulmoides* Oliv. (Eucommiaceae) 3.75 grams
2. *Boswellia carterii* Birdwood (Burseraceae) 6.24 grams
3. *Eugenia caryophyllata* Thunb. (Myrtaceae) 6.24 grams
4. *Cinnamomum cassia* Blume. (Lauraceae) 6.24 grams

Decoct in rice wine, strain, and drink when your stomach is empty.

Monkey Time *(3-5 p.m.) Medicine*

1. *Triticum aestivum* L. (Gramineae) 6.24 grams
2. *Panax ginseng* C.A. Mey. (Araliaceae) 6.24 grams

Decoct in half a cup of water to prepare 2.48 grams *(8 fen)*. Drink when your stomach is empty.

Cock Time *(5-7 p.m.) Medicine*

Same as Monkey Time Medicine.

Dog Time *(7-9 p.m.) Medicine*

1. *Crocus sativus* L. (Iridaceae) 6.24 grams
2. *Murraya paniculata* L. (Rutaceae) 6.24 grams
3. *Rubia cordifolia* L. (Rubiaceae) 3.75 grams
4. *Wan du hu* 3.75 grams
5. *Artemisia argyi Levl* et Vant. (Compositae) 3.75 grams

Make it into a powder, decoct in rice wine, strain, and drink.

Boar Time *(9-11 p.m.) Medicine*

Same as Dog Time Medicine.

Article 22: Twelve-Hour Green Herbal Remedies

These herbs should be ground into a powder, mixed with rice wine, and drank every three hours to quickly remedy related injuries.

SHICHEN	CHINESE PRONUNCIATION (MANDARIN)	CHINESE IDEOGRAM
1. Rat (11 p.m.-1 a.m.)	*wan du hu*	萬 毒 虎
2. Ox (1-3 a.m.)	*ma di xiang*	馬 地 香
3. Tiger (3-5 a.m.)	*mu guang yin*	暮 光 陰
4. Rabbit (5-7 a.m.)	*qingyu lian*	青 魚 蓮
5. Dragon (7-9 a.m.)	*bai gen cao*	白 根 草
6. Snake (9-11 a.m.)	*wu bu su*	烏 不 宿
7. Horse (11 a.m.-1 p.m.)	*hui sheng cao*	回 生 草
8. Ram (1-3 p.m.)	*tu niu qi*	土 牛 七
9. Monkey (3-5 p.m.)	*bu hun cao*	不 魂 草
10. Cock (5-7 p.m.)	*da hu si*	打 不 死
11. Dog (7-9 p.m.)	*yi zhi xiang*	一 枝 香
12. Boar (9-11 p.m.)	*zui xian cao*	醉 仙 草

1. *wan du hu*   2. *ma di xiang*   3. *mu guang yin*   4. *qing yu lian*

5. *bai gen cao*   6. *wu bu su*   7. *hui sheng cao*   8. *tu niu qi*

9. *bu hun cao*   10. *da bu si*   11. *yi zhi xiang*   12. *zui xian cao*

The herbs above are so obscure that we were not able to identify all the English names for them. As such I will list only their Chinese names. (TR)

Article 23: Crystal Statue Diagram

SHICHEN	LOCATION
Rat (11 p.m.-1 a.m.)	Top of the Skull
Ox (1-3 a.m.)	Temples
Tiger (3-5 a.m.)	Ears
Rabbit (5-7 a.m.)	Throat and Carotid
Dragon (7-9 a.m.)	Chest
Snake (9-11 a.m.)	Ribcage
Horse (11 a.m.-1 p.m.)	Arms and Solar Plexus
Ram (1-3 p.m.)	Stomach
Monkey (3-5 p.m.)	Pelvis and Knees
Cock (5-7 p.m.)	Ankles
Dog (7-9 p.m.)	Upper Back
Boar (9-11 p.m.)	Lower Back

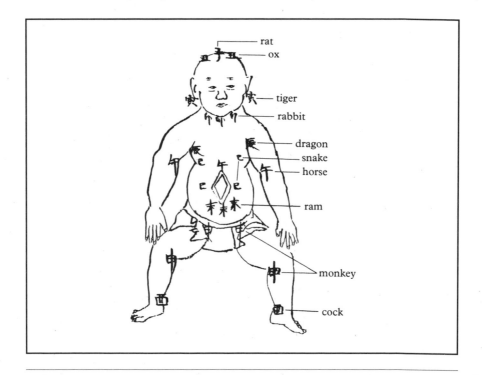

Article 23 refers only to group one and group two herbs; fresh and green plants (sometimes referred to as the master and servant principle). Group one and two herbs are part of four classes of Chinese medicinal herbs used: group one are master herbs, group two are subordinate herbs, group three are enhancing herbs, and group four are function herbs.

Complications arising from injuries to the preceeding locations must be treated with the medicinal herbs listed in Article 22 (see p. 187).

Article 25: Shaolin Herbal Medicine and Injuries Diagram

LOCATION	SHICHEN
The top of the skull	Rat (11 p.m.-1 a.m.)
The temples	Ox (1-3 a.m.)
The ears	Tiger (3-5 a.m.)
The throat and carotid artery	Rabbit (5-7 a.m.)
The chest area	Dragon (7-9 a.m.)
The rib cage	Snake (9-11 a.m.)
Both arms and the solar plexus	Horse (11 a.m.-1 p.m.)
The stomach	Ram (1-3 p.m.)
The pelvis and knees	Monkey (3-5 p.m.)
The ankles	Cock (5-7 p.m.)
The upper back	Dog (7-9 p.m.)
The lower back	Boar (9-11 p.m.)

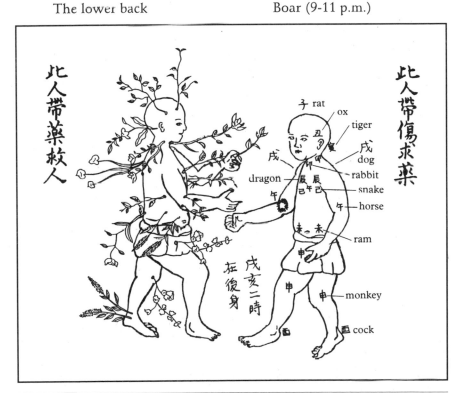

The left figure illustrates a Chinese medicine hawker with the kind of herbs available for injuries or illnesses that correspond to the 12 *shichens,* illustrated by the right figure. The times and locations of this illustration are the same as in the Crystal Statue and Bronze Man diagrams (see Article 23, p. 188 and Article 24, p. 246). The medicine hawker is giving the injured man the herb *wu bu su (Zanthoxylum avicennae* Lam. DC. (Rutaceae)) to treat his injured arm. This herb is used to reduce swelling caused by a traumatic injury.

Article 30: Valuable Ointment for Treating Weapon Wounds and Chronic Head Pain

Herbs must be chopped into small rough pieces and soaked in five kilograms of sesame seed oil. Note that the herbs should be soaked for three days during spring weather, six days during summer weather, seven days during autumn weather, and ten days during winter weather. Decoct in rice wine until herbs turn black. Strain through a linen fabric to clean off unnecessary residue. Do not decoct or treat herbs again until you add two kilograms of minium. Stir continuously with the branch of a willow tree while decocting over a strong flame until solution evaporates. Continue stirring over a low flame until the solution turns to a thick paste. To get the maximum potency from medicinal herbs it is important to understand the different times required to properly decoct plants, flowers, leaves, stalks, roots, minerals, etc. The effectiveness of each ingredient depends entirely upon the length of time you have decocted it. For example, an ingredient that is decocted for too long may have a reverse effect upon its user.

Ingredients
1. *Ligusticum wallichii* Franch. (Umbelliferae) 1.55 grams
2. *Angelica dahurica* Benth. et Hook. (Umbelliferae) 1.55 grams
3. *Asarum heterotropoides* Fr. Schmidt. Var. Mandshuricum (Maxim.) Kitag. (Aristolochiaceae) 1.55 grams
4. *Angelica sinensis* (Olive.) Diels (Umbelliferae) 1.55 grams
5. *Atractylodes macrocephala* Koidz. (A. Ovata A.P. DC.) (Compositae) 1.55 grams
6. *Atractylodes lancea* (Thunb.) DC. (Compositae) 1.55 grams
7. *Citrus reticulata* Blanco (Rutaceae) 1.55 grams
8. *Cyperus rotundus* L. (Cyperaceae) 1.55 grams
9. *Citrus aurantium* L. or *Citrus wilsonii* Tanaka (Rutaceae) 1.55 grams
10. *Lindera strychnifolia* Vill. (Lauraceae) 1.55 grams
11. *Pinellia temata* (Thunb.) Breit. (Araceae) 1.55 grams
12. *Citrus reticulata* Blanco (Rutaceae) 1.55 grams
13. *Anemarrhena asphodeloides* Bunge. (Liliaceae) 1.55 grams
14. *Fritillaria verticillata* Willd. (Liliaceae) 1.55 grams
15. *Coptis chinensis* Franch. (Ranunculaceae) 1.55 grams
16. *Prunus persica* (L.) Batsch. (Rosaceae) 1.55 grams
17. *Moms alba* L. (Moraceae) 1.55 grams
18. *Scutellaria baicalensis* Georgi. (Labiatae) 1.55 grams
19. *Phellodendron amurense Rupr.* (Rutaceae) 1.55 grams
20. *Vitex rotundifolia* LF. (Vervenaceae) 1.55 grams
21. *Rheum tanguticum* Maxim. ex Regel. (Polygonaceae) 1.55 grams

22. *Corydalis bulbosa* DC. or *Corydalis Ambigua* Cham. et Schlecht. (Papaveraceae) 1.55 grams
23. *Mentha arvensis* L. (Labiatae) 1.55 grams
24. *Paeonia lactiflora* Pall. (Paeoniaceae) 1.55 grams
25. *Akebia quinata* (Thunb.) Decne. (Lardizabalaceae) or *Aristolochia manshuriensis* Kom. (Aristolochiaceae) 1.55 grams
26. *Manis pentadactyla* L. (Munidae) 1.55 grams
27. *Croton tiglium* (Euphorbiaceae) 1.55 grams
28. *A. kusnezoffii* Reich. 1.55 grams
29. *Hydnocarpus anthelmintica* Pierre. (Flacourtiaceae) 1.55 grams
30. *Rhus chinensis* Mill. (Anacardiaceae) 1.55 grams
31. *Anemone raddiana* Regel (Ranunculaceae) 1.55 grams
32. *Leonurus heterophyllus* Sweet (Labiatae) 1.55 grams
33. *Aconitum carmichaeli Debx.* 1.55 grams
34. *Acanthopanax gracilistylus* W. W. Smith. (Araliaceae) 1.55 grams
35. *Dictamnus dasycarpus* Turcz. (Rutaceae) 1.55 grams
36. *Cannabis sativa* L. (Moraccae) 1.55 grams
37. *Arisaema consanguineum* Schott (Araceae) 1.55 grams
38. *Clematis chinensis* Osbeck (Ranuculaceae) 1.55 grams
39. *Bombyx mori* L. with Batrytis Bassiana Bals. 1.55 grams
40. *Sophora flavescens* Ait. (Leguminosae) 1.55 grams
41. *Ledebouriella seseloides* (Hoffm.) (Umbelliferae) 1.55 grams
42. *Schizonepeta tenuifolia* Briq. (Labiatae) 1.55 grams
43. *Lonicera japonica* Thunb. (Loniceraceae) 1.55 grams
44. *Polygonum multiflorum* Thunb. (Polygonaceae) 1.55 grams
45. *Notopterygium incisium* Ting (Umbelliferae) 1.55 grams
46. *Glycyrrhiza uralensis* Fisch. (Leguminosae) 1.55 grams
47. *Artemisia capillaris* Thunb. (Compositae) 1.55 grams
48. *Eucommia ulmoides* Oliv. (Eucommiaceae) 1.55 grams
49. *Dioscorea batatas* Decne. (Deoscoreaceae) 1.55 grams
50. *Polygala tenuifolia* Willd. (Polygalaceae) 1.55 grams
51. *Dipsacus asper* Wall. (Dipsacaceae) 1.55 grams

Article 31: Ointments, Medicines, and Pills
Eight Immortals Crossing the Sea Internal Healing Pills

Use about 3.75 grams of each ingredient and grind into a fine powder. Take 3.75 grams and mix with rice wine for one dose to treat internal bleeding, or the medicine can be wrapped in rice paper to make individual pills to be taken later. If pills are made, honey should also be used.

1. *Pinellia ternata* (Thunb.) Breit. (Araceae)
2. *Croton tiglium* (Euphorbiaceae)

3. *Angelica sinensis* (Oliv.) Diels (Umbelliferae) for frost
4. *Boswellia carterii* Birdwood (Burseraceae)
5. *Commiphora myrrha* Engler. (Burseraceae)
6. Borax
7. *Daemonorops draco* Blume. (Palmae)
8. *Eupolyphaga sinensis* Walk. (Blattidae)

An alternative is to use the following "Herbal Brew" recipe that helps the heart and promotes blood flow. Decoct in a bowl-and-a-half of water until eight-tenths of a bowl remain.

1. *Prunus armeniaca* L. var. ansu Maxim. (Rosaceae) 3.75 grams
2. *Prunus persica* (L.) Batsch. (Rosaceae) 3.75 grams
3. *Citrus reticulata* Blanco (Rutaceae) 3.75 grams
4. *Akebia quinata* (Thunb.) Decne. (Lardizabalaceae) or *Aristolochia manshuriensis*
5. Kom. (Aristolochiaceae) 25 grams
6. *Commiphora myrrha* Engler. (Burseraceae) 25 grams
7. *Drynaria fortunei* (Kze.) J. Sm. (Polypodiaceae) 9.36 grams
8. *Saussurea lappa* Clarke (Compositae) 9.36 grams
9. Amber 9.36 grams

Rooster Crowing Powder Medicine (Ji Ming San)

Grind ingredients into a powder, decoct in rice wine, and drink it when the rooster crows at dawn.

1. *Rheum tantguticum* Maxim. et Rgl. (Polygonaceae) 18.75 grams soaked rice wine
2. *Angelica sinensis* (Oliv.) Diels (Umbelliferae) 2.5 grams
3. *Prunus persica* (L.) Batsch. (Rosaceae) 2.5 grams

Pain Killer for Treating Weapon Wounds

Grind ingredients into a fine powder, soak in rice wine, and prepare 11.25 gram dosages for each treatment, which is to be taken with rice wine.

1. *Boswellia carterii* Birdwood (Burseraceae) 3.75 grams
2. *Commiphora myrrha* Engler. (Burseraceae) 3.75 grams
3. *Paeonia lactiflora* Pall. (Paeoniaceae) 3.75 grams
4. *Angelica dahurica* Benth. et Hook. (Umbelliferae) 3.75 grams
5. *Ligusticum wallichii* Franch. (Umbelliferae) 3.75 grams
6. *Rehmannia glutinosa* (Gaertn.) Libosch. (Scrophulariaceae) 3.75 grams
7. *Angelica sinensis* (Oliv.) Diels (Umbelliferae) 3.75 grams
8. *Paeonia suffruticosa* Andr. (Paeoniaceae) 3.75 grams
9. *Glycyrrhiza uralensis* Fisch. (Leguminosae) 3.75 grams

Alternative Treatment for Weapon Wounds

Grind ingredients into a fine powder, mix in warm rice wine, and prepare 11.35 gram dosages for each treatment. Drink for 3-4 days until you are fully recovered.

1. *Caesalpinia sappan* L. (Leguminosae) 11.25 grams
2. *Carthamus tinctorius* L. (Compositae) 11.25 grams
3. *Angelica sinensis* (Oliv.) Diels (Umbelliferae) 11.25 grams
4. *Rheum tanguticum* Maxim et Rgl. (Polygonaceae) 11.25 grams

Vein and Blood Vessel Tonic

Used to restore damaged or weak muscle tissue; stimulate vitality; promote kidney and liver function. Also used to contract blood vessels and check the flow of blood.

After soaking in rice wine, roast ingredients dry before grinding into a powder to make 2.5 gram dosages. Take it when your stomach is empty for optimal results.

1. *Polygonum multiflorum* Thunb. (Polygonaceae) 3.75 grams
2. *Achyranthes bidentata* Blume. (Amaranthaceae) 11.25 grams
3. *Angelica sinensis* (Oliv.) Diels (Umbelliferae) 7.5 grams
4. *Vitex rotundifolia* L.F. (Vervenaceae) 3.75 grams
5. *Lycopus lucidus* Turcz. (Labiatae) 3.75

Effective Herbal Plaster Ointment for Treating Bone Fractures

Crush class one ingredients into a paste (ointment) and apply directly to damaged area.

1. *Boswellia carterii* Birdwood (Burseraceae) 9.36 grams
2. *Saussurea lappa* Clarke (Compositae) 9.36 grams
3. *Commiphora myrrha* Engler. (C. molmol Engler.) (Burseraceae) 9.36 grams
4. *Panax pseudo-ginseng* Wall. (Araliaceae) 15.6 grams
5. Paulownia, 20 seeds
6. *Bletilla striata* (Thunb.) Reichb. F. (Orchidaceae) 9.36 grams
7. Pyritum 9.36 grams

Herbal Ointment for Treating Bone Bruises

Grind ingredients together, roast until color changes to black, add rice wine, and cook into a paste before applying to bruised area.

1. *Aconitum carmichaeli* Debx. 3.75 grams
2. *A. kusnezoffii* Reich. 6.24 grams
3. *Angelica dahurica* Benth. et Hook. (Umbelliferae) 3.75 grams
4. *Paeonia lactiflora* Pall. (Paeoniaceae) 6.24 grams
5. *Acanthopanax gracilistylus* W. W. Smith. (Araliaceae) 25 grams
6. *Rheum tanguticum* Maxim. et Rgl. (Polygonaceae) 15.6 grams
7. *Lycium chinense* Mill. (Solanaceae) 12.48 grams
8. Pyritum 3.75 grams
9. *Drynaria fortunei* J. Smith. (Polypodiaceae) 3.75 grams

10. *Boswellia carterii* Birdwood (Burseraceae) 6.24 grams
11. *Commiphora myrrha* (C. molmol Engler.) (Burseraceae) 3.75 grams
12. *Bletilla striata* (Thunb.) Reichb. F. (Orchidaceae) 3.75 grams
13. Bracken root starch, 1 pipe full.

Original Herbal Cure for Chronic Suffering
Grind these ingredients into a powder and begin to decoct in one cup of rice wine then add *Curcuma zeadoaria* Rose. (Zingiberaceae) 6.24 grams, and mix in some fresh *Panax pseudo-ginseng* Wall. (Araliaceae).
1. *Angelica sinensis* (Oliv.) Diels (Umbelliferae) 6.24 grams
2. *Rehmanniaglutinosa* (Gaertn.) Libosch. (Scrophulariaceae) 6.24 grams
3. *Carthamus tinctorius* L. (Compositae) 6.24 grams
4. *Paeonia sujfruticosa* Andr. (Paeoniaceae) 6.24 grams
5. *Mylabris phalerata* Pall. (Lyttinadae) 6.24 grams
6. Hanging *Uncaria rhynchophylla* (Miq.) Jacks. (Rubiaceae) 6.24 grams
7. *Lycopus lucidus* Turcz. (Labiatae) 6.24 grams
8. *Panax pseudo-ginseng* Wall. (Araliaceae) 15.6 grams

Five Fragrance Herbal Powder (Wu Xiang San)
Used to treat infections resulting from open (stab) wounds.
   Mix ingredients together, roast until hard, grind into a powder, and mix with native wine before application.
1. *Aquilaria agallocha* Roxb. (Thymelaeaceae) 15.6 grams
2. *Boswellia carterii* Birdwood (Burseraceae) 15.6 grams
3. *Saussurea lappa* Clarke (Compositae) 15.6 grams
4. *Commiphora myrrha* Engler. (C. molmol Engler.) (Burseraceae) 15.6 grams
5. *Panax pseudo-ginseng* Wall. (Araliaceae) 15.6 grams

Promoting the Secretion and Flow of Urine Hampered by Trauma to Testicles
Make an ointment by crushing all ingredients together into a pulp before applying to injured area.
1. *Moschus moschiferus* L. (Cervidae) 6.24 grams
2. Pond snails, 5
3. Dried lamb stool, 5 flakes
4. *Allium fistulosum* L. (Liliaceae), 5 stalks
5. *Artemisia capillaris* Thunb. 3.75 grams

An Alternative Treatment for Promoting Urine Flow
Grind all ingredients together, collect the juice, mix with the urine of a healthy boy under 12 years old, and drink.
1. Bulrush Grass, 1 ounce bundle

2. Bamboo Leaves, 1 small bundle
3. Ginger, 1 lump

The Master and Servant Treatment (Jun Chen Fang)

This refers to the principal herbs being supplemented by secondary herbs to either enhance or decrease the potency of a given prescription. It can also be used for promoting the flow of urine.

Decoct in a bowl-and-a-half of water, until eight-tenths of a bowl remain and apply the sediment directly to the bruised area.

1. *Akebia quinata* (Thunb.) Decne. (Lardizabalaceae) or *Aristolochia manshuriensis* Kom. (Aristolochiaceae) 3.75 grams
2. *Plantago asiatica* L. (Plantaginaceae) 3.75 grams
3. *Rehmannia glutinosa* (Gaertn.) Libosch. (Scrophulariaceae) 3.75 grams
4. *Scutellaria baicalensis* Georgi. (Labiatae) 24.96 grams
5. *Caesalpinia sappan* L. (Leguminosae) 3.75 grams
6. *Carthamus tinctorius* L. (Compositae) 15.6 grams
7. *Citrus aurantium* L. or *Citrus wilsonii* Tanaka (Rutaceae) 3.75 grams
8. *Angelica sinensis* (Oliv.) Diels (Umbelliferae) 3.75 grams
9. *Allium sativum* L. (Liliaceae) 3.75 grams
10. *Glycyrrhiza uralensis* Fisch. (Leguminosae) 9.36 grams

A Cure for Internal Bleeding and Trauma-Related Injuries

Before taking this prescription one should first eat some fresh *wu ye mei*.

Decoct in water until eight-tenths of a bowl remain. If bleeding does not subside, prepare herbs in ground grain and eat.

Honey should be used with nearly all internal medicines, and all ball-or-pill-form dosages. If honey is not used, there is a strong possibility that the effectiveness of the medicine will be reduced by 50%, if not 100%.

1. *Rehmannia glutinosa* (Gaertn.) Libosch. (Scrophulariaceae) 24.96 grams
2. *Carthamus tinctorius* L. (Compositae) 3.75 grams
3. *Prunus persica* (L.) Batsch. (Rosaceae) 3.75 grams
4. *Caesalpinia sappan* L. (Leguminosae) 3.75 grams

A Cure for Internal Bleeding and Left-Sided Pleurisy

Decoct in a bowl-and-a-half of water until eight-tenths of a bowl remain.

1. *Rehmannia glutinosa* (Gaertn.) Libosch. (Scrophulariaceae) 3.75 grams
2. *Lycopus lucidus* Turcz. (Labiatae) 3.75 grams
3. *Carthamus tinctorius* L. (Compositae) 24.96 grams
4. *Mylabris phalerata* Pall. (Lyttinadae) 3.75 grams
5. *Angelica sinensis* (Oliv.) Diels (Umbelliferae) 3.75 grams
6. *Vitex rotundifolia* L.F. (Vervenaceae) 3.75 grams fried
7. *Citrus aurantium* L. or *Citrus wilsonii* Tanaka (Rutaceae) 3.75 grams

8. *Areca catechu* L. (Palmae) 3.75 grams
9. *Corydalis bulbosa* DC. or *Corydalis ambigua* Cham. et Schlecht (Papaveraceae) 3.75 grams
10. *Citrus reticulata* Blanco (Rutaceae) 3.75 grams
11. *Phellodendron amurense* Rupr. or *Phellodendron chinense* Schneid. (Rutaceae) 3.75 grams
12. *Glycyrrhiza uralensis* Fisch. (Leguminosae) 3.75 grams

A Cure for Restoring Qi and Right-Sided Pleurisy

Decoct in a cup-and-a-half of water and prepare 2.5 gram dosages
1. *Rheum tanguticum* Maxim et Rgl. (Polygonaceae) 6.24 grams with rice wine
2. *Citrus reticulata* Blanco (Rutaceae) 3.75 grams
3. *Scirpus yagara* Ohwi. (Cyperaceae) 3.75 grams
4. *Curcuma zedoaria* Rose. (Zingiberaceae) 3.75 grams
5. *Boswellia carterii* Birdwood (Burseraceae) 3.75 grams
6. *Commiphora myrrha* Engler. (Burseraceae) 3.75 grams
7. *Perilla frutescens* Var. Crispa Dcne. (Labiatae) 3.75 grams
8. *Ophiopogon japonicus* (Thunb.) Ker-Gaw. (Liliaceae) 3.75 grams
9. *Crataegus pinnatifida* Bunge. (Rosaceae) 3.75 grams
10. *Scutellaria baicalensis* Georgi (Labiatae) 3.75 grams
11. *Citrus aurantium* L. or *Citrus wilsonii* Tanaka (Rutaceae) 3.75 grams
12. *Saussurea lappa* Clarke (Compositae) 3.75 grams powdered
13. *Aquilaria agallocha* Roxb. (Thymelaeaceae) 3.75 grams powdered
14. *Glycyrrhiza uralensis* Fisch. (Leguminosae) 3.75 grams

The Light Body Way (Qing Yu Gao) Vitality Elixir

This medicine will make your body strong and lively. It especially promotes blood circulation and invigorates the internal organs; it will even make gray hair black again. Taking this medicine will make people feel so young, light, and vigorous that they will feel as if they can fly. Contained in a valuable book, this prescription has been handed down for generations and describes how we must care for ourselves, so that our fortune is not squandered nor precious lives wasted. These are the precepts handed down from the Daoist ascetics. It is the Way.

Steam the ingredients nine times then sun them nine times. Eat 9-12 grams every morning. This will promote good blood circulation and provide abundant energy.
1. *Rehmannia glutinosa* (Gaertn.) Libosch. (Scrophulariaceae) 28 grams (big size)
2. Steamed fatty meat 28 grams

Five Herb Medicine Powder (Wu Gin San)

Used to prevent infectious diseases. Also called *Xiao Yu Wan*.

Mix together all ingredients and decoct in water. Blend with powdered rice and cook into a paste to make pills.

1. *Atractylodes macrocephala* Koidz. (A. Ovata A.P.DC.) (Compositae) 9 grams
2. *Poria cocoes* Wolf. (Polyporaceae) 18 grams
3. *Grifola umbellata* (Pers.) Pilat (Polyporaceae) 9 grams
4. *Alisma plantago-aquatica* L. Var. Orientale Sam. (Alismataceae) 6 grams
5. *Cinnamomum cassia* Blume. (Lauraceae) 6 grams

Yellow Texture Medicine (Huang Li Tang or Zai Zao Wan)

Used to treat blood loss and anemia.

Crush fresh ingredients together, mix with glutinous rice, and simmer over low flame. Make pills from the paste.

1. *Atractylodes macrocephala* Koidz. (A. ovata A.P.DC.) (Compositae) 15.6 grams
2. *Poria cocos* (Schw.) Wolf. (Polyporaceae) 15.6 grams
3. *Zingiber officinale* Rose. (Zingiberaceae) 15.6 grams, fried & roasted
4. *Coptis chinensis* Franch. (Ranunculaceae) 15.6 grams
5. Broiled *Glycyrrhiza uralensis* Fisch. (Leguminosae) 6.24 grams
6. *Evodia rutaecarpa* Benth. (Rutaceae) 6.24 grams

Medicine Worth Ten Thousand Gold Pieces (Wan Jin Dan)

1. The extract from 1.125 kg of *Acacia catechu* Wild. (Leguminosae)
2. *Santalum album* L. (Santalaceae) 3.75 grams
3. *Eugenia caryophyllata* Thunb. (Myrtaceae) 3.75 grams
4. *Cinnamomum cassia* Bl. (Lauraceae) 3.75 grams
5. *Moschus moschiferus* L. (Cervidae) about 25 grams
6. *Dryobalanops aromatica* Gaertn. F. (Dypterocarpaceae) or *Blumea balsamifera* DC. (Compositae) about 25 grams
7. *Aquilaria agallocha* Roxb. (Thymelaeaceae) 3.75 grams
8. *Glycyrrhiza uralensis* Fisch. (Leguminosae) 3.75 grams

The remedy for Rooster Crowing Powder Medicine appears in Motobu Choki's 1926 book *Okinawan Kempo Karate-jutsu Kumite* on p. 73 of Seiyu Oyata's English translation, or p. 57 of the original Japanese version. The two remedies that follow (i.e, Pain Killer for Treating Weapon Wounds and Alternative Treatment for Weapon Wounds) also appear in that book on the same page. No recipe is given for Medicine Worth Ten Thousand Gold Pieces except "hot water half cup." (TR)

子時用藥 澤首一分沈香不乳香不　老酒一杯煎午杯服下

丑時 射香一不茯苓不住花不午七不　酒一杯真午杯服下

寅時 射香不沈香一分澤首二分肉桂二不午七二分　酒一碗一杯服

卯時 真珠一分射香二分万毒虎之分浸酒服

辰時 紅曲一分白釉一分青桃仁五小地批根二紅花二酒煎服下

巳時 上支用紅花二分下步用牛七二分　沖酒服下

午時 蛇胆二分度香頭二香州子七个紅工糸二酒三砥煎一砥服

未時 社仲一乳香二丁香二肉桂二沖酒空心服

申時 介麦二右朱心三分水砥半煎八分空心服

戌亥時 紅二満山紅不紅土糸一万生母発二橘未沖酒服下

Early hand-written portion of Article 19.

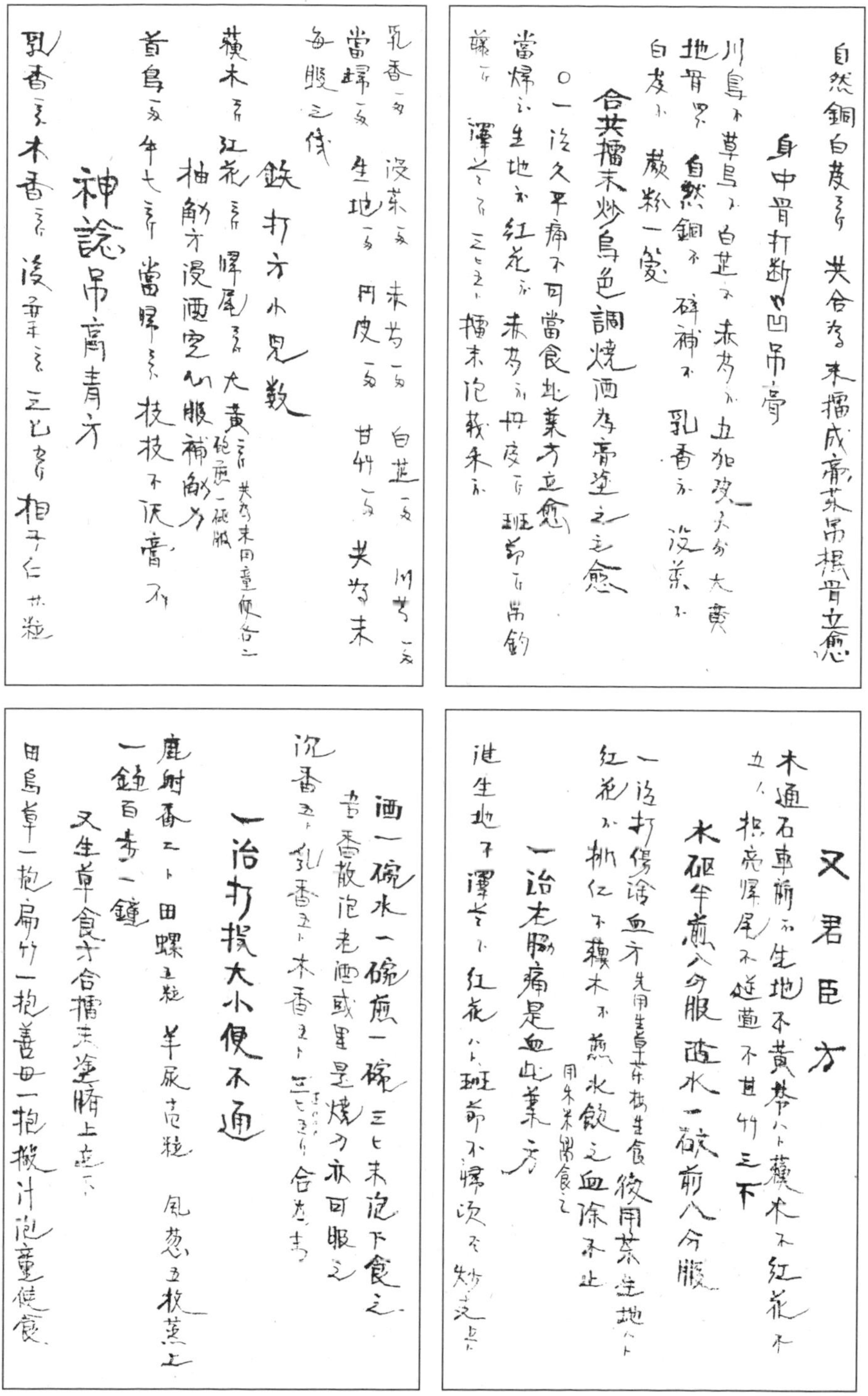

Early hand-written portions of Article 31

PART THREE

THE VITAL POINTS

"The Bubishi is an Enigma"

by Evan Pantazi
Kyusho International
www.kyusho.com

After first reading Hanshi McCarthy's epic rendition of the Bubishi, it became an enigma or a puzzle... one that continually unfolds into deeper understanding once the keys are known.

To the first-time reader or novice, Hanshi McCarthy's historical input is invaluable, as so much confusion and misconception is in the arts today. Many traditions observed or initiated are based on false or misunderstood dogma. But the true base is revealed in this "Bible of Karate" that Hanshi McCarthy painstakingly assembled and documented as a must for any martial artist.

For those that have been in the arts for a longer time, or have read the book already, the ancient treaties within this manual may seem confusing in its cryptic terminology or contents, but I urge you to read, re-read and visit it often. These are what the martial arts are all based upon, taking advantages of the weaknesses of the opposition in anatomical, tactical and strategical advantage.

Admittedly I did not grasp its full worth at first reading, yet it kept calling me to dig deeper, as there had to be worth in such a time honored text. But by continually returning to the treaties within, so many answers were found regarding these hidden realities (secrets as many would claim), that unleashed unlimited possibilities for the study, practice and use of Kyusho especially and the martial arts as a whole. I still do not claim to fully understand this manual; I only know what it has unlocked for me and tens of thousands around the world regarding the inner anatomical weaknesses of the human body and how to best take advantage of these against the opponent.

Instead of only reading through or even studying this manual and its concepts, we took it to the mat and laboratories to prove its validity: we researched deeply using many scientists and medical professionals around the world, to better understand the science, affects, possibilities and their ramifications on the human body. What has occurred over the decades of this extensive research, development and actualization on living beings, is that each new discovery could also already be found in the Bubishi. And so this amazing compilation continuously reveals more information, which again reveals even more… and all document-ed cryptically centuries ago. A source or perpetual knowledge, as the reader grows so does this text.

The key that unraveled this ancient compilation is held in the Six Ji Hands, which I urge the reader to fully investigate. From this single key—not revealed in the scrolls of Fujita, the 23 included Ryu, other ancient Chinese documents like the White Crane Cutting Veins, or even the supposed notes of Hohan Soken—has come many profound discoveries. They give the practitioner the maximum control and skill in focused power, leverage, torque, penetration (into the vital targets) and energetic transfer through physics, not myth or folklore. Not only has the physical aspects and the results been studied, they have been validated by medical specialists and scientists, from experiential use, research and rigorous testing. But, more importantly, they are fully ap-plicable in real training and have also been validated from hundreds of real encounters in countries around the world.

The Ji Hands in turn unlocked the attributes of Dim Mak, Kyusho, Iron Shirt, "metaphysical" as well as physical methods, and a differ-ent method of "Body Change" (not to be confused with the Yi Jin Jing Muscle & Tendon Changing)… or Sanchin (although these principles are within certain styles of this ancient kata). They are expanded upon in the two hand-to-hand combative methods prominently discussed and depicted—Tiger method of Body Change and the Crane method of Body Change. These two methods (purposefully not referred to as styles), have within them the "Body Change" dynamics that yield certain physical skills and mental acuity as they develop a specialized spirit or tactical approach. This occurs with actual changes in the neuro functionality of the body as well as the mental processes and cross neu-ral programming—these are deeper physiological changes, not the more rudimentary physical processes.

We have all seen the elite athletes in any sport possessing something remarkable that even their high level counterparts do not have. They tapped into a higher degree of physical attribute that makes their phys-ical performance enhanced and ultimately superior to conventional physiology and functionality. These attributes, processed and produced in the several cortexes of the brain, are natural for these elite—how-ever, within the Body Change methods of the Bubishi lay the method to understand and develop by anyone. This information can, and will, give the committed practitioner the specialist physical attributes to not only affect themselves, but also the opposition.

Whereas many readers may be attracted to this manual by the tar-gets of *dim mak* (attacks on the blood systems as well as the organs) included in this ancient compilation, they remain confusing and enigmatic unto themselves. These essential vital targets have and would have been highly prized and trained in any military unit for the best areas in which to kill, or assure that result, in a given time period (please note time is an important element in this manual). This was actualized when the body would either bleed out or become fatally septic from piercing, slicing, exploding or impeding blood vessels and or organs at their most vulnerable areas. The primary concern in any attack was to prevent the fallen from living or recuperating and once again confronting the victors at a later time. It may also be in part why herbs are included, to remedy these battlefield wounds and their many other health damaging developments (as well as all illness that befalls armies in strange lands, from dysentery to tetanus and beyond).

Reading the Bubishi from a historical perspective gives the reader not only the correct foundational understanding and abilities, it also yields the vital capabilities for modern times. As the Bubishi was intentionally a record of the more destructive applicational methods against the blood and organ system of the opponent along with the tactical deployment in weapon and hand-to-hand combative use, these are no longer an acceptable possibility due to the ethics, modern laws, societal advancement and other such factors. With the insights provided in the Bubishi, the nerve system and neurological functionality of the human body (Kyusho) can easily be deployed for safer and more instantaneous control of an opponent, even by a smaller, weaker individual. Whereas this manual was originally intended for combat on an ancient battlefield, the times have changed, but the need has not—this manual still serves its original purpose.

By leveraging the deeper principles and methodologies contained in this text, any martial artist can gain great skill and improved effect. Hand-to-hand combative skills are still as necessary in our modern times, and perhaps even more so, as the governments of the world work to disarm the public. Gaining and especially retaining hand-to-hand advantage with larger, younger, stronger and more aggressive opponents is the Vital Point (Kyusho) of this manual. Even if you are a larger, younger, stronger and more aggressive individual now, time will eventually take its toll and or you will encounter someone of greater capacity in these areas... we all need the advantages that the Bubishi reveal.

This text is not full of fantasy, it is comprised of real, time-tested and battle-proven skills. If you are a serious martial artist, no matter what your current level or background, this text is vital for you. There is a good reason it retains higher value today than hundreds of years ago and why it has lasted through the centuries. It will last for centuries more, due to the efforts of Hanshi Patrick McCarthy.

There are several renditions of this ancient work, all coming to the market after Hanshi Patrick McCarthy's original publication. But none have the depth of research painstakingly compiled by him, and none have been able to relate the insights of this text you now read. As Mc-Carthy still continues his campaign to enrich us with the ancient methods, traditions and intrinsic value contained in this book, we all stand to benefit. There is no comparison.

Thank you to Hanshi Patrick McCarthy for the dedication and continuous efforts to keep this epic martial arts document available for all who seek its value.

During the Song dynasty (960–1279 A.D.) China suffered numerous military defeats and occupied a relatively small territory. Rather than encouraging militarism, the Song rulers placed emphasis upon civil endeavors. Thus, during this period great advances were made in the arts, literature, and medicine, especially acupuncture and moxibustion.

The Bronze Man Statue

Chinese historical records recount Emperor Ren Zong instructing the imperial medical officer, Wang Wei, in 1026 A.D., to cast two bronze models of men that would accurately disclose the location of every meridian point, so as to establish a standard for all acupuncture and moxibustion students in China. When completed, one of the models was placed at the Imperial Doctors' Bureau, and the other at the Ren Ji Prayer Hall in the Xiang Guo Temple.

The Bronze Men were exact three-dimensional models of the human body that displayed precise locations of the meridian points in relation to their corresponding internal organs. The Bronze Men were used in official examinations during that time by students of acupuncture. This development marked a significant breakthrough in medical science; before the Song dynasty, all anatomical representations had been two-dimensional. Accordingly, reproductions of the Bronze Men were duplicated and diagrams printed and distributed throughout the medical community. As such, knowledge of the anatomy and its meridian locations increased greatly during that time.

It is said that by the end of the Song dynasty one of the original Bronze Men was lost in central China's Hubei Province, and the other taken as plunder by the Jin army during their invasion of Song territory. It was only after the Mongols defeated the Jin dynasty that the Bronze Men were safely returned.

In the Ming dynasty during the reign of Emperor Jia Jing (1522–67), a private physician of acupuncture and moxibustion named Gao Wu cast three of his own Bronze Men. Discovering the anatomical differences between a man, a woman, and a child, he recognized the need for such an analysis. With the Bronze Man statues enabling physicians to study the external vital point locations, the development of the Crystal Man statue further enabled scholars to study the internal organs while observing the circulatory system.

Through the thousands of years of acupuncture and moxibustion practice, many locations on the human body not suitable for needling or cautery were discovered. Pricking at these points would worsen the disease rather than curing it, and at certain points, needling could cause immediate death.

Zhang Sanfeng

One man to explore and record the results of his vital point analysis was the Daoist martial arts expert and acupuncturist Zhang Sanfeng (b. 1270). Fascinated by the fighting traditions, and proficient in the Shaolin hard styles, Zhang sought to create the ultimate form of self-defense; one that would allow him to subjugate an opponent with only minimal force by traumatizing weak parts of the human body. To corroborate his hypotheses, it is said that Zhang traveled extensively and experimented on both animals and humans.

During his analysis, Zhang and his associates discovered that by striking specific vital points, alternative areas became much more vulnerable to even less powerful attacks; thus by pressing, squeezing, or traumatizing one point, striking other points would have a critical effect. Chinese folklore maintains that Zhang Sanfeng corroborated his lethal suppositions by bribing jailers and experimenting on prisoners on death row.

It is said that Zhang Sanfeng later produced his own Bronze Man to facilitate the teaching of his theories. Using wax, the special attack points (i.e., the tiny orifices of the Bronze Man) were blocked and hidden, and the body was filled with mercury. If his disciples succeeded in pricking the correct vital point(s) with a needle while blindfolded, liquid oozed from the hole.

Legend maintains that Zhang Sanfeng developed a series of continuous postures *(quan)* based upon his knowledge of hard Shaolin and soft Daoist *gongfu,* through which the principles of his vital point theory could be disseminated. Remaining disguised within the abstract postures, the combat applications were only disclosed to his most trusted disciples. Although there is opposition to this hypothesis, folklore maintains that Zhang's unique development later became known as *taijiquan,* the "grand ultimate fist."

The Forbidden Vital Points

During the Ming dynasty, acupuncturists recorded dozens of vital points where needling and cautery were forbidden. These forbidden points located on the head include: *Naohu Xue, Xinhui Xue, Shenting Xue, Louque Xue, Yuzhen Xue, Jiaosun Xue, Luxi Xue, Chengzhu Xue, Chengling Xue, Chengguang Xue, Yamen Xue, Fengfu Xue, Jingming Xue, Zuanzhu Xue, Yingxiang Xue, Tianqu Xue, Shanglinzhu Xue, Ermen Xue, Sizhu Kong, Douwei Xue,* and the *Xiaguan Xue.* Forbidden points on the trunk include: *Jianzhen Xue, Tianchuang Xue, Xinshu Xue, Jiuwei Xue, Ruzhong Xue, Jizhong Xue, Baihuashu, Yuanye Xue, Zhourong Xue, Fuai Xue, Shendao Xue, Lingdai Xue, Shanzhong Xue, Shuifen Xue, Shenque Xue, Huiying Xue, Shimen Xue, Quepen Xue,* and the *Jianjing Xue.* The forbidden points on the four limbs include: *Hegu Xue, Sanyinjiao Xue or Yunhao, Chongyang Xue, Sanyanglou Xue, Shaoshang Xue, Yuji Xue, Jingqu Xue, Tianfu Xue, Zhongchong Xue, Yangchi Xue, Yangguan Xue, Diwanghui, Lougu Xue, Yinlingquan Xue, Tiaokou Xue, Yinmen Xue, Zhongmai Xue, Chengfu Xue, Futu Xue, Biguan Xue, Weizhong Xue, Yinshi Xue,* and the *Dubi Xue.*

By the middle of the Ming dynasty, with generations of empirical analysis and an intimate understanding of these vital points, acupuncturists developed their own remarkably effective method of self-defense, intended for doctors and scholars. Some carried women's sewing needles in their pockets so that if attacked, they could prick the attacker's vital points. Others wrapped five poison-soaked needles together in a bundle, referring to them as "plum blossom needles," and stored them in a slender bamboo tube ready for use. Some scholars preferred to strike the enemy's forbidden vital points with writing brushes or fans made of iron or bamboo. However, these weapon-usable objects were often inconvenient to carry and therefore few became skillful with them.

A Ming dynasty Daoist, Feng Yiyuan, developed a method of attacking the forbidden vital points using only bare hands. It is believed that the vital point striking information in the Bubishi is based on Feng's analysis. Feng, like Zhang Sanfeng, discovered which points on the human body induced optimum injury when pressed, squeezed, or traumatized. Feng also came to understand how the lunar and solar cycles of each day influenced the blood flow and at what times of the day it was more vulnerable than others. Hence, if certain areas were pressed, squeezed, or traumatized during those periods, the vital points were more likely to be damaged, which could cause a number of internal disorders, ranging from great pain and paralysis, to a neurological shutdown (knockout), or a thrombosis (the obstruction of a blood vessel) which, without treatment, could impair the circulatory system, cause an organ to dysfunction, and ultimately lead to death.

Composed of 36 variations, Feng used this method to fight monks, generals, and other Daoists, and was never defeated. He passed his unique method onto several disciples who propagated it. Sought out by many, the principles of Feng Yiyuan's "vital-point striking" quickly became protected by an iron-clad ritual of secrecy. According to legend, the 36 major vital points developed by Feng Yiyuan were divided into nine death points, nine neurological shutdown points, nine pain points, and nine paralyzing points.

Over time, many misinterpretations were introduced by illiterate adherents. As such, the locations of many vital points were disregarded and Feng's discipline became obscure as its practice was maintained only by reclusive mountain Daoists.

In 1638, during the last days of the Ming dynasty, a Chinese martial artist from Hangzhou named Chen Yuanbin (1587–1671) arrived in Nagasaki, Japan, where he ultimately served at the castle of the Owari Daimyo. Also an expert in the art of seizing *(qin na)* and striking vital points, Chen Yuanbin (Chin Gempei in Japanese) taught his art to Fukuno Shichiroemon, Miura Yojiemon, and Isogai Jirozaemon, who in turn created three schools of ju-jutsu. Though it may be incorrect to call Chen the "father of ju-jutsu," from that time on, all ju-jutsu schools used vital-point striking, a practice, however, which only a few ju-jutsu traditions understand today.

Hoards of ex-Ming dynasty officials also sought refuge in neighboring countries and surrounding islands. Annan (the old name for Vietnam), Siam (Thailand), Burma (Myanmar), Malaysia, Korea, and Taiwan accommodated many. The Ryukyu Kingdom, which was then a tributary principality of the Middle Kingdom, also became an ideal sanctuary for freedom fighters waiting to liberate their country. Just how many of China's civil fighting traditions were taught in those countries remains the subject of intense curiosity. During the Qing dynasty, the great scholar Huang Zongxi and his son Huang Baijia learned the secrets of vital points striking from eminent *gongfu* master Wang Zhengnan. Together, they were indirectly responsible for passing on this knowledge to the Southern Shaolin Temple (as contrasted to the Northern Shaolin Temple in Heman), which some sources claim was located on Mount Jiulian (Nine Lotus Mountain), while other sources claim it was located near Putian in Fujian Province. Complicating matters is the fact that the Jiulian mountains are located in the area where Guangdong and Jiangxi province border one another. The temple's actual location has not yet been discovered.

This Shaolin Temple (often described as the Shorei Temple in Japanese) had an enormous impact upon the growth and direction of the civil fighting traditions in the area south of the Yangtze River during the Qing dynasty. From that time on, all records passed down over the generations contained the secrets of vital point striking.

It is regrettable that in some of these diagrams the locations of the vital points are not identical or complete. These drawings illustrate points but don't say how to strike the point to get the desired effect.

Daoist Feng Yiyuan's discipline utilized attacks to 36 points on the body. Zhang Zhuanyi was a prodigy of Feng, who was said to have increased the number of targets to 72. By the time the Southern Shaolin School was established, the number of vital points had been increased to 108 and the Shaolin recluses used a special name to describe each of the techniques. In order to maintain robust health and to memorize defensive procedures and corresponding vital points, continuous attacking postures (complete with individual names to identify the attack) were brought together to form new set routines *(quan)* and given such names as: *Seisan* (Thirteen), *Seipai* (Eighteen), *Niseishi* (Twenty-four), *Nepai* (Twenty-Eight), *Sanseiru* (Thirty-six), *Useishi* (Fifty-four), *Peichurrin* (108). Some of these sets served as the foundation upon which alternative styles unfolded in Fujian.

Other *quan* often bore abstract names, which corresponded with their founder, place of origin, pugilistic intention, specialty, or some unique characteristic of the *quan,* etc. All *quan* promoted physical health and mental well-being. It was through the *quan* that the secrets of self-defense were taught: joint-locks; chokes; take-downs; throws; hand and leg maneuvers; grappling; escapes; ground-work; the pressing, squeezing, or traumatizing of vital points; organ-piercing blows (designed to shock those organs not protected by the ribcage); blood gate attacks (rupturing veins or arteries through unprotected cavities); traumatizing nerve plexus; and combinations thereof. The *quan* taught how to defend oneself by injuring, incapacitating, or even killing. Notwithstanding, studying the *quan* became the accepted custom through which the secret applications of self-defense were disseminated.

To govern the behavior of those who studied the deadly secrets of the *quan,* the various *gongfu* schools embraced the philosophical teachings of the sages, and hence were profoundly affected by Daoist, Confucian, and Buddhist thought.

After the Boxer Rebellion of 1900 and the fall of the Qing dynasty in 1911, little emphasis was placed on the complex art of striking vital points or even on learning the unarmed fighting arts. The development and widespread use of firearms had reduced the effectiveness of hand-to-hand self-defense. Moreover, the stagnant economy and the sweeping social changes that took place under the new Republic of China (1912-49) left few with the time or money needed to seriously pursue the fighting traditions. After that time most, but not all, who learned the fighting traditions studied them for recreational interest, artistic performance, and/or personal improvement. That is why so few people today understand the secrets of striking the vital points.

Vital Point Analysis

I would like to conclude this analysis by discussing the skill of striking the 12 *shichen* (bi-hourly) vital points as developed and passed down through the Ming dynasty Daoist Wu Liuyuan. I would also like to present a related section of Jin Yiming's *Secrets of Wudang Boxing (Wudang Quanshu Mijue)*. Combined with Feng Yiyuan's principles and Wu's analysis, the *Secrets of Wudang Boxing* is a crucial addition to gaining a deeper understanding of the Bubishi.

The correlation between the vital points and intervals to traumatize them are as follows:

1. *Shuigou Xue* during the Time of the Rat (11 p.m.-1 a.m.)
2. *Dianyan Xue* during the Time of the Ox (1-3 a.m.)
3. *Jiaogong Xue* during the Time of the Tiger (3-5 a.m.)
4. *Zisai Xue* during the Time of the Rabbit (5-7 a.m.)
5. *Daiying Xue* during the Time of the Dragon (7-9 a.m.)
6. *Jiangdai Xue* during the Time of the Snake (9-11 a.m.)
7. *Maiguan Xue* during the Time of the Horse (11 a.m.-1 p.m.)
8. *Jigan Xue* during the Time of the Ram (1-3 p.m.)
9. *Xuanhai Xue* during the Time of the Monkey (3-5 p.m.)
10. *Baihai Xue* during the Time of the Cock (5-7 p.m.)
11. *Donghudilou Xue* during the Time of the Dog (7-9 p.m.)
12. *Yongquan Xue* during the Time of the Boar (9-11 p.m.)

Comparing these 12 vital points with the corresponding points of the original Bronze Man statue for acupuncture, we discover that the locations are similar but, other than two, all the names are different. These variations surfaced from an attempt to keep the locations a secret through oral tradition and misunderstandings.

It is maintained that ancient Daoist recluses used the polarity theory developed by Xu Wenbo and Xi Yuan and the opening and closing of vital points when they developed the methods of striking them and interrupting meridians. Cutting off the breath and the blood at a certain meridian or vital point during a corresponding two-hour interval prevents the meridian from receiving its nourishment, resulting in tissue and blood degeneration that reduces *qi* energy. Meridians carry breath, blood, and nutrients to the organs.

The blocking or intercepting of energy could cause neurological shutdown or death. The length of time it would take someone to die from this kind of injury would depend entirely upon how severely the point was struck and what, if any, medical attention was administered. For example, after one of the temporal, ethmoidal, or frontal arteries had been ruptured, it might take several days for the head to fill with blood and death to result. Such was often the case in old China, where medical attention was scarce, and physical conflict frequent.

Chinese characters for vital point manipulation.

The Thirty-Six Vital Points

LOCATION	MERIDIAN POINT	ENGLISH NAME
1. Coronal Suture	GV 22	Brain House
2. Frontal Fontanel	GV 24	Temple of God
3. Temples		Great Yang
4. Eyes		
5. Ears		
6. Mastoid Process	TH 17	Wind Screen
7. Philtrum	GV 26	Water Drain
8. Chin (indentation)	CV 24	Containing the Fluid
9. Neck (both sides)	SI 16	Heavenly Window
10. Throat (also larynx)	ST 9	Man Welcomes
11. Suprasternal Fossa	CV 22	Appearing To Disappear
12. Supraclavicular Fossa	ST 12	Small Bowl
13. Posterior Midline	GV 16	Wind Palace
14. Seventh Cervical Vertebra	GV 14	Grand Hammer
15. Breast Bone	CV 18	Jade Palace
16. Xiphoid Process	CV 15	Tail of the Dove
17. Axilla (armpit)	HT 1	Extreme Fountain
18. Fourth Thoracic Vertebra	BL 43	Hollow of the Vital

19. First Lumbar Vertebra	BL 51	Door of the Vital
20. Tip of the Coccyx	GV 1	Long Strength
21. Below the Umbilicus	CV 4	Gate of Origin
22. Testicles (and Prostate Nerve)	CV 1	Meeting of Yin
23. Seventh Intercostal Space	GB 24	Sun and Moon
24. Tip of the Eleventh Rib	LIV 13	Door of the Shelter
25. Inguinal Region	LIV 11	Yin Passage
26. Biceps (lateral side)	LU 3	Celestial Palace
27. Forearm	LI 10	Three Miles
28. Wrist Crease	HT 5	Communication With The Interior
29. Wrist Crease	LU 8	Meridian Gutter
30. Hand (between the Thumb and Forefinger)	LI 4	Joining of the Valleys
31. Hand (web between the Baby and Ring Finger)	TH 2	Door of the Fluids
32. Lower Thigh	GB 31	City of Wind
33. Back of the Knees	BL 40	Perfect Equilibrium
34. Ankle (inside)	KD 6	Sea of Luminescence
35. Ankle (outside)	BL 62	Vessel of the Hour of Shen
36. Foot (crease between the second and third Metatarsal phalangeal joint)	LIV 3	Big Surge

---

The following indicates the abbreviations for the meridian channels: LU = lung, LI = large intestine (or CO = colon), ST = stomach, SP = spleen, HT = heart, SI = small intestine, BL = bladder, KD = kidney, PC = pericardium (heart constrictor), TH = three heater (triple heater), GB = gall bladder, LIV = liver, CV = conception vessel, GV = governor vessel, m = muscle, t = tendon, 1 *cun* = 3 cm.

The English names given for the pressure points are the standard translations used by the Australian National Acupuncture College, as they appear in the *Point Location and Point Dynamics Manual* by Drs. Carole and Cameron Rogers.   (TR)

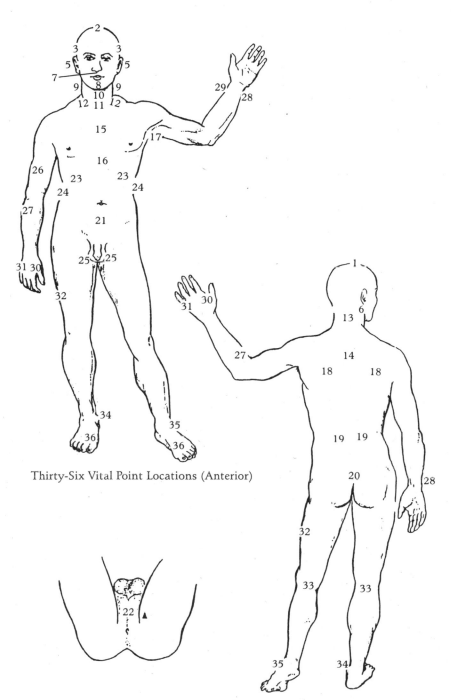

Thirty-Six Vital Point Locations (Anterior)

Thirty-Six Vital Point Locations (Posterior)

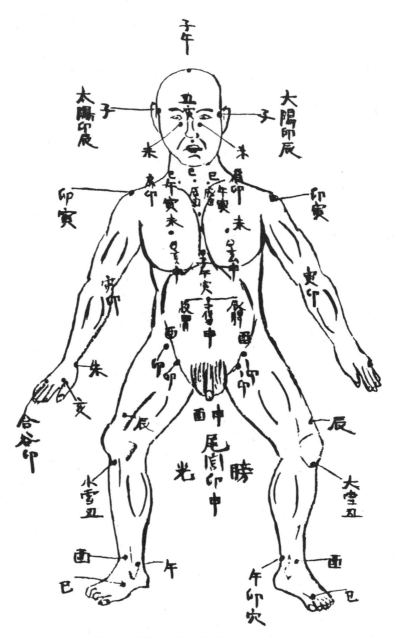

Original Thirty-Six Vital point Locations

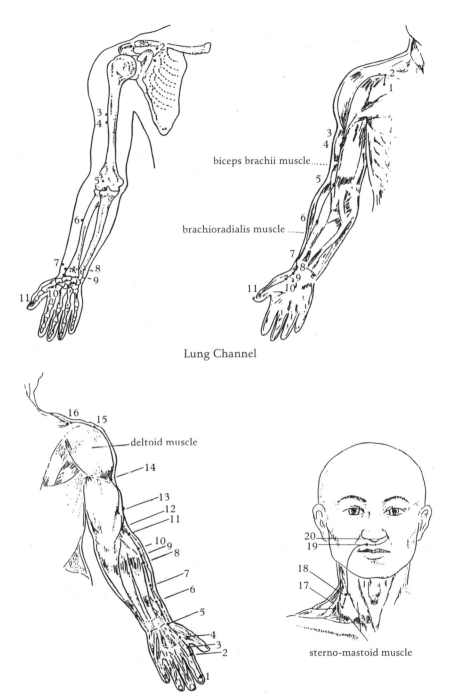

biceps brachii muscle

brachioradialis muscle

Lung Channel

deltoid muscle

sterno-mastoid muscle

Large Intestine (Colon) Channel

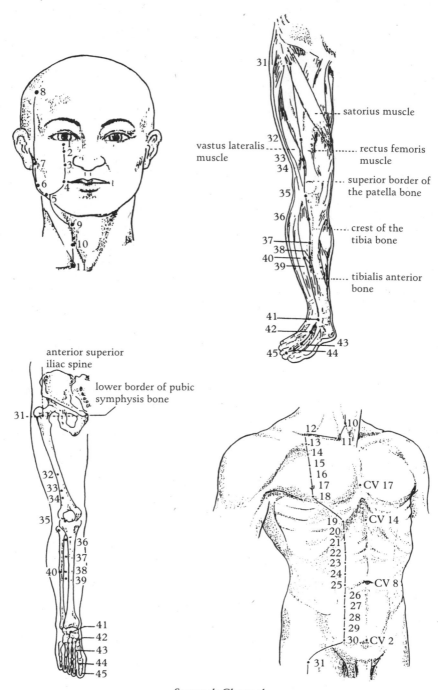

satorius muscle

vastus lateralis
muscle

rectus femoris
muscle

superior border of
the patella bone

crest of the
tibia bone

tibialis anterior
bone

anterior superior
iliac spine

lower border of pubic
symphysis bone

CV 17

CV 14

CV 8

CV 2

Stomach Channel

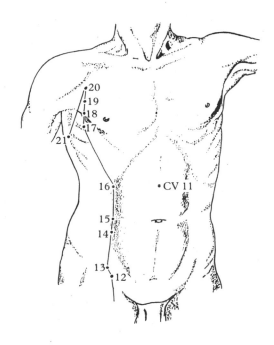

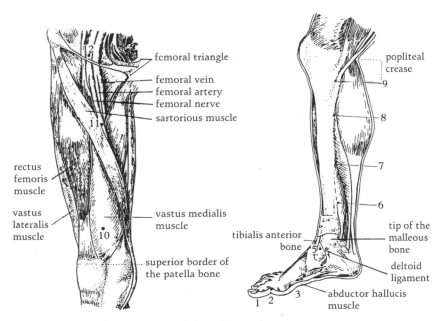

Spleen Channel

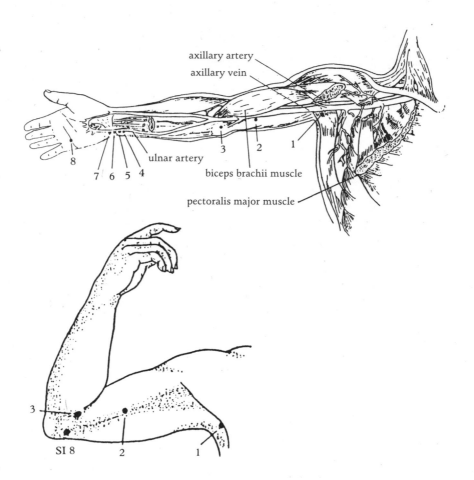

axillary artery
axillary vein
ulnar artery
biceps brachii muscle
pectoralis major muscle

8 7 6 5 4 3 2 1

3 SI 8 2 1

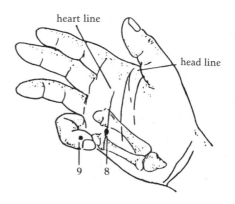

heart line
head line

9 8

Heart Channel

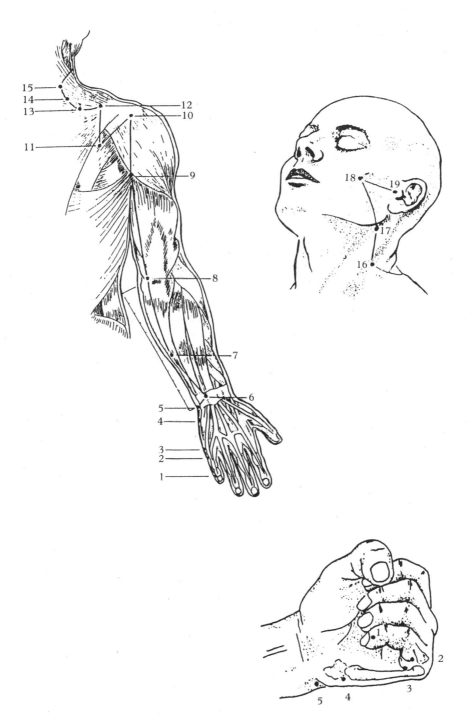

Small Intestine Channel

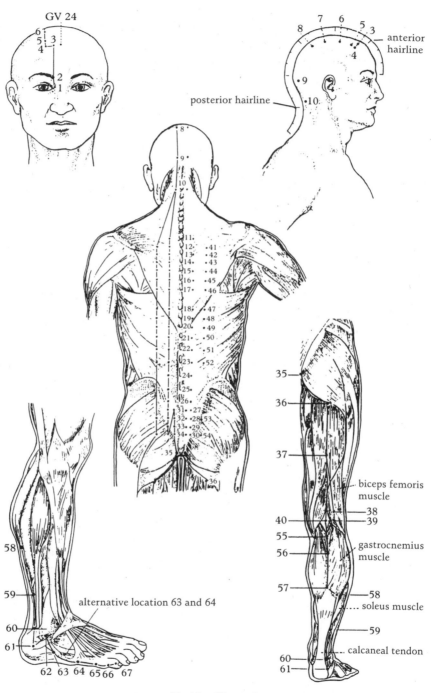

GV 24

anterior hairline

posterior hairline

biceps femoris muscle

gastrocnemius muscle

soleus muscle

calcaneal tendon

alternative location 63 and 64

Bladder Channel

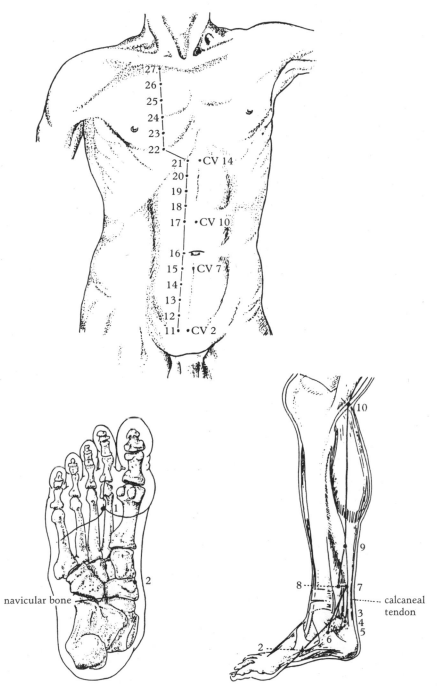

Kidney Channel

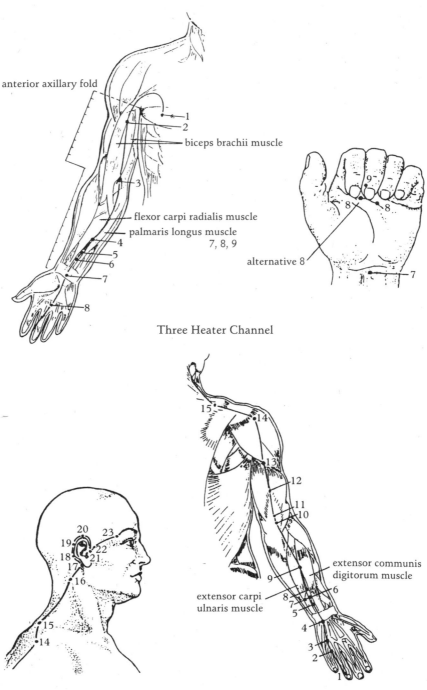

anterior axillary fold

1
2

biceps brachii muscle

3

flexor carpi radialis muscle
palmaris longus muscle
7, 8, 9

4
5
6
7
8

9
8
8

alternative 8

7

Three Heater Channel

15
14

13

12

11
10

extensor communis
digitorum muscle

9

extensor carpi
ulnaris muscle

8
7
6
5
4
3
2
1

20
23
19
18
22
17
21
16

15
14

Pericardium (Heart, Constrictor) Channel

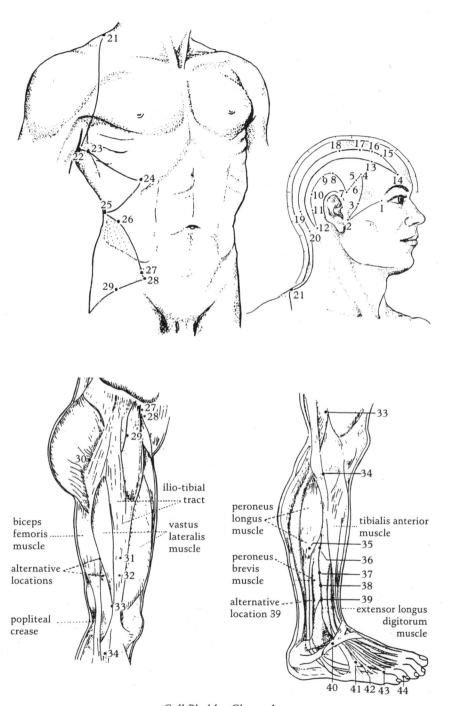

Gall Bladder Channel

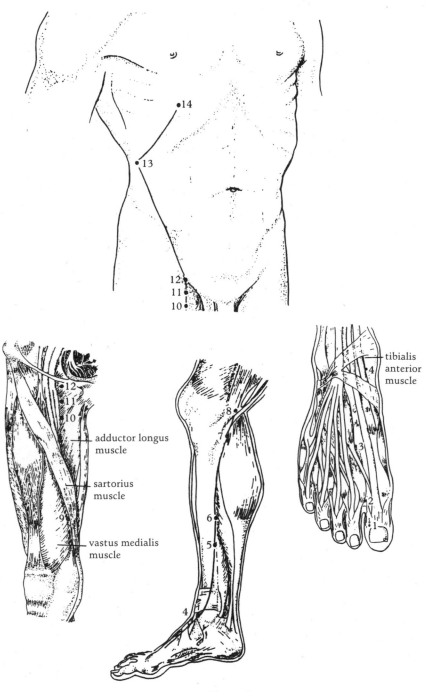

Liver Channel

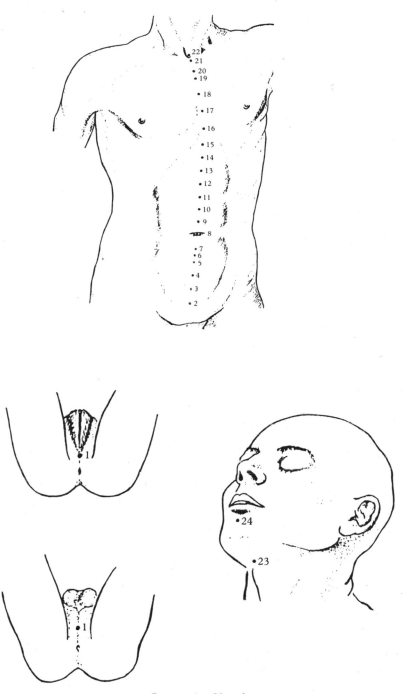

Conception Vessel

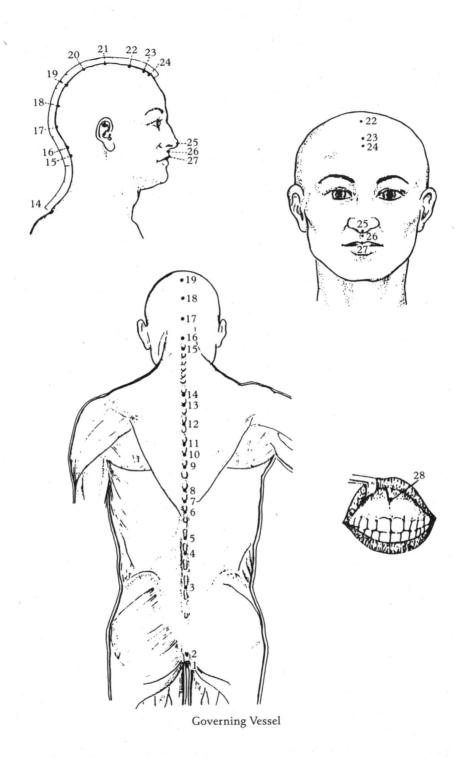

Governing Vessel

The Secrets of Wudang Boxing

This 1928 book was written by Jin Yiming and is similar to the Bubishi in that it includes a series of tables on vital point striking. What is significant about it is that although it concerns the soft, or internal, Chinese fighting systems, the vital points and techniques described are remarkably similar to those presented in the Bubishi, a text concerning the hard, external fighting arts. This would indicate that although the hard and soft styles appear radically different, at their nucleus, they are identical.

In the following section I will present several relevant sections of the text. I have edited it down considerably for use in this text.

What Does Striking the Vital Points Mean?

Striking the vital points means closing the lines of internal bodily communication by cutting off their transportation function. The human body (i.e., head, limbs, and the five *zang* and six *fu* organs or viscera) is connected by tendons and collaterals that are irrigated by arteries and veins. A man cannot move if his tendons and collaterals have been injured; and if the blood, arteries, or veins stop functioning, he will lose consciousness. Tendons and collaterals start at the fingertips, gather at the knees, and converge in the head and face. *Qi* energy governs the activities of the tendons and collaterals. Hence, when training one's tendons, it is necessary to cultivate *qi*. *Qi* runs outside one's tendons and collaterals, and blood flows inside the channels and collaterals. To better understand the blood flow and the vital points, try to imagine one's blood functioning as flowing water, and the vital points serving as a spring. When unobstructed, the flow is free and easy. However, if obstructed, stagnation will ensue.

Blood flow follows the *qi* and originates in the heart. It circulates throughout the 12 main meridians during the *shichen,* starting from the time of the Rat (11 p.m.-1 a.m.). If the blood flow is cut off, it will have an adverse effect.

How to Identify Vital Points

Master Tang Dianqing said that Zhang Sanfeng first learned how to strike the vital points from Daoist Feng Yiyuan. His 36 vital points included death, paralyzing, neurological shutdown, and respiratory points. I know that a man can be dazed by lightly striking a vital point. A heavy trauma can be fatal.

Of the 36 vital points, 22 are located on the anterior (p. 230), and the other 14 are on the posterior (p. 231). I conditioned my fingers for years but seldom have struck vital points.

However, my own experience has taught me that striking vital

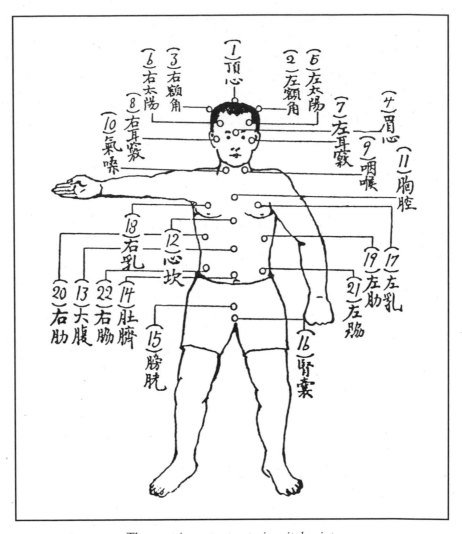

The most important anterior vital points

1. *Dingxin* (top of the head)
2. *Zuojiuo* (left forehead)
3. *Youjiao* (right forehead)
4. *Meixin* (center of eyebrows)
5. *Zuotaiyang* (left temple)
6. *Youtaiyang* (right temple)
7. *Zuoerjiao* (hole of left ear)
8. *Youerjiao* (hole of right ear)
9. *Yanhou* (larynx)
10. *Qisang* (larynx)
11. *Xiongyang* (chest)
12. *Xinkan* (bottom of heart)
13. *Dafu* (large intestine)
14. *Duji* (umbilicus)
15. *Pangguang* (urinary bladder)
16. *Shennang* (kidney bladder)
17. *Zuoru* (left breast)
18. *Youru* (right breast)
19. *Zuolei* (left rib)
20. *Youlei* (right rib)
21. *Zuoxie* (left oblique)
22. *Youxie* (right oblique)

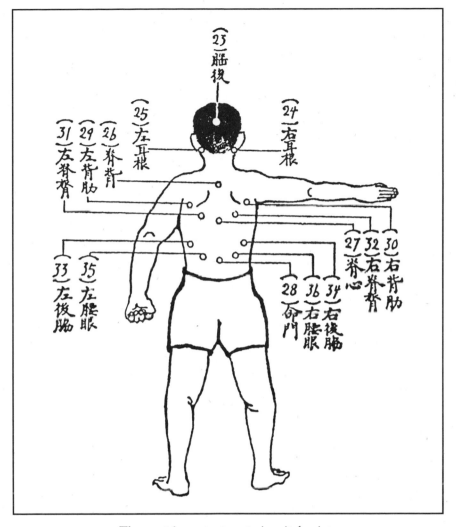

The most important posterior vital points

23. *Naohu* (back of head)
24. *Youergen* (under right ear)
25. *Zuoergen* (under left ear)
26. *Jibei* (back)
27. *Jinxin* (center of back)
28. *Mingmen* (life-gate)
29. *Zuobeilei* (left shoulder blade)

30. *Youbeilei* (right shoulder blade)
31. *Zuojilu* (left upper back)
32. *Youjilu* (right upper back)
33. *Zuohouxia* (left floating rib)
34. *Youhouxia* (right floating rib)
35. *Zuoyaoyan* (left kidney)
36. *Youyaoyan* (right kidney)

points in the head render a man unstable; striking points in the throat can paralyze; striking the upper torso impairs the respiratory system, which results in coughing; and striking the lower part of the body injures the waist, which causes a tingling sensation. The 36 vital points refer to 36 separate locations.

I consulted Master He Fengming about striking vital points. He said that he had not heard of vital point striking for many years, but once knew of a man named Eagle Claw Wang. Wang was a courageous swordsman from the Huaibei district in Anhui. After learning how to strike the vital points from Zhang Sanfeng, he then developed his grappling skills. There are five ways to attack the vital points: chopping (using the side of the palm), thrusting (using the fingers), slapping (using the palm), hitting (using the hand), and seizing (using the fingers to grab).

It is said that, from head to toe in the human body, in each area of about five *cun,* there is a large vital point area, and that each area of five *fen* (one *fen* equals approximately one-tenth of an inch) has a small vital point area. If the vital points are attacked in conjunction with the blood-flow theory, then a trauma to a small vital point will damage a person, and a trauma to a large vital point will kill him.

The blood-flow theory is divided into 12 equal periods, and the vital points are located along 12 channels. When attacking the anterior *Ren* (conception vessel: one of the eight extra meridians) or posterior *Du* (governing vessel: another of the eight extra meridians) vital points, the effect is immediate.

Time Periods for Attacking the Vital Points

SHICHEN	MERIDIAN
1. Rat (11 p.m.-1 a.m.)	Gall Bladder
2. Ox (1-3 a.m.)	Liver
3. Tiger (3-5 a.m.)	Lung
4. Rabbit (5-7 a.m.)	Large Intestine
5. Dragon (7-9 a.m.)	Stomach
6. Snake (9-11 a.m.)	Spleen
7. Horse (11 a.m.-1 p.m.)	Heart
8. Ram (1-3 p.m.)	Small Intestine
9. Monkey (3-5 p.m.)	Bladder
10. Cock (5-7 p.m.)	Kidney
11. Dog (7-9 p.m.)	Pericardium
12. Boar (9-11 p.m.)	Three Heater

This table is identical to one that appears in Article 8 (see p. 235) of the Bubishi. (TR)

It is said that Eagle Claw Wang had 108 hitting and seizing techniques that coincided with the 108 vital points of the anatomy. Conversely, by manipulating the vital points, Wang could also revive victims who had their vital points injured. This method is based upon manipulating the course of various vital points where the blood flow had been shut down. Restoring the body to its normal condition meant stimulating the circulation by manipulating those points where the blood flow originated. Hence, making the blood flow again through the shut down area.

One concept that remains today supports conducting experiments on a live ox after the fingers have been conditioned. Although the animal's anatomy is different from a human's, they share corresponding locations with respect to principal vital points.

My colleague, Zhao Haiping from the Qiyang district in Hunan Province, was the principal disciple of Jiang Xiuyuan, the famous *wushu* master. Master Jiang was a scholar who excelled in Shaolin *wushu*. Zhao studied directly under Jiang and became an expert in vital point attacking. On the day that Qiyang's *wushu* hall opened, Zhao happened to be there with his army. He gave a demonstration of hitting and seizing vital points that was well received by all.

From the time we met, we began to visit each other. Zhao disclosed illustrations that explained the vital areas and told me of the 36 vital points. He said that if I did not believe him I could experiment on a horse. With that, a horse was brought in and when Zhao struck the horse's vital points it took effect immediately.

The following diagram and explanation have been included so that the reader may more easily locate the exact attack points referred to in the "Time Periods for Attacking the Vital Points" table that appears in the *Secrets of Wudang Boxing* and the *shichen* table that appears in Article 8 of the Bubishi (see p. 235). The following table lists the *shichen,* the specific meridian point for attacking, and a translation of the point's Chinese name. (TR)

———— ❧❦❧ ————

SHICHEN	POINT NUMBER	POINT NAME
1. Rat (11 p.m.-1 a.m.)	GB 41	Lying Down to Weep
2. Ox (1-3 a.m.)	LIV 1	Large Hill
3. Tiger (3-5 a.m.)	LU 8	Meridian Gutter
4. Rabbit (5-7 a.m.)	LI 1	Merchant of Yang
5. Dragon (7-9 a.m.)	ST 35	Nose of Calf
6. Snake (9-11 a.m.)	SP 3	Supreme Whiteness
7. Horse (11 a.m.-1 p.m.)	HT 8	Small *Fu*
8. Ram (1-3 p.m.)	SI 5	Valley of Yang
9. Monkey (3-5 p.m.)	BL 66	Bursting the Valley
10. Cock (5-7 p.m.)	KD 10	Valley of Yin

11. Dog (7-9 p.m.)	PC 6	Inner Gate
12. Boar (9-11 p.m.)	TH 6	Branch Ditch

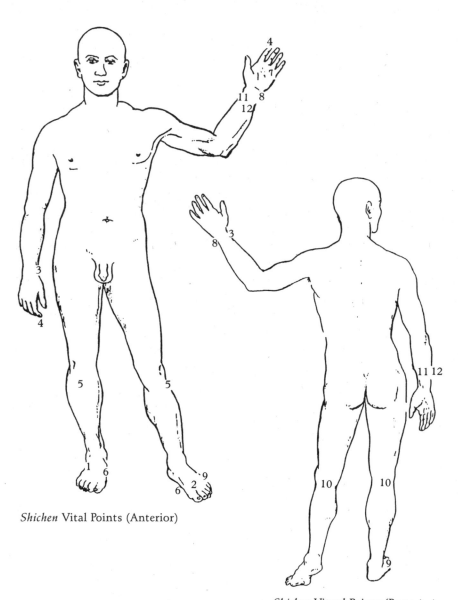

Shichen Vital Points (Anterior)

Shichen Vitual Points (Posterior)

Articles on Vital Points

Article 8: Discussions on Seizing and Striking Veins and Tendons Using the Hard Fist Method

While discussing the values of the fighting traditions, one must not overlook the importance of the "hard-fist" technique. It is said that if one's vital points are forcefully struck with this secret technique, the results can be fatal. On the other hand, attacking a muscle or joint with a well-placed blow can paralyze a person.

I have heard that by using this technique one can also directly terminate a person's *qi*. When correctly used, even if only to a minor point, the result can be fatal. The only variation is the interval of time in which death occurs.

The time of death depends entirely upon how and when the vital points are attacked. For example, a severe trauma might kill someone instantly, whereas other, less concentrated attacks are said to cause dementia.

This obscure method may sound fantastic, and while I have never seen it practiced, I cannot rule out its existence. In fact, until now, I have never expressed my opinion about this matter.

While examining this subject, I discovered, in secret "vein books," theories concerning the human body and how it is influenced by the positive and negative forces of nature. Responsible for the function of our anatomy, the 12 organs also have corresponding passages, located all over the body, through which currents of energy flow in both ascending and descending streams. Described as meridians, there are special points located along each of these passages that are known as single or bilateral points. Each of our internal organs systematically experiences a high and a low energy point corresponding with the time of day. Much in the same way that the principles of acupuncture work to cure a patient, it is entirely possible to reverse the process and impair the function of an organ by traumatizing these points and others.

It is possible that this information may vary from school to school, but this is the way that I have received it. I am sorry that I am not able to provide a more conclusive analysis.

In my experience, some of the most responsive vital points on the human body are as follows:

1. The eyes
2. The xiphoid process (CV 15)
3. The middle of the arms (LI 10)
4. On the artery at the base of the axilla under the armpits (HT 1)
5. The tip of the tailbone (BL 35)
6. The tip of the free end of the eleventh rib on either side of the body (LIV 13)
7. The lumbar region and two sides of the eleventh thoracic vertebra (BL20).

Considering how the elements of nature affect our body, we must always monitor our lifestyle to comply with the cold of winter and heat of summer. Respecting others begins by respecting oneself. Be considerate but prudent.

As with using herbal medicines to treat diseases that result from organ dysfunction, by taking the prescription during the corresponding active time, intervals one can insure maximum curative benefit. Employing the same principles, one can reverse damage to an organ by manipulating certain points during their active intervals.

MERIDIANS	SHICHEN
1. Gall Bladder	Rat (11 p.m.-1 a.m.)
2. Liver	Ox (1-3 A.M.)
3. Lung	Tiger (3-5 a.m.)
4. Large Intestine	Rabbit (5-7 a.m.)
5. Stomach	Dragon (7-9 a.m.)
6. Spleen	Snake (9-11 a.m.)
7. Heart	Horse (11 a.m.-1 p.m.)
8. Small Intestine	Ram (1-3 p.m.)
9. Bladder	Monkey (3-5 p.m.)
10. Kidney	Cock (5-7 p.m.)
11. Pericardium	Dog (7-9 p.m.)
12. Three Heater	Boar (9-11 p.m.)

Article 9: Twelve-Hour Vital Points Revealed

SHICHEN	POINT NUMBER	POINT NAME
1. Rat (11 p.m.-1 a.m.)	GB 24	Sun and Moon
2. Ox (1-3 a.m.)	LIV 14	Door of the Period
3. Tiger (3-5 a.m.)	LU 1	Central Palace
4. Rabbit (5-7 a.m.)	LI 10	Three Miles
5. Dragon (7-9 a.m.)	ST 25	Celestial Axis
6. Snake (9-11 a.m.)	SP 14	Abdominal Knot

7. Horse (11 a.m.-1 p.m.)	HT 8	Small *Fu*
8. Ram (1-3 p.m.)	CV 6	Sea of Energy
9. Monkey (3-5 p.m.)	CV 2	Crooked Bone
10. Cock (5-7 p.m.)	BL 52	Lodge of the Will
11. Dog (7-9 p.m.)	BL 14	Pericardium *Shu*
12. Boar (9-11 p.m.)	CV 1	Meeting of Yin

Article 9 lists the *shichen,* and a vital point description, which, according to some sources, is not always consistent with other theories—a point corroborated by both Dr. Wong Chung Ying and Mr. Li Yiduan. Notwithstanding, Article 9, like Article 8 (see p. 235), reveals both blood vessel and nerve point attack locations. See the diagram below to locate the attack points, or refer to the meridian diagrams presented earlier. As with the previous article, I have included a chart and a diagram to better illustrate the *shichen,* their corresponding times, and the attack points along with their Chinese to English name translations. (TR)

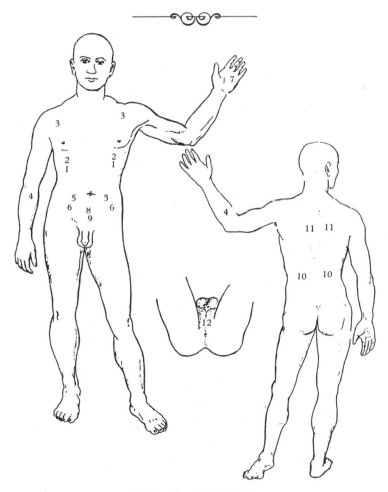

Twelve-Hour Vital Points

Article 17: Seven Restricted Locations

LOCATION	EFFECT
1. Coronal Suture	Line of juncture of the frontal bone and the parietal bones. Death is caused by a severe trauma to the cerebrum and disruptive stimulation of cranial nerves.
2. The Third Intervertebral Space	Loss of consciousness is caused by a severe trauma to the cerebrum, cranial nerves, and spinal cord, producing a loss of sensory and motor function.
3. The Concavity Behind both Ears	Between the mastoid process and the lower jaw. Loss of consciousness is caused by a trauma to the cranial nerves and spinal cord, resulting in a loss of sensory and motor function.
4. Suprasternal Notch	The concavity on the ventral surface of the neck above the sternum. Death or loss of consciousness is caused by a trauma that results in blocking the windpipe.
5. Tip of the Eleventh (Floating) Rib	Loss of consciousness is caused by a severe trauma to the stomach and spleen on the left side, producing a loss of nerve function associated with the heart and lungs. Severe trauma to the right side affects the liver, resulting in the loss of nerve function associated with the liver and lungs.
6. Testicles	Loss of consciousness is caused by a severe trauma to the nerves and arteries in this delicate area, causing the testicles to rise, producing a loss of motor function and ability to breathe. A penetrating trauma to the prostate nerve can cause death.
7. Heart	Severe trauma to any heart-related vital point has a disruptive effect upon other internal organs and the nervous system that leads to the loss of consciousness and/or breathing.

This article advises against striking these seven locations, as the trauma caused may be lethal. Rather than literally translating the crude descriptions that appear in this section, I have described the locations and detailed effects of trauma to these seven areas using modern medical terminology. The diagram accompanying this description does not appear in the original Bubishi.

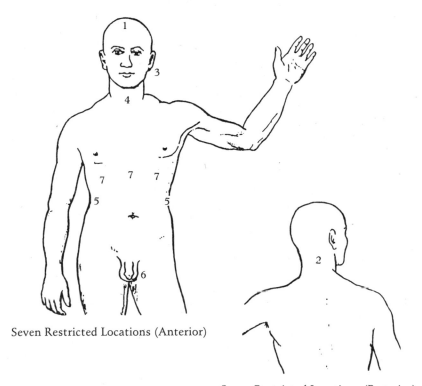

Seven Restricted Locations (Anterior)

Seven Restricted Locations (Posterior)

The Chinese characters for the
Seven Restricted Locations

Article 21: Delayed Death Touch Twelve-Hour Diagrams

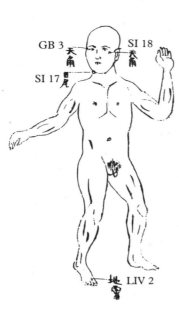

Rat *Schichen* Vital Points

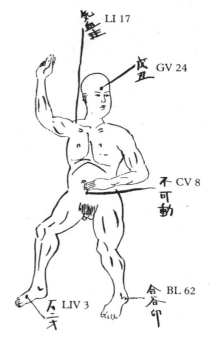

Ox *Shichen* Vital Points

SHICHEN	EFFECT
Rat (11 p.m.-1 a.m.)	Death in one day can be caused by a severe trauma to the medial portion of the instep between the tendons of the big and second toe on the dorsalis hallucis artery (LIV 2), the carotid artery (SI 17), the temporal maxillary arteries at the superior border of the zygomatic arch, in the depression that can be felt by the bone (GB 3), or at the cheekbone directly below the outer canthus (SI 18).
Ox (1-3 a.m.)	Death within 14 days can be caused by traumatizing the carotid artery and sublingual nerve, which is located between the sternomastoid muscle and the clavicle bone (LI 17) (but only when the head is being tilted back by pulling the hair), the external calcanean artery on the outer ankle directly below the lateral malleolus (BL 62), the tibial artery and deep fibular nerve (LIV 3), the coeliac axis aorta at the umbilicus (CV 8), or the anterior temporal artery just below the hairline (GV 24).

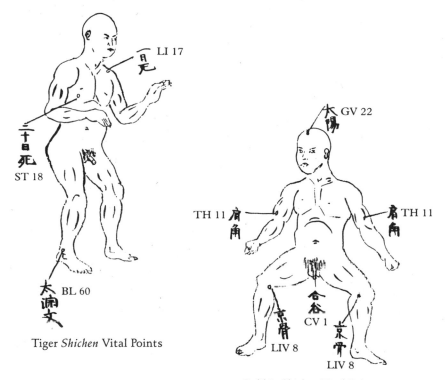

Tiger *Shichen* Vital Points

Rabbit *Shichen* Vital Points

Tiger (3-5 a.m.)

Death within 20 days can be caused by traumatizing the carotid artery and sublingual nerve between the sterno-mastoid muscle and the clavicle bone (LI 17) (but only when the head is being tilted back by pulling the hair), the internal mammary artery just under the nipple (ST 18), or the external malleolar artery at the ankle (BL 60).

Rabbit (5-7 a.m.)

Death in one day can be caused by a severe trauma to the anastomotica magna of the femoral artery in the depression anterior to the semimembranosus and semitendinosus muscles posterior to the medial condyle of the tibia (LIV 8), the transverse perineal artery, between the anus and the scrotum in the male (CV 1), the brachial artery (TH 11), or the anterior ethmoidal artery or cranial nerve at the frontal fontanel (GV22).

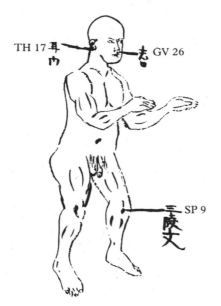

Dragon *Shichen* Vital Points

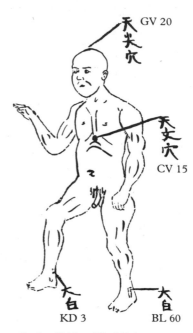

Snake *Shichen* Vital Points

Dragon (7-9 a.m.)	Death before a person can even take seven steps can be caused by a severe trauma to the articular artery at the inferior border of the medial condyle of the tibia (SP 9), the superior coronary artery at the philtrum (GV 26), and the carotid artery or concavity behind the ear in the depression between the mastoid process and the ramus bone (TH 17).
Snake (9-11 a.m.)	Death within three years can be caused by traumatizing the posterior tibial artery (KD 3), or external malleolar artery (BL 60), to the coronal suture (GV 20), or the tip of the xiphoid process (CV 15).

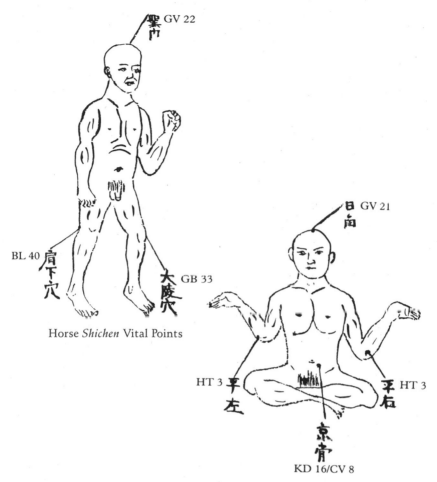

Horse *Shichen* Vital Points

Ram *Shichen* Vital Points

Horse (11 a.m.-1 p.m.)	Indefinite paralysis can be caused by a severe trauma to the popliteal vein exactly between the tendons of the biceps femoris and semitendinosus muscles (BL 40), the inferior external articular artery in the depression superior to the lateral epicondyle of the femur bone (GB 33), or the coronal suture (GV 22).
Ram (1-3 p.m.)	Death within one year can be caused by a severe trauma to the basilic artery (HT 3), co-eliac axis artery lateral to the umbilicus (KD 16/CV 8), and the coronal suture (GV 21).

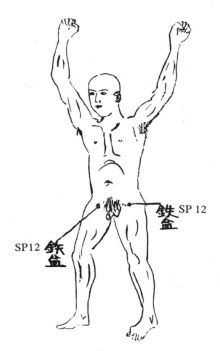

Monkey *Shichen* Vital Points

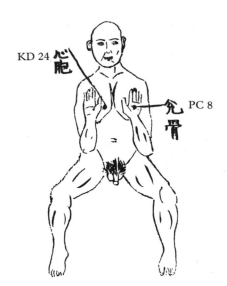

Cock *Shichen* Vital Points

Monkey (3-5 p.m.)	Death within two weeks is caused by a severe trauma to the underlying femoral artery and nerve lateral to the midpoint border of the symphysis pubis bones (SP 12).
Cock (5-7 p.m.)	Death within two days can be caused by a severe trauma to the left innominate vein at the third intercostal space (KD 24), while depressing the deep ulnar artery in the center of the palm between the third and fourth metacarpal (PC 8).

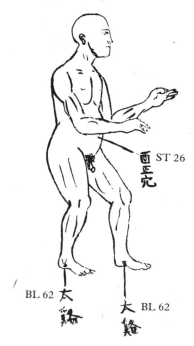

Dog *Shichen* Vital Points

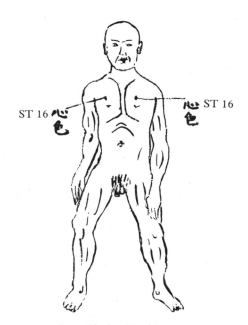

Boar *Shichen* Vital Points

Dog (7-9 p.m.)

Death within three days can be caused by a severe trauma to the hepatic artery lateral to the midline at the level of CV 7 and one *cun* below the level of the umbilicus (ST 26), the external calcanean artery on the outer ankle directly below the lateral malleolus (BL 62), or the plantar artery in the depression on the anterior medial edge of the foot at the distal and inferior border of the navicular bone.

Boar (9-11 p.m.)

Death within one week can be caused by severe simultaneous trauma to the area above the nipple located on the third intercostal space (ST 16).

Article 24: Bronze Man Statue
Anterior:

SHICHEN	VITAL AREA
Rat (11 p.m.-1 a.m.)	The frontal fontanel (GV 22) is most vulnerable to a hammer fist strike
Ox (1-3 a.m.)	The temples (GB 3) are most vulnerable to a single knuckle thrust
Tiger (3-5 a.m.)	The ears are vulnerable to being slapped simultaneously
Rabbit (5-7 a.m.)	The carotid artery behind the clavicle (ST 12 and ST 9), along with inside of the suprasternal notch (CV 22), are vulnerable to forceful finger pressure
Dragon (7-9 a.m.)	The chest area between the second intercostal space (ST 15) and the third intercostal space closer to the midline (ST 16) are most vulnerable to a downward palm thrust
Snake (9-11 a.m.)	Just below the nipple, between the sixth and seventh intercostal space (LIV 14)
Horse (11 a.m.-1 p.m.)	The xiphoid process (CV 14) is vulnerable to a palm thrust, as is the lower biceps and elbow area (HT 3, TH 10, SI 8, LI 10, 11, and 12, LU 5)
Ram (1-3 p.m.)	The umbilicus area (CV 4) and pelvic basin are vulnerable to an upward kick
Monkey (3-5 p.m.)	The femoral triangle (vein, artery, and nerve) and popliteal crease (SP 9) are vulnerable to thrusting kicks
Cock (5-7 p.m.)	The ankle and Achilles tendon area are vulnerable to being kicked, stomped on, or squeezed
any time	The philtrum (GV 26) is extremely vulnerable to a single knuckle thrust, chop, palm heel, or squeeze

Posterior:

Rat (11 p.m.-1 a.m.)	The coronal suture (GV 20) is most vulnerable to a hammer fist strike
Tiger (3-5 a.m.)	The ears are most vulnerable to being slapped simultaneously
Dog (7-9 p.m.)	The seventh thoracic vertebra (GV 9) is vulnerable to an upward trauma
Boar (9-11 p.m.)	The (life gate) second and third lumbar vertebra (GV 4) are vulnerable to an upward trauma
Monkey (3-5 p.m.)	The popliteal crease (SP 9) is vulnerable to thrusting kicks

Cock (5-7 p.m.)   The ankle and Achilles tendon areas are vulnerable to being kicked, stomped on, or squeezed

As mentioned earlier, the Bronze Man statue was first forged nearly a thousand years ago to establish a nationwide standard for the science of acupuncture in ancient China (see below). Although originally produced to illustrate the 12 bilateral meridians and two centerline vessels used in acupuncture, the Bronze Man diagram featured in the Bubishi was drawn with a completely different purpose in mind. Illustrating the vital point principles of Feng Yiyuan, this old diagram, unlike the Crystal Statue diagram (see Figure 23, p. 188), focuses upon those fundamental locations most vulnerable to trauma during the 12 *shichen*.   (TR)

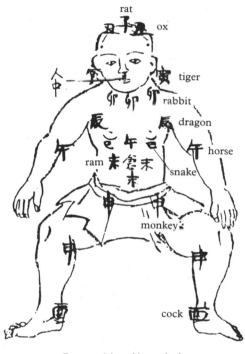

Bronze Man (Anterior)

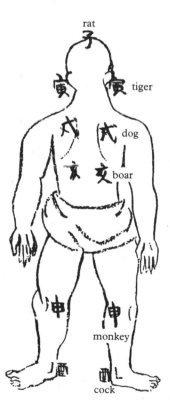

Bronze Man (Posterior)

The Chinese character for *dao* (*do* in Japanese).

PART FOUR

FIGHTING TECHNIQUES

Strategy and Technique in the Bubishi

The Bubishi is a text primarily on Yongchun White Crane and Monk Fist Boxing, two of the primary forms of Chinese *gongfu* that served as the foundation upon which modern karate-do was developed. As such this text contains a considerable amount of data on the self-defense techniques, forms, and strategies used in those arts.

Gongfu Quan

The *quan (kata* in Japanese) of Chinese *gongfu* is the ritualized method through which the secrets of self-defense have been customarily transmitted for generations. Each *quan* addresses a myriad of conceivable self-defense scenarios, but is more than just a long combination of techniques. Rather, each *quan* is a unique tradition unto itself with distinct principles, strategies, and applications. The applications of the forms were intended for use in life-and-death self-defense situations and as such can be used to restrain, hurt, maim, or even kill one's opponent when necessary.

A second but equally important aspect of the *quan* is its therapeutic use. The various animal-imitating paradigms and breathing patterns used were added to improve blood circulation and respiratory efficiency, stimulate *qi* energy, stretch muscles while strengthening them, strengthen bones and tendons, and massage the internal organs. Performing the *quan* also develops coordination as one vibrates, utilizes torque, and rotates the hips. This in turn will improve one's biomechanics and allow one to have optimum performance while utilizing limited energy.

Through regulating the breath and synchronizing it with the expansion and contraction of muscular activity, one oxygenates the blood and learns how to build, contain, and release *qi* energy. *Qi* can have a significant therapeutic effect on the body both internally and externally.

Master Wu Bin of China's Gongfu Research Institute describes the *quan* as vitally important for mobilizing and guiding the internal circulation of oxygen, balancing the production of hormones, and regulating the neural system. When performing the *quan* correctly one should energize the body and not strain excessively. In rooted postures, the back must be straight, shoulders rounded, chin pushed in, pelvis tilted up, feet firmly planted, and the body kept pliable, so that energy channels can be fully opened and the appropriate alignments cultivated.

Many people impair their internal energy pathways through smoking, substance abuse, poor diet, inactivity, and sexual promiscuity.

The unique group of alignments that are cultivated by orthodox *quan* open the body's pathways, allowing energy to flow spontaneously. The *qi* can then cleanse the neural system and regulate the function of the internal organs.

Whooping Crane Grandmaster
Jin Jingfu with the author in
Fuzhou.

In short, regular practice of the *quan* will develop a healthy body, fast reflexes, and efficient technique, helping to prepare one to respond more effectively in potentially dangerous situations.

Qin Na

Before the stylistic methods of *gongfu* were ever codified in China, *qin na* (meaning to catch or seize and hold or control) served as the very first form of self-defense. Although a compilation of self-defense skills that includes many lethal techniques, *qin na* is an art that strives to control an adversary without seriously injuring or killing him. *Qin na* practitioners will hurt rather than be hurt, maim rather than be maimed, and kill rather than be killed.

Qin na brings together techniques of twisting bones, locking joints, and separating tendons from bone; the seizing, manipulation, and striking of nerve plexuses, arteries, and other anatomically vulnerable locations; chokes and strangles; organ-piercing blows; grappling, takedowns, throws, counters, escapes, and combinations thereof. *Qin na* applications were not developed for use in the sports arena or in many cases against experienced trained warriors. In fact many of the *qin na* applications were designed for use on attackers unaware of the methods being used on them.

The hallmark of any orthodox *gongfu* style is the characteristics of their animal *quan* and the interpretation of its *qin na* principles. Based on the self-defense experiences of the style's originator, the application of *qin na* principles vary from style to style. In *gongfu, qin na* represents the application for each technique in each *quan*. In *toudi-jutsu* these techniques came to be called *bunkai*.

Modern Japanese karate-do has popularized other terms to describe specific components of *bunkai* in recent times: *torite (tuidi* in Okinawan Hogan), to seize with one's hands; *kyusho-jutsu,* vital point striking; *tegumi,* grappling hands; *kansetsu waza,* joint locks and dislocations; *shime waza,* chokes and strangulations; and *atemi waza,* general striking techniques.

Before commencing with the presentation of the articles related to fighting techniques and forms, I thought it appropriate to present a capsulized history and study of the distinctive techniques of six systems practiced in Fujian that are relevant to the Bubishi.

Capsule History of Fujian Gongfu Styles

He Quan or Crane Boxing is the general name for five styles of crane-imitating fighting arts. The five styles are: Jumping Crane, Flying Crane, Whooping Crane, Sleeping Crane, and Feeding Crane, all of which have a history of about three hundred years. However, these five styles were not completely stylized until toward the end of the Qing dynasty (1644–1911). I will also include a brief description of Monk Fist Boxing *(Luohan Quan).*

Jumping Crane *(Zonghe Quan)*
During the reign of Emperor Tong Zhi (1861–75) of the Qing dynasty, Fang Shipei, a native of Fujian's Fuqing county, went to learn *gongfu* at the Tianzhu Temple on Mount Chashan. Having studied the principles of fighting for ten years, Fang concluded that the quivering movements of birds, fish, and animals were a natural way of generating more energy. Hence, he employed the principles of body vibration when he developed the Jumping Crane style. His principal disciples included Lin Qinnan and the five brave generals of Fujian: Fang Yonghua, Chen Yihe, Xiao Kongepei, Chen Daotian, and Wang Lin.

Jumping Crane *gongfu* is a perfect example of a style that best utilizes the principles of *qin na.* Jumping Crane Boxing, like Monk Fist Boxing, also hides its intentions in its *quan,* and it includes the seizing and dislocating of opponent's joints, grappling, strangulations, and striking vital points. It is fast and slow, hard and soft, and makes use of the open palm and tips of the fingers. Like Whooping Crane Boxing, it advocates leg maneuvers and body movement to avoid direct assaults, and predetermined responses are aimed at traumatizing specific vulnerable areas of an opponent's body. Breathing exercises *(qigong),* and vigorous shaking of the hands and torso, representing the quivering of birds, fish, and animals, are readily apparent in Jumping Crane Boxing.

Whooping Crane *(Minghe Quan)*

The history of *Minghe Quan* can be traced back to *Yongchun He Quan* or Crane Boxing. In the later part of the Qing dynasty, Lin Shixian, a master of White Crane *gongfu* from Yongchun village, relocated to Fujian's thriving port city of Fuzhou, where he taught this style. Among his most noted disciples was Pan Yuba, the man responsible for teaching Xie Zhongxiang. It is said that Xie, in addition to mastering the rudiments of Yongchun White Crane *gongfu,* was also proficient in several other kinds of boxing. Combining the central elements of *Yongchun He Quan* with his own concepts of fighting, Xie developed a hybrid form of Crane Boxing called *Minghe Quan,* or Whooping Crane *gongfu,* also referred to as Singing or Crying Crane *gongfu.*

Whooping Crane Boxers derive their name from the high-pitched sound that they emit when performing some of their *quan.* The style also emphasizes forceful palm techniques, the 72 Shaolin seizing techniques, striking the 36 vital points, the use of *qi* energy, and body movement.

Sleeping Crane *(Suhe Quan)*

Becoming a recluse, Lin Chuanwu from Fuzhou's Chengmen district studied Crane Boxing at Shimen Temple in Fujian. After five years of dedicated training under Monk Jue Qing, he went back to Fuzhou and established his own school.

Sleeping Crane Boxing stresses deceiving the opponent by pretending to be half asleep. Its actions are meant to be fast and hidden, its hand techniques forceful, and footwork steady and sound. Sleeping Crane imitates the sharp clawing actions of the crane and uses the strength of the opponent against him.

Feeding Crane *(Shihe Quan)*

Ye Shaotao of Fuzhou's Changshan district had studied Feeding Crane *gongfu* from Fang Suiguan, master boxer of Beiling, at the end of the Qing dynasty and the beginning of the Republic of China (1912–49). Enhancing his overall understanding of how to attack the 36 vital points, Ye also learned from the prominent Tiger Boxer Zhou Zihe before he declared himself the master of the Feeding Crane style.

Feeding Crane Boxers pay special attention to hooking, clawing, and striking with the fingertips and palms. Principally employing the steady three-point and five plum blossom stances, Feeding Crane focuses upon single-handed attacks.

Flying Crane *(Feihe Quan)*

In the middle of the Qing dynasty, Zheng Ji learned the rudiments of

Yongchun White Crane *gongfu* from third-generation Master Zheng Li. Later Zheng Ji became well known in and around the Fuqing and Qingzhou districts for his skills in *gongfu*.

Flying Crane Boxers rove around in circles with their bodies and arms relaxed, building power and energy before passing it to their shivering hands, which are held out straight. Imitating the flight of the crane, Flying Crane Boxers also leap about, stand on one leg, and extend their arms like the bird flapping its wings. Flying Crane Boxers use pliability to overcome strength; when an opponent is powerful, they employ power to the contrary.

Monk Fist *(Luohan Quan)*

Because Monk Fist *gongfu* (sometimes referred to as Arhat Boxing) has had such a profound impact upon the evolution of karate-do I have decided to also include its capsule history. Based on the embryonic Indian exercises introduced by the Buddhist missionary monk Bodhidharma at the Shaolin monastery, *Luohan Quan* is based upon 24 defensive and offensive techniques contained in 18 combative exercises cultivated and practiced by Shaolin recluses. Monk Fist Boxing emphasizes physical strength, and knuckle and forearm development.

Basic training centers around cultivating *qi* and strength by training in hourglass *(saam chien)* and horse stances. In addition to fostering a

The author at the Henan Shaolin Temple with Abbot Si Yanpu.

healthy body and thwarting illness, Monk Fist *gongfu* has six *quan* that specialize in striking vital points with the fist, two for striking with the palms, one for using one's elbows, four *quan* for foot and leg maneuvers, and five grappling *quan*. Over the generations nine more exercises evolved from the original 18 *quan*, forming a total of 27, which were further divided into two parts constituting 54 separate skills. Disciples were required to master the application of these 54 skills on both sides, thus totaling 108.

Arhat Boxers hide their intentions in their *quan*, but are proficient in striking vital points, dislocating joints, grappling and strangulations, breathing exercises, and learn other related concepts, including herbal medicine and moral precepts. The nucleus of the system includes 72 seizing and grappling techniques and how to strike the 36 vital points.

The historical information above has been corroborated by Wu Bin, director of the Wushu Research Institute of China, Li Yiduan and Chen Zhinan of the Fuzhou Wushu Association, Tokashiki Iken, director of the Okinawan Goju-Tomari-te Karate-do Association, Otsuka Tadahiko, director of the Gojukensha, and Master Liu Songshan of Feeding Crane *gongfu*. (TR)

Articles on Fighting Techniques

Article 6: Four Quan of Monk Fist Boxing
Techniques of the First Quan

1. The way of pulling arrows
2. Putting on a necklace
3. Stamping your hand seal
4. Carrying a hoe on your shoulder
5. Carrying an iron rod on your shoulder
6. Clanging cymbals when drunk
7. Swirling in a stream
8. Scissors takedown
9. Carrying a shield
10. Place a shield in your cloak
11. Bundle and send
12. Shaking your sleeves
13. Striking the *Huai* (Chinese scholar tree)
14. Drunken man rolling like a ball
15. Dragon winding up a pole
16. Ferocious tiger
17. Strike like an iron ball
18. Strike like a mallet
19. Kick with the bottom of the foot
20. Escaping monkey
21. Evasive jumping
22. Pulling up a bamboo screen
23. Jump up from the ground
24. Swim like a frog
25. Playing in the water
26. Putting on a mask
27. Sealing the elbow

Techniques of the Second Quan

1. Playing with a ball
2. Strike like a mallet
3. Casting a net
4. Pecking with the beak
5. Throwing small stones
6. Going through the target
7. Pretend to give in
8. Powerful tiger
9. Crouching tiger
10. A school of fish swimming
11. Sweeping tail
12. Searching palm
13. Stick to the summit
14. See what can't be seen
15. Putting on clothes
16. Young tiger
17. Sticky hands
18. Strike like a mallet
19. Leg maneuvers
20. Both crescent moons
21. Strike like twin shooting stars
22. Double horn hammer thrust
23. Suspending small stones
24. Strangle
25. Knock down the bridge
26. Vibrating palm
27. Soft fist
28. Sun and moon fist

Techniques of the Third Quan

1. Flowing fists
2. Yin-yang fist
3. Escaping palm
4. Playing with a ball
5. Striking like a mallet
6. Cross block
7. Leg maneuver
8. Shaggy tiger's head
9. Soft fist
10. Left and right escaping palms
11. Thrusting the sword, grasp the ball
12. Augmented sweeping hands
13. Crossing three pagoda
14. Monkey pulls out a gimlet
15. Stick to the summit
16. Twins jumping
17. Feint with the feet
18. Iron chisel
19. Open the castle gate
20. Cat washing its face
21. Double thrust
22. Important double mallet
23. Circling tigers
24. Short pull
25. Spreading your beard
26. Sticky hands
27. Guarding the gate
28. Hanging up an ink stamp
29. Searching tiger

Techniques of the Fourth Quan

1. Putting on a necklace
2. Mrs. Jiang looking in the mirror
3. Clipping your nails
4. Right and left calm tiger
5. Take-down using the dragon and tiger hand
6. Twin crescent moons
7. Knuckle thrust with clasped hands
8. Escaping palm
9. Striking like a mallet
10. Sticky hands
11. Blue dragon in flowing water
12. Searching palm
13. Tiger stands up to kick
14. Morning heaven fist
15. Hitting with a mallet like two bull's horns
16. Hanging a curtain
17. Three-legged frog
18. General's hand
19. Three-level ball
20. Pushing palm
21. Side block
22. Pulling palm
23. Shaking palms
24. Pull out opponent's legs
25. Bat's feet
26. Break the *koto* (zither)
27. Trap a tiger in a pit covered with bamboo

If you have a teacher, you should build a training place where you can invite him to discuss his secrets and guide the disciples. Disciples should obey and do their best to provide for the teacher's needs.

The application of a number of these techniques can be found in Article 29 (see p. 268). (TR)

走外盤式

將人打一片右手一閃而我
將右脚進右肩脚即
必必從片從人射手進右肩
邊從人腰腕進邊
醫手必一從此遯實
也虛必從此會擊
邊此會悟

破打邊盤式

左脚一點右邊騰起
斜進肩必在敵人胸
下手必在敵人腿邊
眼必在敵人腿邊
醫必要緊貼敵人胸
又敵人脚窩後而我
兩脚俱開住即為雙
開法以中盤打邊盤
即為雙關此法更妙
不可岳傳進步法須
要伺斜去

中盤式此破法

左手將人右肘下
托起須從肘下
進右一手與身
緊貼腿血一法
脚窩必一團射進人
亦破敵人雖為手用片
心窩高繁脚從右手
打措掌入腿必進人
破以措掌破敵無能
矢而以身夾步不走
開而進虚法夾進
下也進球法破身
蓋以進者此能石者
法敗者法勝破身
故以進身者法

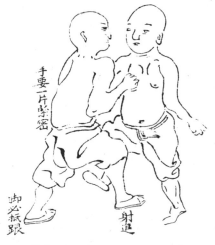

Rakanken two-person practices

Article 7: Nepai Quan

1. Salutation
2. Grab, step in, pull, and right back knuckle
3. Pivot forward, check, wrist release, and hammer fist
4. Step back and check, seize, elbow press, and thrust
5. Trap and wrist lock
6. Step back, jerk down, and kick
7. Elbow smash, back knuckle, and thrust
8. Hook, pull and outside hammer fist, seize, twist, pull, and lock
9. Pivot, check, wrist release, hammer fist, seize, and pull down
10. Pivot around, double rising block and simultaneous inside hammer fists
11. Pivot to the front, shuffle in and drop to one knee, rising block, and downward single knuckle strike
12. Stand up, uppercut and back knuckle, thrust
13. Hook, trap, pull and outside hammer fist, seize, twist, and lock
14. Pivot to the left 270 degrees, wrist release, grab and seize, pivot to the right, and augmented block
15. Pivot to the left, inside middle block, and single knuckle thrust
16. Step to the front, crane on a rock
17. Three-directional windmill hands
18. Shift back to the center, release, seize and chop
19. Pivot around to the front, check, middle block, seize, pull and lock (repeat on other side)
20. Step forward, hammer fist, and double spear-hand thrust (repeat on other side)
21. Pivot to the right, hook, snake finger thrust, trap, and palm strike
22. Pivot to the front, hook, crescent kick, and hammer fist
23. Step in, seize, wrist release, pull, and single-knuckle uppercut
24. Pivot left 270 degrees, inside middle block, and three group fists
25. Pivot to the right, middle block, and thrust
26. Pivot to left, palm check, grab, slap, crescent kick, and hammer fist (repeat on other side)
27. Slide to the left, simultaneous block and thrust (repeat on other side)
28. Shift back, deflect, grab, slide and thrust, seize, twist and lock, turn, and salutation

---

A principal *quan* of Xie Zhongxiang's *Minghe Quan gongfu*, *Nepai*, in Chinese characters, means "Twenty-Eight Strikes." It emphasizes grappling and the striking of anatomical vulnerable points. *Nepai* was first introduced to Okinawa by Go Genki when he taught it to Kyoda Juhatsu and Mabuni Kenwa. To-on-ryu was the only Okinawan style that preserved and passed on *Nepai*. Mabuni's version of *Nepai*, considerably different from the To-on-ryu version, is called *Nipaipo*, and is practiced by some sects of Shito-ryu. *Nepai* is still practiced by several styles of Fujian White Crane *gongfu*. The explanation on this page represents the original Whooping Crane version as taught to me by the great-grandson of Ryuru Ko, Xie Wenliang. (TR)

Article 13: The Eight Precepts of Quanfa

1. The human mind is one with heaven and earth.
2. Our blood circulation parallels the solar and lunar cycles of each day.
3. Inhaling represents softness while exhaling characterizes hardness.
4. Adapt to changing conditions.
5. Response must result without conscious thought.
6. Distancing and posture dictates the outcome of the meeting.
7. See what is unseeable.
8. Expect what is unexpected.

This is the only written explanation about the eight precepts in the Bubishi. However, in more current reproductions of the Bubishi, karate teachers in Japan have elaborated on these precepts. (TR)

Article 14: The Principles of Ancient Law

Once again I would like to reemphasize the importance of these ancient principles. By doing so, I hope to clear up any confusion regarding the rules of polarity and meridian flow theory. Because this law influences all people, one should practice early in the morning when the *qi* is peaceful.

If everyone learned these methods there would be less violence. These methods are intended to foster peace and harmony, not violence. If you know someone with these special skills you should ask them to teach you. The rewards of training are immeasurable for those who remain diligent and follow the correct path. However, this does not apply to those of immoral character.

When forced to fight, theory and technique are one in the same; victory depends upon who is better prepared. When engaging the adversary, respond instinctively. Movement must be fast and materialize without thought. Never underestimate your opponent, and be careful not to waste energy on unnecessary movement. If you recognize or create an opening, waste no time in taking advantage of it. Should he run, give chase but be prepared, expect the unexpected, and do not get distracted. You must evaluate everything when fighting.

Quanfa Strategies

A person may observe your fighting skills and compare them to his own. However, remember each encounter is different so respond in accordance to fluctuating circumstances and opportunity. Utilize lateral and vertical motion in all conceivable gates of attack and defense. Refrain from using an elaborate defense and remember that basic technique and common sense go a long way. I cannot emphasize enough the importance of taking advantage of an opening, and do not forget that the opposite also applies to you; always be aware of openings you present to your opponent.

If seized above the waist by an adversary, use your hands to "flutter all over him like a butterfly." If attacked below the waist, use your hands to hook him up "like a flapping fish in the water." If confronted by an adversary you must appear as confident and powerful as a wolf or tiger pursuing its prey.

Learn well the principles of "hard" and "soft" and understand their application in both the physical and metaphysical realms. Be pliable when met by force (also be a modest and tolerant person), but use force to overcome the opposite (be diligent in the pursuit of justice).

The more you train (in *quanfa*), the more you will know yourself. Always use circular motions from north to south and do not forget that there is strength in softness. Never underestimate any opponent, and be sure never to use any more force than is absolutely necessary to assure victory, lest you be defeated yourself. These are the principles of ancient law.

Article 15: Maxims of Sun Zi

1. Know both yourself and your adversary and you will not know defeat.
2. Knowing only yourself and not your adversary reduces your chances by 50%.
3. Knowing neither yourself nor your adversary means certain defeat.
4. Be serious but flexible, employing elusiveness so as not to become a victim of habit.
5. To win without fighting is the highest achievement of a warrior. Never forget this wisdom and live your life according to the principles of the warrior.

Article 16: Grappling and Escapes

1. Body language and feinting are important points in fighting. Read your adversary and make openings.
2. By taking away your adversary's balance, you will have greater opportunities for victory. Awareness and perception are strong weapons.
3. If attacked from the front, consider attacking the groin.
4. When defending against a rear hair grab, sink and turn quickly into the adversary with your hands protecting your face, then charge in, taking away his balance.
5. Should someone try to stomp on your foot, be prepared to counter with your hands.

6. Against a forceful hair pull, attack the thumb joint and take him down.
7. Low counters are the rule for high attacks.
8. Use high counters against low attacks.
9. Strategy is important in handling a skillful kicker. Do not limit yourself to only sweeping out his balance. Try to anticipate his intention, intercept the kick and scoop up the leg.
10. Be quick to take advantage of an adversary who becomes emotional, overexcited, or confused by always evaluating his mental condition.
11. When attacked from the rear, use your sense of touch and his body language to try to anticipate his intentions. Do your best to maneuver behind your opponent.
12. If you want to attack the east, first move west. Never reveal your true intentions. If you decide to move in a straight line, know what is behind you.
13. If an adversary bites you, attack his throat right away.
14. When being strangled, counter by slapping his ears or striking deeply into his ribs.
15. When dodging a stomping kick, sidestep and counter with the same technique.
16. Never execute a technique when off balance, as a skillful fighter will most certainly take advantage of the situation.
17. A superior strategist uses multilevel attacks to his advantage, rather than single kicks or punches.
18. If someone seizes your clothing, strike him with your knee.
19. Inhaling represents softness and exhaling represents hardness. Always be aware of this balance and use it to your advantage.
20. Maintain your balance while and after throwing the adversary, as it is critically important to follow up with the finishing blow.
21. Special attention must be taken fighting an opponent using the Drunken Fist method because of its unpredictability. Employing very deceptive leg maneuvers, this unorthodox style embraces limitless techniques.
22. While an opponent's low posture may reduce mobility and hamper his kicking skills, be careful as it enhances hand power. Try to get inside an opponent's high posture.
23. There is a degree of danger to oneself, and in particular to the genitals, when kicking high. Be careful not to lean too far forward or too far backward, and protect your genitals at all times.
24. If you trap your adversary's foot with your own foot, strike with your hands right away. Then run your hands from top to bottom, pulling his legs out from under him.
25. If you are taken down, make every attempt to attack the adversary's genitals.

26. Should someone attack you from behind with a bear hug, smash his face with the back of your head before counterattacking.
27. A sure way to stop other people from killing themselves in a fight is by attacking the neck artery.
28. If an adversary charges into you and grabs your lower body, use both hands to slap the ears or attack the top of his head.
29. If you want to take down an adversary, keep moving, and before initiating the throw, feint to his shadow.

Article 20: Six Ji Hands of the Shaolin Style

Injuries sustained from these special hand techniques must be treated immediately or else the consequences could be fatal.

1. The Iron Bone Hand technique can only be developed through relentless physical training. After thrusting the bare hand into a container filled with hot sand on a daily basis for many weeks, the fingers gradually become conditioned enough to initiate the second stage of training. After thrusting the bare hand into a container filled with gravel on a daily basis for many weeks, the fingers will become even more conditioned so that the final stage of conditioning can be initiated. The final stage of conditioning requires one to thrust the bare hand into a container of even larger stones. This special kind of conditioning will lead to hand deformity and the loss of one's fingernails. Alternative training methods often include thrusting the bare hand into bundles of wrapped bamboo in an effort to condition the fingers for lethal stabbing and poking. This technique is very effective for striking between the eyes. The Bone Hand technique will most certainly cause internal bleeding, especially if one is struck before mealtime. If one is struck with the Bone Hand after mealtime, the results could be fatal.

2. The Claw Hand is an effective technique and is especially effective for dislocating the jaw. Used in a circular and hooking fashion, it is a multipurpose technique. Medical treatment must be quickly rendered if struck with the Claw Hand. If not, internal hemorrhaging will be followed by three days of vomiting blood, and death within one month.

3. The Iron Sand Palm is developed in much the same way as the Iron Bone Hand. Using a wok filled with hot sand, training involves a slapping-type practice until the desired effect is accomplished. This technique is sometimes called the "Vibrating Palm." The Iron Sand Palm is an effective weapon used against many vital areas. When used against the back of the skull, it is especially lethal and could kill someone instantly.

4. The Blood Pool Hand is used to twist and pull at the eyes, throat, head, hair, and genitals. Victims of this technique must be treated with

a ginger and water solution. After applying cold water to the injured area, the victim must refrain from lying face down.

5. The Sword Hand technique is used to attack bones, tendons, and joints. It is an effective way to traumatize and subjugate an adversary. When struck by the Sword Hand a victim can experience a wide range of effects, including temporary loss of speech, unconsciousness, and seizures.

6. The One Blade of Grass Hand technique is sometimes called the "half-year killing technique," but is more popularly referred to as the "death touch." It is generally used to attack the spine and the vital points. Medical attention must be rendered immediately to anyone struck by this special technique.

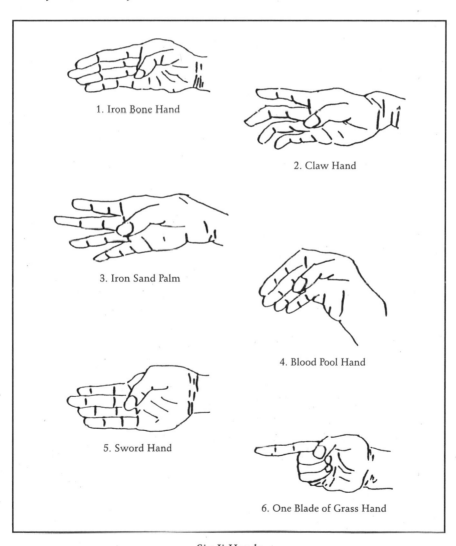

1. Iron Bone Hand

2. Claw Hand

3. Iron Sand Palm

4. Blood Pool Hand

5. Sword Hand

6. One Blade of Grass Hand

Six Ji Hands

Article 27: Zheng's Twenty-Four Iron Hand Applications and White Monkey Style

There is no explanation to accompany this illustration. However, it does say "Aunt and Uncle Zheng." I assume that they are in some way related to Zheng Lishu (see Article 1, p. 157). In the Chinese ranking system, terms like big brother and uncle are used to denote seniority. (TR)

Article 28: Eighteen Scholars White Crane Fist and Black Tiger Style Fifty-Four Step Quan

Like Article 27 (see p. 266), there is no detailed explanation to accompany this illustration. I believe that they are the names of two significant *quan*. However, they are also labeled "She Ren," which means that the two people are low-level public officials, and could mean that they were either employed by the Emperor, or an aristocrat's family. People of wealth and/or position often engaged the services of those who were skilled in medicine and also experts in the fighting arts to be bodyguards, personal self-defense teachers, and in-house doctors.

Article 29: The Forty-Eight Self-Defense Diagrams

The 48 self-defense illustrations, unlike other parts of this text, do not describe striking nerve plexus or blood canals, instead focusing on simple practical applications. These 48 self-defense illustrations can be divided into seven categories: defenses against fixed techniques, defenses against straight punches, defenses against various kinds of hand attacks, defenses against kicking techniques, how to react when grabbed, handling special circumstances, and defending against combinations.

After comparative analysis, one is easily able to recognize the remarkable similarity between these old illustrations and the many *kata* of traditional Okinawan karate-do. When comparing these 48 self-defense illustrations with other old Chinese and Japanese combative documents, I discovered a remarkable likeness with those of the Monk Fist style. I believe that this is an important discovery that brings us that much closer to locating one of the original Chinese sources from which karate-do came. Some of the names describing the applications in this segment correspond directly with the techniques in Article 6 (see pp. 257–258), on the four Monk Fist *quan*. Matsuda Takatomo *Sensei, gongfu* expert and author of *Rakan Ken (Monk Fist Boxing)* described the unidentified "hand and foot postures" of Article 32 as a typical "old-style *quan*" from his style.

In the following section I will first give the literal translation of the Chinese names for the techniques depicted in the illustrations, then I will describe the actual techniques. (TR)

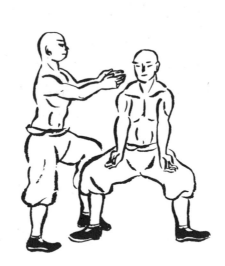

WINNING TECHNIQUE
One thousand pounds falls to the ground

LOSING TECHNIQUE
Bell and drum sounding together

1. To defend against someone who has you in a bear hug *(left),*
escape by dropping down in your stance *(right).*

白猿盜菓手敗　　黑虎出欄手勝

WINNING TECHNIQUE
Black tiger rushing out from the cage

LOSING TECHNIQUE
White monkey stealing fruit

2. If an attacker attempts to lunge out to strike you *(left)*,
jam the attack, cutting off the assault in its midst *(right)*.

落地交剪刀手勝　　撥水求魚手敗

WINNING TECHNIQUE
*Dropping to the ground and
capturing legs like scissors*

LOSING TECHNIQUE
*Trying to catch a fish by moving
hands in the water*

3. If an attacker is vigorously trying to grab you *(right)*,
quickly drop to the ground and scissor his leg *(left)*.

LOSING TECHNIQUE
Child holding a lotus flower

WINNING TECHNIQUE
General holding a seal/stamp

4. Against a smaller attacker who grabs you *(left)*,
counter by grabbing the back of the head (or hair) with one hand while lifting
the chin with the other and twisting the head *(right)*.

LOSING TECHNIQUE
Climbing mountain to hunt tigers

WINNING TECHNIQUE
Bowing to cut onions

5. It is often a good strategy to seize an attacker's leg *(right)* if he
follows a hand technique with a high kick that compromises his balance *(left)*.

雙叉炉並灭手勝

單刀破竹手敗

WINNING TECHNIQUE
Gathering around a fire

LOSING TECHNIQUE
Breaking bamboo

6. If an attacker telegraphs his intentions by using long swinging motions *(right)*, make use of your distancing with evasive body movements while blocking with your hands to position yourself for an effective counter *(left)*.

羅漢開門手敗

小鬼拔闖手勝

LOSING TECHNIQUE
Arhat opening the door

WINNING TECHNIQUE
Small demon trying to remove door bar

7. When attacked by a downward overhead strike *(left)*, step in and counter with a simultaneous block and counterpunch *(right)* to the midsection.

WINNING TECHNIQUE
One hand holding up a golden lion

LOSING TECHNIQUE
Twin dragons playing in the water

8. In the midst of a grappling encounter where a person is trying to strike your head *(right)*, block the attack *(left)*, seize the arm, and apply a joint lock at the elbow to defeat him.

WINNING TECHNIQUE
Scissors on ground, pretending to fall over

LOSING TECHNIQUE
Using cymbals

9. If an attacker tries to grab you with both hands *(right)*, drop to the ground, capture his leg *(left)* and take him down.

LOSING TECHNIQUE
White monkey breaking bamboo

WINNING TECHNIQUE
Twin dragons playing with a pearl

10. If an attacker tries to take you down by grabbing your leg *(left)*,
counter by striking the temples *(right)* or slapping the ears.

LOSING TECHNIQUE
Four horses on the loose

WINNING TECHNIQUE
Tiger pulling down a boar

11. In the heat of grappling, you can win by scooping up
the opponent's legs *(right)* and flipping him over.

LOSING TECHNIQUE
Butterfly fluttering

WINNING TECHNIQUE
Moving one thigh

12. If an attacker assaults you with a vigorous combination of punches *(left)*, you can defeat him by going low and scooping up either leg and attacking the inside of the thigh, taking him down *(right)*.

LOSING TECHNIQUE
Phoenix facing the sun

WINNING TECHNIQUE
Blue dragon going out to seize

13. If someone fakes a punch with one hand to hit you with the other (especially an uppercut) *(left)*, you should check the feint, move in, and trap the second while seizing his larynx *(right)*.

進步單機手存要節敗

身化辺門用三角戰手勝

LOSING TECHNIQUE
Advancing single ji hand

WINNING TECHNIQUE
One-sided triangular horse-ride step

14. If an attacker reaches out to grab, push, or punch you *(left),*
redirect his energy and apply a joint lock *(right).*

扭髮撞脑手敗

鎖喉寒陽手勝

LOSING TECHNIQUE
Grab hair to push

WINNING TECHNIQUE
Seize the larynx and testicles

15. If an attacker grabs you by the hair *(left),*
seize both his larynx and testicles *(right).*

WINNING TECHNIQUE
Drunken arhat

LOSING TECHNIQUE
Single ji *hand*

16. Often it is essential to deceive an attacker to make an opening. Use the
Drunken Fist method to feign intoxication, weakness, or cowardice *(left)*
and when he lets down his guard, immediately counterattack.

LOSING TECHNIQUE
Golden carp facing the sky

WINNING TECHNIQUE
Beautiful woman wearing make-up

17. In a grappling encounter when an attacker chambers his hand to
strike you *(left),* reach out and seize his larynx and hair *(right)*
to manipulate the head and defeat him.

獅戲珠手敗

虎撲地手勝

LOSING TECHNIQUE
Lion playing with a ball

WINNING TECHNIQUE
Tiger strikes the earth

18. Regardless of an attacker's size or strength, you can take him
down by seizing the leg with one hand and pushing the
inside of the knee or hip joint with the other *(right).*

孩兒抱蓮手敗

短打穿心手改之勝

LOSING TECHNIQUE
Child holding a lotus flower

WINNING TECHNIQUE
Short hit through heart

19. In a grappling encounter in which you have little room to move,
you must attack the weak areas like the eyes, ears, nose, and larynx *(right).*

WINNING TECHNIQUE
Seizing ox, sweeping leg

LOSING TECHNIQUE
Two tigers

20. By twisting an attacker's wrists *(left)*, his balance is weakened, which permits you to follow up by sweeping his legs out from under him.

LOSING TECHNIQUE
Going through small gate with one side then hitting

WINNING TECHNIQUE
Squatting with legs wider than shoulders and seizing the leg

21. Another way to defeat an attacker is by seizing one leg *(right)* and kicking the other out from under him.

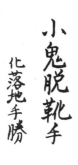

WINNING TECHNIQUE
*Little demons remove their boots
and squat down*

LOSING TECHNIQUE
Big step, hold up

22. By capturing an attacker's leg, either when he is moving or attempting a high kick, you can lift it up beyond its limit, causing him to fall on his head.

LOSING TECHNIQUE
Iron ox hits stone

WINNING TECHNIQUE
*Catching ribs like a carp jumping
out of the water*

23. The art of deception is a powerful tool. If you can make an
attacker think that you have mistakenly left a target undefended,
it will be easy to anticipate his attack and counter it.

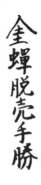

WINNING TECHNIQUE
Golden cicada slipping out of its shell

LOSING TECHNIQUE
Carp jumping into a well

24. If an attacker reaches out to grab you *(top),* you can surprise him by dropping to the ground and throwing him over your body *(bottom).*

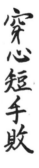

LOSING TECHNIQUE
Short piercing attack

WINNING TECHNIQUE
Using cymbals

25. If a person pushes, shoves, or tries to poke you in the eyes *(left),* you can overpower him by shifting just outside the attack and simultaneously striking behind the ear and the lower ribs *(right).*

羅漢播身手勝

手足齊到敗

WINNING TECHNIQUE
Arhat turns his body

LOSING TECHNIQUE
Hands and feet arrive simultaneously

26. Against someone who throws a one-sided, punch-kick combination *(right)*, utilize the evasive principles of Monk Fist Boxing by checking the punch and sliding outside the attack to defeat the attacker *(left)*.

後亭採標手勝

後背伏虎手敗

WINNING TECHNIQUE
Seize testicles behind

LOSING TECHNIQUE
Tiger crouching behind

27. Against a rear bear hug *(right)*, take one step forward, raising an arm to destroy the attacker's balance, while seizing his testicles with the other hand *(left)*.

WINNING TECHNIQUE
Carp turning its body

LOSING TECHNIQUE
Mount Tai pushing down an egg

28. If an attacker tries to strike down on your head *(right),* counter with an "X-block," twist his arm *(left),* and throw him.

WINNING TECHNIQUE
Child picking up a lotus

LOSING TECHNIQUE
Golden turtle lying on the ground

29. You can defeat an attacker by scooping up one leg *(left)* and flipping him over on his back.

LOSING TECHNIQUE
Tiger mauls its prey

WINNING TECHNIQUE
Monkey threading a needle

30. By checking a punch or pulling a push and striking a vital point *(right)*, it is easy to defeat an inexperienced attacker *(left)*.

WINNING TECHNIQUE
Going to fight with one knife

LOSING TECHNIQUE
Fighting alone at the gate of an official residence

31. If an attacker reaches out to punch or grab you *(right)*, step to his outside *(left)*, grab his lead arm, and apply an arm-bar, foot-sweep combination to defeat him.

鳳展翅手勝

龍吐珠手敗

WINNING TECHNIQUE
Phoenix spreads its wings

LOSING TECHNIQUE
Dragon spits pearls

32. If a person throws a short punch at you *(right)*,
trap the attack and gouge his eyes *(left)*.

麒麟擺口手敗

金獅搖頭手勝

LOSING TECHNIQUE
Qilin *(Chinese unicorn)* opens
its mouth to eat

WINNING TECHNIQUE
Golden lion shakes its mane

33. When a person tries to trip you *(left)*, check his attack, seize his hair, poke his
eyes, grab his groin *(right)*, then pull his hair down to throw him to the ground.

WINNING TECHNIQUE
Phoenix pecking at a pearl

LOSING TECHNIQUE
White crane folds its wings

34. If a person tries to smash his hand into your torso *(right)*,
move in and use your arms (palms twisted out) to reduce the impact of
his attack, and then counter with the phoenix fist *(left)*.

WINNING TECHNIQUE
Raindrops on flower petals

LOSING TECHNIQUE
Thunder hitting a tree

35. If a person abruptly seizes you *(right)*,
be pliable, go with the flow, and strike his eyes *(left)*.

佛座蓮手勝

虎偷心手敗

WINNING TECHNIQUE
Buddha sitting on a lotus

LOSING TECHNIQUE
Tiger steals heart

36. An overconfident attacker *(right)* can be defeated by checking an attack and dropping down to seize the testicles *(left)*.

獨角牛手敗

存一柔手勝

LOSING TECHNIQUE
One-horned ox

WINNING TECHNIQUE
Keeping a flower

37. When attacked with a fierce straight punch *(left)*, move outside and check the attack before countering *(right)*.

WINNING TECHNIQUE
Two hands worshipping the Buddha

LOSING TECHNIQUE
Rain wet through to body

38. If a person grabs you in an effort to throw you *(right)*, shift back a little to offset his balance, chop down on his arms to loosen the grip, and then by coming outside and then looping up and under his arms, lock his elbow joints *(left)*.

WINNING TECHNIQUE
Pulling then hitting back

LOSING TECHNIQUE
Twisting the head

39. By grabbing an attacker's wrist and pulling him off balance, you can strike his armpit or throat with your elbow *(left)* before locking his arm to throw him down.

獨壺戰手勝

準合掌手敗

WINNING TECHNIQUE
Fighting alone

LOSING TECHNIQUE
Closing the hands in prayer

40. You can defeat a person who tries to grab you *(right)*
by sinking down and striking a single vital point *(left)*.

日月足手勝

風雲拳手敗

WINNING TECHNIQUE
Sun and moon hand

LOSING TECHNIQUE
Wind cloud boxing

41. If an attacker gets inside your engagement distance and tries to attack your
ribs with both hands *(right)*, be sure to distance yourself precisely before
attempting to counter *(left)*.

WINNING TECHNIQUE
Press blossoms down

LOSING TECHNIQUE
Straight plum blossoms strike

42. Lateral body movement *(left)* will present you with the precise space needed to defeat an attacker *(right)* if you can accurately determine his distance.

WINNING TECHNIQUE
Flag and drum gesture

LOSING TECHNIQUE
Sword and shield posture

43. If an attacker remains locked in his posture too long *(right)*, he will be unable to prevent a powerful hand attack *(left)*.

LOSING TECHNIQUE
Tiger hitting waist

WINNING TECHNIQUE
Leopard shows its fangs

44. If a person's offense is hampered because of poor coordination *(left)*,
you can avoid his attack by shifting your body to the side *(right)* and defeat him.

WINNING TECHNIQUE
Left and right wings

LOSING TECHNIQUE
Front and back twisting

45. At close range, if a person tries to punch your body
(especially with an uppercut) *(right)*, trap the attack and thrust your
fingers into his throat to defeat him *(left)*.

伸猿背手勝

出戰機手敗

WINNING TECHNIQUE
Monkey stretches its arms

LOSING TECHNIQUE
Going to fight ji *hand*

46. Be quick to seize an opportunity *(left)* if your attacker
loses his balance after missing his intended target *(right)*.

化鉄牛手勝

存節度手敗

WINNING TECHNIQUE
Charging iron bull

LOSING TECHNIQUE
Keeping strength

47. In the case of a person who hesitates during his attack *(right)*,
quickly close the distance and counter with the vertical
downward palm strike to defeat him *(left)*.

十文打手敗

獨拳鼎手勝

LOSING TECHNIQUE
Cross gesture

WINNING TECHNIQUE
Single hand holding up a vessel

48. If a person is trying to inch his way inside your engagement distance and presents a large target *(left),* feint an attack with one hand horizontally, and when he reacts, come down on top of his head with the other hand *(right).*

This calligraphy by Grandmaster Hokama Tetsuhiro means "auspicious crane" and was brushed as a congratulatory keepsake for this publication.

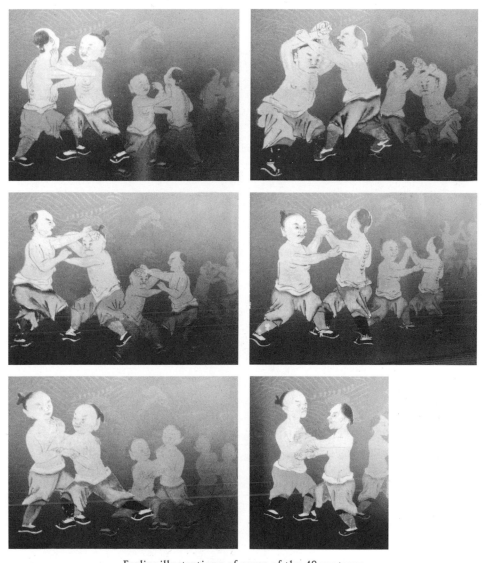

Earlier illustrations of some of the 48 postures

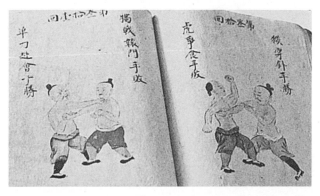

Two pages from the
original Bubishi

Article 32: Shaolin Hand and Foot, Muscle and Bone Training Postures

There is no descriptive text accompanying the illustrations that follow. The illustrations represent the individual combative postures of an original *gongfu quan*. The name of each movement and its self-defense application has been lost in the sands of time. Therefore, the exact details surrounding the origins and purposes of this particular *quan* are not available. However, by analyzing each of the illustrations, one can observe crane stances, crescent kicks, one-fingered thrusts, open-handed techniques, all of which are used in Monk Fist and Crane Boxing. (TR)

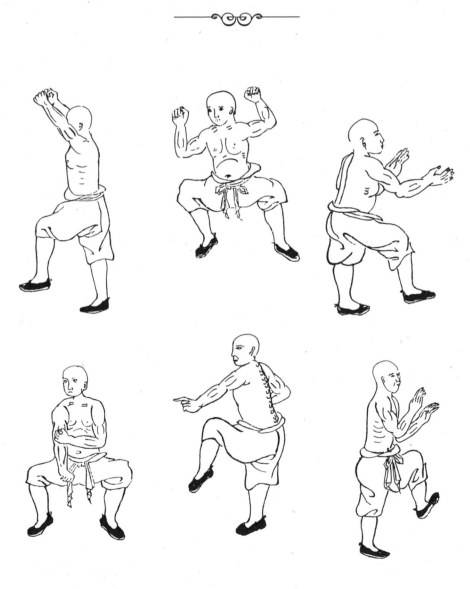

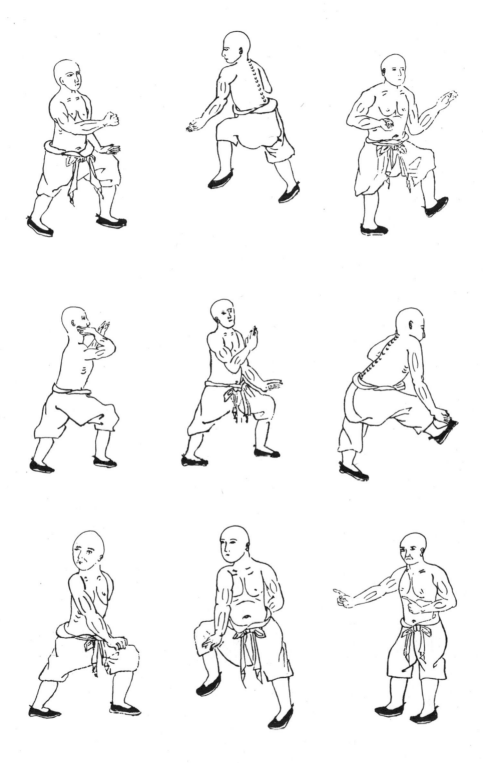

The Chinese characters for *toudi-jutsu* (or *karate-jutsu*), the first character of which refers to the Tang dynasty, and karate-do, "the way of the empty hand."

✺ Conclusion ✺

The Bubishi is a work of great breadth in terms of its subject matter and great depth academically and philosophically. As we have seen, its impact on karate-do has been significant both in terms of philosophy and technique. When Miyagi Chojun said that the Bubishi was "the Bible of karate-do," his choice of words was particularly appropriate. Just as Christians use the Bible as a textual guide for their lives, the Bubishi is a text to assist karateka as they tackle the challenges of life and begin on the path to perfection in its physical, psychological, and spiritual forms. The Bubishi is a key that opens the door to a new dimension of karate training and to understanding the universe and one's place in it.

Those familiar with the power of combining rigorous physical discipline with philosophical study can readily testify to the self-conquests made possible through karate-do. However, before the light inside each of us can ever be turned on we must balance physical with the nonphysical by mastering the ritual of silence and breathing, meditation.

The methodical and protracted introspection made possible by meditation is of vital importance to the growth and maturity of each and every individual who studies karate-do, regardless of how ignorant or skeptical they may at first be. It is ritual performance that draws our attention inward, to where a lifelong journey of harmony is pursued. Performing orthodox *kata* is a form of ritual meditation that develops power and strength and, as contradictory as it sounds, it is through this process that one learns humility and gentleness. In so doing, karate-do becomes a fascinating vehicle of inner exploration through which untold personal rewards are made possible.

However, it takes a long time to understand that there is something beyond the immediate results of physical training. Insight takes place slowly and is the product of personal sacrifice and diligent effort. To be the best one can be, whether in fighting, sports, business, or school, requires resolve and inner strength. A mind tempered in the tradition of true karate-do will remain impervious to worldly delusion and illuminate the darkness of selfishness and ignorance. With greater control over our minds, we have greater control over our bodies, lives, and the exterior world of which we are a part. It is by putting this power to work every day that our lives are enriched and fulfilled in ways we never thought possible.

Through adhering to the precepts of karate-do, one also comes face to face with one's weaknesses. It is through this process that weaknesses are turned into strengths, and strengths into even greater strengths. The indomitable fortitude created by karate training insulates us against the forces of immoral temptation and irresponsible action while providing the resilience to withstand the personal failures that test each of us along life's unrelenting path.

Life presents us with many issues we must all address sooner or later, a few of which include: aging, the way we think, our urges and sexuality, the necessity to know ourselves, the need to find a reason for existence, and coming to terms with our mortality. As such there will always be a need for traditions that have the answers to these questions. Karate-do is one such tradition. It teaches us to understand that everything in the circle of life is seasonal, changing, dying, and being reborn. A microcosm of the *dao,* karate-do teaches us to understand these changes, accept them, and live in harmony with them. In so doing we need no longer fear the mysterious or inevitable as we embrace the circle of life.

The beginning of wisdom starts with a desire for discipline. Through studying the past we are brought closer to understanding the present. My analysis of the Bubishi has had a profound affect upon not only my art, but upon my life in general. I hope that the glimpse of the past provided by the Bubishi and its profound teachings will have as positive an influence on you as it has on me, and that it has brought you closer to that which you have yet to discover.

≪ Bibliography ≫

IN ENGLISH:

Beijing Medical College. *Dictionary of Traditional Chinese Medicine.* Hong Kong: The Commercial Press, 1987.

Ellis, Andrew, Nigel Wiseman, and Ken Boss. *Grasping the Wind.* Brookline: Paradigm Books, 1989.

Flaws, Bob. *Hit Medicine.* Boulder: Blue Poppy Press, 1983.

Funakoshi Gichin. *Karate-do Kyohan.* Translated by Tsutomu Oshima. Tokyo: Kodansha International, 1973.

Fuzhou Wushu Association. *Fuzhou Wushu.* Fuzhou: 1993.

Haines, Bruce. *Karate's History & Traditions (Revised Edition).* Tokyo: Charles E. Tuttle Publishing Company, 1995.

Haring, Douglas. *Okinawan Customs: Yesterday and Today.* Tokyo: Charles E. Tuttle Publishing Company, 1969.

Hsieh, H.Y. *Advanced Dim Mak.* China: Meadea Enterprises, 1991.

_____. *Dim Mak (Dim Hsueh) the Poison Hand Touch of Death.* China, Meadea Enterprises, 1993.

Jin, Yiming. *Secrets of Wudang Boxing.* Translated by Patrick and Yuriko McCarthy. Yokohama: International Ryukyu Karate Research Society, 1994.

Kerr, George H. *Okinawa: History of an Island People.* Tokyo: Charles E. Tuttle Publishing Company, 1958.

Keys, John D. *Chinese Herbs.* Tokyo: Charles E. Tuttle Publishing Company, 1976.

Manaka, Yoshio, and Ian A. Urguhart. *The Layman's Guide to Acupuncture.* Tokyo: Weatherhill, 1972.

McCarthy, Patrick. *Classical Kata of Okinawan Karate.* Burbank: Ohara Publications, 1987.

Miyagi, Chojun. *Outline of Karate-do.* Translated by Patrick McCarthy. Fujisawa: International Ryukyu Karate Research Society, 1993.

Montaigue, Erle. *Dim-Mak.* Boulder: Paladin Press, 1993.

Motobu, Choki. *Okinawan Kempo Karate-jutsu.* Translated by Seiyu Oyata. Olathe: Ryukyu Imports Inc., 1977.

Nagamine, Shoshin. *The Essence of Okinawan Karate-do.* Translated by Shinzato Katsuhiko. Tokyo: Charles E. Tuttle Publishing Company, 1976.

Rogers, Carole and Cameron Rogers. *Point Location and Point Dynamics Manual.* Sydney: Acupuncture Colleges (Australia), 1979.

Smith, Robert W. *Chinese Boxing: Masters and Methods.* Tokyo: Kodansha International, 1974.

Van Wolferen, Karel. *Enigma of Japanese Power.* London: MacMillan, 1989.

Wu, Bin. *Essentials of Chinese Wushu.* Beijing: Foreign Language Press, 1992.

Yang, Jwing-Ming. *Analysis of Shaolin Chin Na.* Jamaica Plain: YMAA Publication Center, 1991.

IN JAPANESE:

Funakoshi, Gichin. *Karate-do Kyohan.* Tokyo: Kobundo, May 1935.

——.*Ryukyu Kempo Toudi.* Tokyo: Bukyosha, 1922.

Hokama, Tetsuhiro. *Karate-do no Ayumi.* Naha: IKO, 1984.

Imamura, Yoshi. *Nihon Budo Zenshu,* Vol. 5. Tokyo: Jinbutsu Oraisha, 1967.

Itoman, Seishin. *Toudi-jutsu no Kenkyu.* Tokyo: Shinkokaku, July 1934.

Kinjo, Hiroshi. *Shashin de Oboeru Karate no Naraikata.* Tokyo: Yuki Shobu, 1967.

Liu, Yinshan. *Hakutsuru Mon: Shokutsuru Ken.* Tokyo: Narumido, 1983.

Mabuni, Kenwa. *Kobo Jizai Karate Kempo Seipai no Kenkyu.* Tokyo: Nakasone Genwa Kobukan, 1934.

Matsuda, Takatomo. *Rakan Ken.* Tokyo: Tsuchiya Shoten, 1990.

Miki, Nisaburo and Takada Mizuho. *Kempo Gaisetsu.* Tokyo: Tokyo Teikoku Daigaku Kempobu, January 1930.

Miyagi, Tokumasa. *Karate no Rekishi.* Naha: Hirugisha, 1987.

Nagamine, Shoshin. *Okinawa no Karate Sumo Meijin Den.* Tokyo: Shinjinbutsu Oraisha, 1986.

Nakasone, Genwa. *Karate-do Taikan.* Tokyo: Tosho Kabushiki Kaisha, 1938.

Otsuka, Tadahiko. *Chugoku Kempo Dai Koza.* Tokyo: Chugoku Kempo Shinko Kai, 1978.

——.*Goju Kensha Karate-do Kyo Hon.* Tokyo: Goju Kensha Karate-do Renmei, 1977.

——.*Jintai Kyushozu.* Tokyo: Chugoku Kempo Shinko Kai, 1975.

——.*Okinawa Den* Bubishi. Tokyo: Baseball magazine, 1986.

Sakagami, Ryusho. *Karate-do Taikan.* Tokyo: Nichibo Shuppansha, 1978.

Uechi, Kanei and Takamiyagi Shigeru. *Okinawa Karate-do Sono Rekishi to Gihon.* Ginowan: Uechi-ryu Karate-do Kyokai, 1977.

Yamaguchi, Gogen. *Goju no Ibuki.* Tokyo: Eiko Shuppansha, 1966.

IN CHINESE:

Cheng, Chi Fuwang. *Fujian Shaolin Gou Quan.* Taiwan: Hua Lian, 1988.

Hou, Ji Hwaun, Sun Zong Shun, and Yen Bao Sheng. *He Quan Fujian Nan Quan.* Fuzhou: Fujian Renrenda Banshe, 1982.

Huang, Ti. *Nei Ching.* Translated by Wu Hong Cho. China: Ba Shu, 1987.

Hwaung, Tsun Ming. *Shaolin Luohan Quan.* Taiwan: Hua Lian, 1987.

Qi, Jiguang. *Ji Xiao Xin Shu.* Reproduced by Chang Hi and Rour Yei Shio. Taiwan: Hua Lian, 1986.

Li, Yi Chung. *Nan Quan Pai.* Taiwan: Hua Lian, 1987.

Li, Yingang. *Tan Tui Fa Ru Men.* Taiwan: Hua Lian, 1972.

Wei, Qiqi, Hu Jinhuan, and Sun Chongxiong. *Hu Xing Quan Fujian Nan Quan Cong Shu.* Fuzhou: Fujian Renrenda Banshe, 1985.

Yang, Chin Chi. *He Quan.* Taiwan: Hua Lian, 1987.

Yeer, Chinghi, and Shu Jingdong. *Wu Zu Quan.* Taiwan: Hua Lian, 1976.

Zhou, Huanzong. *Nan Pat Shaolin Quan.* Taiwan: Hua Lian, 1986' *WuBeiZhi.* Fuzhou: 1834.

MAGAZINES:

Lee, Toon. "*Dian-Xue:* Hitting the Vital Points." *Secrets of Gongfu Magazine,* no. 15 (1977).

Wong, Chun-Ying. "The Relationship Between Acupuncture and *Gongfu.*" *Secrets of Gongfu Magazine,* nos. 6 and 7 (1986).

——."The Science of the Chinese Martial Arts." *Secrets of Gongfu Magazine* nos. 2, 3, and 4 (1977).

⊰ List of Chinese and Japanese Terms ⊱

aji 按司
Anhui 安徽
anji 安司
Aragaki Seishō 新垣世璋
Arhat Boxing 羅漢拳
Ason アソン
atemi waza 当身技

Beiling 北嶺
Ben Cao Gang Mu 本草綱目
Black Tiger Fifty-Four Step Quan
　　黑虎五十四步
Blood Pool Hand 撒攬手
bō-jutsu 棒術
Bronze Man 銅人
Bubishi 武備志
budō 武道
Bunbu Ryōdō 文武両道
bunkai 分解
bushi 武士
bushidō 武士道

Chen Yuanbin 陳元斌
Chengmen 城門
chikusaji pechin 筑佐事親雲上
chikudun pechin 筑登之親雲上
Chūkyō 中框
Chūzan 中山
Claw Hand 爪手
Confucius 孔子
Crane Boxing 鶴拳
Crystal Man 琉璃人

Dai Nippon Butokukai 大日本武徳会
daimyō 大名
dan-kyū 段級
Dao De Jing 道德經

dao 道
di 手
dian xue 點穴
dim mak 點脉
dō 道
Dog Boxing 犬拳
Doonquan 十三步連
Dragon Boxing 龍拳

Eagle Claw Wang 鷹爪王
Edo 江戸
Eighteen Scholar Fists 十八学士拳
eku (kai) 櫂

Fang Huishi 方慧石
Fang Shipei 方世培
Fang Zhonggong 方種公
Fang Suiguan 方水官
Fang Qiniang 方七娘
Feeding Crane 食鶴拳
Feng Yiyuan 馮一元
Five Fragrance Herbal Powder 五香散
Fu Xi 伏羲
Fujian 福建
Funakoshi Gichin 富名腰義珍 (船越
　　義珍）
Fuqing 福清
Fuzhou 福州

Gao Wu 高武
*General Outline and Division of Herbal
　　Medicine* 本草綱目
Gōjū-ryū 剛柔流
Gokenki 呉賢貴
gongfu 功夫
Guangdong (province) 廣東

Hanashiro Chomo　花城長茂
Hanshi　範士
Happoren　八歩連
He Fengming　何鳳鳴
He Quan　鶴拳
Hebei (province)　河北
Heian (period)　平安
Henan (province)　河南
Higashimura　東村
Higashionna Kanryō　東恩納寛量
Higashionna Kanryū　東恩納寛裕
Higashionna Kanyō　東恩納寛用
Hogen Monogatari　保元物語
Hong Wu　洪武
Hua Tuo　華陀
Huang Baijia　黄白家
Huang Di　黄帝
Huang Li Tang　黄理湯
Huang Zongxi　黄宗義
Hunan (province)　湖南

Iron Bone Hand　鉄骨手
Iron Sand Palm　鉄沙手
Isshin-ryū　一心流
Itosu Anko　糸州安恒
Iwah　イワー

Ji Ming San　鶏鳴散
Jia Jing　嘉靖
Jiang Xiuyuan　蔣修元
Jigen-ryū　示現流
Jin Yiming　金一明
jō　杖
Jue Qing　覺清
Jumping Crane　蹤鶴拳
Jun Chen Fang　君臣方
Jūanporen　十三歩連
Jūsen　柔箭

kai　櫂
kama　鎌
Kanō jigorō　嘉納治五郎
kansetsu waza　関節技
karate (Chinese hand)　唐手

karate (Empty hand)　空手
karate-dō　空手道
karate-jutsu　空手術
keimochi　系持
keisatsu　警察
Kempō Karate-jutsu Hiden　拳法空手術秘伝
kempō　拳法
ken-jutsu　劍術
kentōshi　遺唐使
ki　氣
Kinjō Hiroshi　金城裕
Kyoda Jūhatsu　許田重発
kobu-jutsu　古武術
kobudō　古武道
Kojō Kaho　湖城嘉宝
Kojō Taitei　湖城大韻
kokutai　国体
Konishi Yasuhiro　小西康裕
Kume　久米
kumiai-jutsu　組合術
Kuninda　久米村
Kusankun　公相君
Kyōshi　教士
Kyōho-jutsu　急所術

Lao Zi　老子
Li Shizhen　李時珍
Li Yiduan　李一端
Light Body Way Vitality Elixir　輕身法
Lin Chuanwu　林傳務
Liu Songshan　劉嵩山
Luohan Quan　羅漢拳

Mabuni Kenwa　摩文仁賢和
magiri　間切り
Maki-minato　牧港
Mao Yuanyi　茅元儀
Master and Servant Treatment　君臣方
Matsumura Sokon　松村宗棍
Medicine Worth Ten Thousand Gold Pieces　萬金丹

Meiji (era)　明治
menkyo　免許
Minamoto Tametomo　源為朝
Ming dynasty　明朝
Minghe Quan　鳴鶴拳
Miyagi Chōjun　宮城長順
Monbusho　文部省
Monk Fist Boxing　羅漢拳
Motobu Chōki　本部朝基
Mount Chashan　茶山

Naha　那覇
Nakaima Norisato　仲井間憲里
Nepai　二十八
Nijūhiho　二十四歩
Nipaipo　二十八歩
Niseishi　二十四
Nishimura　西村
niya　仁屋

Okinawa Kempō Karate-jutsu
　Kumite　沖縄拳法空手術組手
okumiza　大与座
One Blade of Grass Hand　一路草技手
Ōshima Hikki　人島筆記
Ōshima Incident　大島筆記
Ōtsuka Hironori　大塚博紀
Ōzato　大里

Paipuren　八歩連
Pan Yuba　潘嶋八
pechin　親雲上
Peichurrin　壱白零八手

Qi jiguang　戚繼光
qi　氣
qigong　氣功
Qijing　七景（錦）
qin na　擒拿
Qing dynasty　清朝
Qing Shen Fa　輕身法
Qiyang　祁陽
Qixiao Xinshu　起効新書
quan　拳

quanfa　拳法
Quan Kui　全魁

Ren Zong　仁宗
Riyu　利勇
rokushaku bō　六尺棒
Rooster Crowing Powder　鶏鳴散
Roujin　柔箭
Ruei-ryū　劉衛流
ryūakusei　留学生
Ryūyū　琉球
Ryūyū *kempō toudi-jutsu*　琉球拳法
　唐手術
Ryūyū *kempō* karate-jutsu　琉球拳法
　唐手術
Ryuru Ko　如如哥

Saam Chien　三戦
Sakugawa Kanga　佐久川寛賀
Sanchin　三戦
Sanseim　三十六手
Sanshikan　三司官
sapposhi　冊封使
Satsuma　薩摩
Satto　察度
satunushi　里主（里之子）
Secrets of Kempō Karate-jutsu　拳法空
　手術秘伝
Secrets of Wudang Boxing　武當拳術
　秘訣
seipai　十八手
seiru　十六手
Seisan　十三手
Sekigahara　関ケ原
senpai　先輩
Sensei　先生
Sha Lian Liu　沙蓮流
shakuhachi　尺八
Shaolin Bronze Man Book　少林銅人簿
Shaolin Temple　少林寺
Shen Nong　神農
shichen　時辰
Shichikei　七景（錦）
Shifu　師父

Shihan 師範

Shihe Qunn 食鶴拳

Shimabukuro Tatsuo 島袋龍夫

Shimazu Yoshihisa 島津義久

shime waza 閉技

Shimen Temple 石門寺

Shiohira 潮平

Shitō-ryū 糸東流

shizoku 士族

Shō Nei 尚寧

Shō Shin 尚真

Shōei-ryū 昭霊流

Showa (era) 昭和

shugyō 修行

Shunten 舜天

Shuri 首里

Six *Ji* Hands 六機手

Sleeping Crane 宿鶴拳

Sōke 宗家

Song dynasty 宋朝

Suhe Quan 宿鶴拳

Sui dynasty 隋朝

Sun Zi 孫子

Suparinpei 壱白零八手

taijiquan 太極拳

Taiki 泰期

Taishō (era) 大正

Tales of Hogen War 保元物語

Tang Daji 唐大基

Tang Dianqing 唐殿卿

Tang dynasty 唐朝

te 手

tegumi 手組

Teijunsoku Uekata 程順則親方

"Teng Shan" Wang Foudeng 藤山王缶登

Teruya Kanga 照屋寛賀

Thirty-Six Families 三十六姓

Tianzhu Temple 天竹寺

Tiger Boxing 虎拳

Tobe Ryōen 戸部良熙

Tōgō Bizen no Kami Shigekata 東郷肥前守重方

Tomoyose Ryuru 友寄隆優

Tong Zhi 同治

Tori Hori 鳥堀

Tosa 土佐

toudi (karate) 唐手

toudi-jutsu 唐手術

Tsuken Koura 津堅幸良

Twenty-Four Iron Hands 二十四鉄沙手

uchideshi 內弟子

Uchinanchu 沖縄人

Uechi Kanbun 上地完文

Uechi-ryū 上地流

Unten 運天

Urazoe 浦添

Wa 和

Wai Xinxian 准振山

Wan Jin Dan 萬金丹

Wang Foudeng 王缶登

Wang Wei 王惟

Wang Zhengnan 王征南

White Monkey Style 白猿手

Whooping Crane 鳴鶴拳

Wu Bin 呉彬

Wudang Quanshu Mijue 武當拳術秘訣

Wu Xiang San 五香散

wu ye mei 五葉梅

Wushu 武術

Xiang Guo Temple 相國寺

Xie Wenliang 謝文亮

Xie Zhongxiang 謝崇祥

Xu Wenbo 徐文伯

Yabu Kentsū 屋部憲通

Yagajijima Island 屋我地島

Yamaguchi Gōgen 山口剛玄

Yang Zai 陽載

Ye Shaotao 葉紹陶

Yellow Texture Medicine 黃理湯

Yongchun 詠春

Yoshimura Udun Chōmei　義村御殿朝明

Zeng Cishu　曾賜叔
Zhang Sanfeng　張三丰
Zhang Zhongjing　張仲景
Zhao Haiping　趙海屏
Zhao Ling Liu　昭霊流

Zhao Xin　趙新
Zheng Ji　鄭紀
Zheng Li　鄭礼
Zheng Lishu　鄭礼叔
Zhong yao　中薬
Zhou dynasty　周朝
Zhou Zihe　周子和
Zonghe Quan　蹤鶴拳

≪ Index ≫

At Shuri Castle dressed in the traditional
Chikudoun Pechin costume.

Patrick McCarthy is one of the few foreigners to actually teach karate-do in Japan. Moreover, he is recognized worldwide as one of the foremost authorities on the civil fighting traditions of Okinawa. He is also the first non-Japanese to ever be awarded the coveted *Kyoshi* 7th Dan Teacher's License from Kyoto's prestigious Dai Nippon Butokukai. He has been practicing karate-do since the 1960s, and also studied a variety of Chinese, Southeast Asian, and western fighting arts.

During the mid-1970s, while pursuing a successful competitive career, McCarthy met the "Harvard Professor of the Martial Arts," Master Richard Kim, a disciple of whose he subsequently became in 1977.

Patrick McCarthy with his awards, Vancouver Karate Centre.

A holder of a Butokukai *Hanshi* 9th Dan Grandmaster's License, Kim *Sensei* emphasized the importance of studying karate's non-utilitarian elements. As a result of Master Kim's influence, McCarthy undertook a deep study of karate's history and philosophy, the research for which continues to this day.

His research has brought him not only to Japan, but also Taiwan, Hong Kong, and the People's Republic of China. With an extensive background in both the Okinawan and Chinese fighting arts, McCarthy was in a unique position to research the most profound and influential document in the history of karate-do, the Bubishi. Since that time, he has interviewed and trained with the world's top masters of *gongfu* and karate-do while unraveling the history of this document and the fighting systems associated with it.

After moving to Japan in the mid-1980s, he became Master Kim's personal representative in Japan, and not long thereafter established the International Ryukyu Karate Research Society (IRKRS) as an outgrowth of his research. The IRKRS is a non-profit, nonpolitical group of researchers and practitioners of budo, dedicated, but not limited, to the analysis, preservation, and promotion of karate-do.

Mr. McCarthy is a frequent contributor to martial arts magazines throughout the world, author of *The Classical Kata of Okinawan Karate, Beyond Physical Training, Kata: Karate's Paragon of Mystery,* and translator of Miyagi Chojun's 1934 *Outline of Karate-do, The Secrets of Wudang Boxing,* Taira Shinken's 1964 *Ryukyu Kobudo Taikan, The Matsumura and Itosu Precepts,* and the 1936 *Meeting of the Okinawan Masters.*

Presently ranked Hanshi, 9th dan, McCarthy sensei travels the world lecturing on the Bubishi, *kata* application, *Yamane Ryu kobudo,* karate history, and philosophy. He can be contacted for such seminars c/o patrick_mccarthy@mac.com.